The French Wars of Religion, 1562–1629

This is a new edition of Mack P. Holt's classic study of the French religious wars of the sixteenth and seventeenth centuries. Drawing on the scholarship of social and cultural historians of the Reformation, it shows how religion infused both politics and the socio-economic tensions of the period to produce a long extended civil war. Professor Holt integrates court politics and the political theory of the elites with the religious experiences of the popular classes, offering a fresh perspective on the wars and on why the French were willing to kill their neighbours in the name of religion. The book has been created specifically for undergraduates and general readers with no background knowledge of either French history or the Reformation. This new edition updates the text in the light of new work published in the last decade and the 'Suggestions for further reading' has been completely rewritten.

MACK P. HOLT is Professor of History at George Mason University. His previous publications include *The Duke of Anjou and the Politique Struggle during the Wars of Religion* (1986) and *Renaissance and Reformation France, 1500–1648* (2002, ed.)

D0145411

NEW APPROACHES TO EUROPEAN HISTORY

Series editors

WILLIAM BEIK, *Emory University*
T. C. W. BLANNING, *Sidney Sussex College, Cambridge*

New Approaches to European History is an important textbook series, which provides concise but authoritative surveys of major themes and problems in European history since the Renaissance. Written at a level and length accessible to advanced school students and undergraduates, each book in the series addresses topics or themes that students of European history encounter daily: the series embraces both some of the more 'traditional' subjects of study, and those cultural and social issues to which increasing numbers of school and college courses are devoted. A particular effort is made to consider the wider international implications of the subject under scrutiny.

To aid the student reader scholarly apparatus and annotation is light, but each work has full supplementary bibliographies and notes for further reading: where appropriate, chronologies, maps, diagrams and other illustrative material are also provided.

For a list of titles published in the series, please see end of book.

The French Wars of Religion, 1562–1629

Second Edition

MACK P. HOLT

George Mason University
Fairfax, Virginia

CAMBRIDGE
UNIVERSITY PRESS

CAMBRIDGE UNIVERSITY PRESS
Cambridge, New York, Melbourne, Madrid, Cape Town, Singapore, São Paulo

Cambridge University Press
The Edinburgh Building, Cambridge CB2 8RU, UK

Published in the United States of America by Cambridge University Press, New York

www.cambridge.org
Information on this title: www.cambridge.org/9780521547505

© Cambridge University Press 1995, 2005

This publication is in copyright. Subject to statutory exception
and to the provisions of relevant collective licensing agreements,
no reproduction of any part may take place without
the written permission of Cambridge University Press.

First published 1995
Reprinted 3 times
Second edition 2005
Reprinted 2007

Printed in the United Kingdom at the University Press, Cambridge

A catalogue record for this publication is available from the British Library

ISBN 978-0-521-83872-6 hardback
ISBN 978-0-521-54750-5 paperback

Cambridge University Press has no responsibility for
the persistence or accuracy of URLs for external or
third-party internet websites referred to in this book,
and does not guarantee that any content on such
websites is, or will remain, accurate or appropriate.

In memory of
J. Russell Major and
Nancy Lyman Roelker

Contents

Illustrations

Maps

Figures

Acknowledgements

I owe a special thanks to the many institutions that have provided financial support for this book. Several friends and colleagues have also given generously of their time and expertise. And while it is invidious to name some and not others, a few deserve special mention. Jonathan Powis was a well-spring of ideas at every stage. Phil Benedict and Jim Farr both read the entire manuscript and made a number of insightful suggestions. Although neither agreed with everything I wrote, they saved me from a number of errors. Bill Beik and Bob Scribner were model series editors. They also spotted a number of slips and made many useful suggestions. And I am especially grateful to Bill Beik's undergraduate students at Emory University, who tried the book out in the Fall semester 1994. They showed me where my arguments needed to be tightened (or in some cases abandoned). I want to thank my colleagues in the History Department at George Mason University, who have been supportive as well as generous with new ideas. Richard Fisher of Cambridge University Press has had the patience of Job waiting for me to finish this book, and I thank him for all his support. My copy-editor, Janet Hall, has also been a model of professionalism, efficiency and helpfulness. And I owe more than I can say to my wife Meg, who has made writing this book so much easier.

Finally, I owe a special debt to two scholars who have strongly influenced me. Russell Major rescued me from the scrapheap of burned out graduate students at a critical point in my career. When I was close to abandoning an academic career altogether, he took me aside and told me that he believed in me. Without that support, I would never have become a historian, much less written this book. And when I was first asked to write this book, I was fortunate enough to spend a year in Cambridge, Massachusetts where I encountered Nancy Roelker. We talked about the book a lot and shared a number of ideas, and she generously supported me in every way thereafter. Although I am saddened that she is unable to see the finished product, I can only hope that she would have been pleased. Thus, it is a privilege as well as a pleasure to dedicate this book in memory of Russell Major and Nancy Roelker.

Preface to the Second Edition

It has been a decade since I wrote the text of the first edition of this book, and I am happy to accept the invitation of Cambridge University Press to produce a revised and updated edition. I wish to thank all those readers and reviewers who took the time to point out several minor errors of fact or interpretation in the first edition, especially Hilmar Pabel and Mark Greengrass, and I have silently corrected these errors in this new edition. Because so much new work has also been published in the last decade, I have also taken the opportunity of this new edition to update the text in order to incorporate much of this recent scholarship. In some cases this has resulted in the expansion of certain passages or the insertion of totally new passages. Finally, I have also rewritten the 'Suggestions for further reading'. Although these revisions have not significantly altered my original approach or the principal argument of the book, they have, I hope, resulted in a more up-to-date and satisfying book.

Chronological table of events

1516	Concordat of Bologna; Guillaume Briçonnet appointed Bishop of Meaux.
1517	Luther posts his 95 theses in Wittenburg.
1525	Circle at Meaux broken up by the Sorbonne and the Parlement of Paris.
1534	Affair of the Placards.
1536	Calvin published the first edition of the *Institution of the Christian Religion*.
1541	Calvinism is established in Geneva.
1545	Pope Paul III convoked the first session of the Council of Trent.
1547	Death of Francis I, who is succeeded by his son Henry II.
1548–50	The *Chambre ardente* is established by Henry II.
1551	The Edict of Châteaubriant bans Protestantism.
1555	The evangelical ministry from Geneva begins in France.
1559	Execution of Anne du Bourg; Treaty of Cateau-Cambrésis; death of Henry II in a jousting accident.
1560	Conspiracy of Amboise; death of Francis II in December.
1561	Colloquy of Poissy.
1562	Edict of Toleration in January; violence at Vassy in March begins first civil war.
1563	Edict of Amboise ends first civil war; Charles IX reaches his age of majority.
1564–66	Royal tour of the kingdom by the court.
1567	Second civil war begins when Huguenots seize several fortified towns.
1568	Edict of Longjumeau ends second civil war in March, quickly followed by the beginning of the third civil war in September.
1569	Battles of Jarnac and Moncontour result in heavy Huguenot defeats, as well as the death of Condé.
1570	Edict of St. Germain ends the third civil war.
1572	St Bartholomew's massacres in Paris and the provinces start the fourth civil war.

1573   Siege of La Rochelle; Peace of La Rochelle ends the fourth civil war; Henry, Duke of Anjou is elected King of Poland.

1574   Death of Charles IX in May.

1575   Escape from court of the Duke of Alençon in September begins the fifth civil war; German mercenaries led by the Duke of Casimir join Protestant army.

1576   Henry of Navarre escapes from court in February; Peace of Monsieur (Edict of Beaulieu) ends the fifth civil war in May; the Estates-General meets at Blois in November.

1577   Sixth civil war begins in March and ends in September with the Peace of Bergerac.

1578–80   Peasant revolts in Provence, the Vivarais, and Dauphiné.

1580   Seventh civil war erupts briefly, ending with the Peace of Fleix in November.

1581–83   Duke of Anjou visits England and the Netherlands.

1584   Death of Anjou in June makes the Protestant Henry of Navarre the heir to the throne and begins the eighth civil war; Treaty of Joinville signed in December between Spain and the Catholic League.

1585   Treaty of Nemours signed by Henry III and the League in July.

1587   Duke of Casimir leads another invasion of German mercenaries into France to support the Huguenots.

1588   Day of the Barricades in May; Edict of Union in July; Estates-General meets in Blois in December; assassinations of the Duke and Cardinal of Guise lead to numerous towns supporting the League.

1589   Death of Catherine de Medici in January; assassination of Henry III in August; Catholic League begins its reign of terror.

1590   Siege of Paris by the army of Henry IV.

1591   The Sixteen in Paris executes Barnabé Brisson in November.

1592   Siege of Rouen by the army of Henry IV.

1593   Estates-General of the League meets in Paris in the spring; Henry IV abjures Protestantism in July.

1593–94   Peasant revolts begin in Burgundy, Limousin, Périgord, and Agenais.

1594   Coronation of Henry IV at Chartres in February; Paris submits to the king in March, as other towns soon follow suit.

1595   Henry IV receives papal absolution in August from Pope Clement VIII; the Duke of Mayenne submits to the king in September; Henry IV declares war against Spain.

1596   Spanish army seizes Cambrai and Calais.

1597   Spanish army seizes Amiens in the spring, which is then liberated by Henry IV in September after a three-month siege.

1598   Duke of Mercoeur submits to the king in January; the Edict of Nantes ends the eighth civil war in April; Henry IV signs peace treaty with Philip II of Spain in May.

1606   The brevets of the Edict of Nantes are renewed.

1610   Assassination of Henry IV in May by François Ravaillac; regency government of the young Louis XIII is headed by Marie de Medici.

1611   Sully resigns from the privy council; Huguenot assembly at Saumur.

1614   Revolt against the regency government led by the Prince of Condé; Louis XIII reaches his age of majority; the Estates-General meets in Paris in October.

1617   Assassination of Concini.

1618   Protestants revolt in Bohemia against the Habsburg Emperor.

1620   Royal military campaign in Béarn; Edict of Restitution restores Béarn to the crown of France in October; Huguenot assembly in La Rochelle opens in November.

1621   Military campaign against the Huguenots begins in the spring; fall of St. Jean d'Angély in June; the siege of Montauban is lifted in November.

1622   Renewal of military campaign against the Huguenots in the spring; Soubise is routed by royal troops at the Ile de Ré in April; Montpellier submits to the king in October after a short siege.

1624   Cardinal Richelieu is admitted to the privy council.

1625   Soubise seizes the islands of Ré and Oléron off the coast of La Rochelle in January; Louis XIII's sister Henrietta marries Charles I of England.

1626   Edict of La Rochelle signed in February; a royal garrison is placed on the Ile de Ré.

1627   English fleet under the command of the Duke of Buckingham attacks the Ile de Ré in July; Buckingham is repelled by royal forces in November; the siege of La Rochelle by the royal army begins in August.

1628   Fall of La Rochelle and submission to the king in October.

1629   Submission of the Duke of Rohan to the king in the spring; Peace of Alais signed in June ending the last civil war.

1685   Revocation of the Edict of Nantes by Louis XIV.

Introduction

Like Michel de Montaigne, perhaps I too ought to have called this book an *essai* in the original sense; for an 'attempt' is about all one can manage in the face of the confusing morass of court factions, countless leading actors and bit players, a seemingly unending series of peace agreements followed by renewed warfare, and the bizarre diplomatic intrigues of nearly every state in western Europe that made up the French Wars of Religion. It is no small wonder, then, that even specialist historians have never found explaining this conflict a particularly easy task. What is a student to make of the problem? Thus, while this book is certainly a trial or attempt to 'make the crooked straight and the rough places plain' for the reader with little background to the French religious wars of the sixteenth and early seventeenth centuries, I hope it is also more than that. Surely any reader who picks up a book claiming to offer 'new approaches to European history' has a right to expect as much. So, perhaps it is best to sketch out exactly what is so novel about this approach right at the start.

To begin with, the pages which follow will argue at some length that the series of French civil wars which began with the massacre at Vassy in 1562 and concluded with the Peace of Alais in 1629 was a conflict fought primarily over the issue of religion. This may startle some readers, used to the generations of historians and not a few sixteenth-century contemporaries who believed steadfastly that the main actors in the religious wars only used religion as a pretext, a 'cloak' in the words of the Parisian diarist Pierre de l'Estoile, to mask their political, dynastic, or personal power struggles. Moreover, other historians (and not just Marxist historians) have interpreted the civil wars as fomented mainly by socio-economic tensions rather than ideology, as urban, skilled, mainly literate, and prosperous merchants, professionals, and artisans turned to Calvinism as a means of combatting the economic and political stranglehold of the landed elites of church and state. While I would be the first to agree that the politicization of religious issues played a significant role in shaping the course of the wars (especially during the wars of the League in the 1590s) and that socio-economic tensions were a permanent feature of early modern French society, occasionally bubbling over into popular violence, it seems to me that religion was nevertheless the fulcrum upon which the civil wars balanced.

I am not suggesting, however, that three generations of French men and women were willing to fight and die just over differences of religious doctrine, whether it be over how to get to heaven or over what actually transpired during the celebration of mass. What this book will propose is that the French Wars of Religion were fought primarily over the issue of religion as defined in contemporary terms: as a body of believers rather than the more modern definition of a body of beliefs.[1] Thus, the emphasis here is on the social rather than the theological. In these terms, Protestants and Catholics alike in the sixteenth century each viewed the other as pollutants of their own particular notion of the body social, as threats to their own conception of ordered society. When a mob of Catholic winegrowers set fire to a barn in Beaune where a clandestine group of Protestants had observed the Lord's Supper in both kinds on Easter Sunday of 1561, for example, their actions went far beyond an expression of discontent and intolerance of the Calvinist theology of the eucharist. Those winegrowers were cleansing the body social of the pollutant of Protestantism, and in the process, preventing a dangerous and threatening cancer from spreading. By setting ablaze the barn where that pollution had taken place, they were purifying by fire the social space those Protestants had desecrated.[2] Huguenots (as French Calvinists came to be called) did perceive Catholics as superstitious believers to be sure, just as French Catholics viewed them as heretics, but the resulting clash was one of cultures as much as theologies. This is hardly a novel approach to the Wars of Religion, as Lucien Febvre pioneered more than fifty years ago the study of what has today come to be called 'religious culture'. And the specialized research of more recent practitioners such as Philip Benedict, John Bossy, Denis Crouzet, Natalie Davis, Barbara Diefendorf, Jean Delumeau, and Robert Muchembled among others, has led to a far greater understanding of what religious difference meant in sixteenth-century France (see the 'Suggestions for further reading' for

---

[1] For a discussion of this transformation of the definition of religion in the seventeenth century, see the perceptive comments of John Bossy, *Christianity in the West, 1400–1700* (Oxford, 1985), passim, but especially pp. 170–1.

[2] This incident is recounted in Theodore Beza, *Histoire ecclésiastique des élises réformées au royaume de France*, ed. G. Baum and E. Cunitz, 3 vols. (Paris, 1883–89), I, 864, and III, 489. For other examples, see the classic interpretation of religious violence during the Wars of Religion, Natalie Zemon Davis, 'The Rites of Violence' in her *Society and Culture in Early Modern France* (Stanford, CA, 1975), pp. 152–87.

bibliographic details). To date, however, no one has attempted to write a general history of the religious wars from quite this perspective.

I should point out, however, that by underscoring the religious nature of the Wars of Religion, as defined above in social terms, I am not implying that political, economic, intellectual or even other social factors ought to be de-emphasised. Not only did politics significantly matter in the sixteenth century, but as will become clear below, it was high politics that largely shaped the beginning and the end of the wars, not to mention how they were fought in between. My point is that there was a religious foundation to sixteenth-century French society that was shared by elites and popular classes alike, and it was the contestation of this essential religious fabric of both the body social and the body politic that led to the French civil wars taking the shape they did. In short, while civil war, popular revolt, and social violence were endemic to pre-modern society, it was the dynamic of religion that distinguished the sixteenth-century civil wars and resulted in the most serious crisis of French state and society before the Revolution.

Secondly, this particular attempt to explain the wars of religion will take a longer chronological perspective than most of its predecessors, which traditionally have depicted the Edict of Nantes in 1598 as the terminus of the wars. The older studies of J-H. Mariéjol, *La Réforme, la Ligue, l'Edit de Nantes, 1559–1598* (Paris, 1904) in the Lavisse series and of J. E. Neale, *The Age of Catherine de Medici* (London, 1943) as well as the more recent works of Georges Livet, *Les guerres de religion, 1559–1598* (Paris, 1962) in the *Que sais-je?* series; J. H. M. Salmon, *Society in Crisis: France in the Sixteenth Century* (New York, 1975); and Michel Pernot, *Les guerres de religion en France 1559–1598* (Paris, 1987) all in various (and by no means similar) ways treat the Edict of Nantes as the *terminus ad quem* of the wars. Although this edict issued in 1598 is a convenient cutoff point, initiating an extended period of peace, it hardly marked the end of the fighting between Protestants and Catholics in France. More seriously, by ending the story in 1598 there is the implicit danger the reader might be persuaded that the Edict of Nantes was meant to establish a permanent settlement of co-existence between the two religions with a measure of toleration on both sides. According to the traditional interpretation, this settlement was brought about by a growing group of 'modern thinking' men in the 1590s called 'politiques', who felt that the survival of the state was more important than ridding the kingdom of heresy, especially as forty years of civil war had not achieved the defeat of the Huguenots. Putting religious differences aside, they turned to the newly converted Henry IV to end the violence and restore law and order. Mariéjol, Neale, and Livet go out of their way to underscore that this was indeed the case, and by implication suggest that had it not been for the less tolerant policies of Louis XIII and Richelieu that Henry IV's edict of 1598 might have survived. 'The wars demonstrated', noted Georges Livet at the end of his brief summary of the conflict, 'that religious unity was an impossibility in late sixteenth-century France. The only solution possible if the country was to survive was the co-existence, albeit regulated and limited, of the two religions.'[3] The perspective presented here, while hardly novel in itself, will suggest that the Edict of Nantes was never intended by Henry IV or his 'politique' supporters to be more than a temporary settlement, to end the violence in order to try to win back by conversion those remaining Huguenots to the Roman Catholic church. Indeed, Henry himself urged his former co-religionnaires to emulate his own example and abjure the Protestant religion. This perspective stresses the continuity in the aims of Henry IV and Louis XIII rather than a dichotomy. Both monarchs had the same goal in mind: the traditional *un roi, une foi, une loi* – that is, one king, one faith, and one law – of their ancestors. Their means of achieving this goal certainly differed – with Louis XIII and Richelieu abandoning Henry's carrot of conversion in favour of a return to the stick of suppression – but an analysis of their policies suggests that their religious aims were not wholly dissimilar. Moreover, this perspective counters the traditional claim that the 'politique' supporters of Henry IV in the 1590s were a more 'modern' group of secular, political men with sceptical attitudes toward religious ideology. 'Liberty of conscience and toleration', Livet concluded, 'the foundation of a secular state, were two ideas dearly bought which defined the originality of Henry IV's French solution [in the Edict of Nantes]'.[4] No matter how hard generations of liberal, Protestant historians have tried to separate 'one faith' from 'one law' and 'one king', in the sixteenth century no such dissolution was possible.

Finally, in order to take account of recent work by historians on both sides of the Atlantic, the most stimulating of which has been in the area of social and cultural history, this perspective will take on a decidedly more popular and provincial look than most histories of the Wars of Religion. I have done my best to write as balanced an account as possible, in view of the many partisan accounts of the wars that still seem to surface. Doubtless much of the polemic is the result of the contemporary sixteenth-century rhetoric in the sources, where partisans of both sides tended to speak out much more often than more moderate voices, which

[3] Georges Livet, *Les guerres de religion* (Paris: Presses Universitaires de France, 1977 edn.), p. 122.
[4] Ibid., p. 123.

were in a distinct minority in any case. As will become apparent, in a clash of cultures such as the religious wars it is easy for the historian to swallow whole the Catholic views of Protestants as 'seditious rebels' and the Huguenot view of French Catholics as 'superstitious idolators'. These perceptions clearly should be treated as stereotypes rather than reflections of social reality, as insiders describing outsiders, members of one culture depicting a counter-culture. As such, they reveal much more about the creator of these images than their intended targets. This is not to suggest that many Protestants were not in fact rebelling against the crown or that some Catholics were not superstitious. Historians such as Peter Burke and Roger Chartier, however, have much to say on how to 'read' these texts. They can reveal a great deal, but about what, or whom? Even self-perceptions need to be treated with care, as the Catholics' view of themselves as 'guardians of law and tradition' and the Protestant perception of themselves as the 'persecuted minority' are stereotypes. None of these stereotypes was wholly fact or fiction, but the point is that the stereotype itself can tell us a great deal about the motivations of its creator whether it reflected social reality very well or not.[5]

Although my goal throughout has been to try to write a balanced account, some readers will be able to detect a distinctly Burgundian flavour to the book. This is explained by the fact that I had already been working for two years on a study of the political and religious culture in Burgundy during the Wars of Religion when I was approached to write this volume. I have made a genuine attempt, however, to balance my perspective with examples from other parts of France, or have only chosen to illustrate my story with episodes from Dijon, Beaune, and Auxonne which I thought were characteristic of France as a whole. Nevertheless, I apologize if some readers still find the aroma of *pinot noir* and *moutarde* too pungent for their palates; perhaps it will whet the appetite of others.

I should also stress that the decision to write a more 'popular' history was not shaped by any political agenda, social cause, or moral duty to write a history of 'the common man' (not to mention woman) in the Wars of Religion. Such attempts often do no more than trivialize or patronize the subjects they are trying to elevate, and they can be just as one-sided as those histories written from the perspective of the elites. Moreover, decisions taken by kings to wage war or raise taxes had just as much a

---

[5] Although many of their works could be cited, see particularly Peter Burke, 'Perceiving a Counter-Culture', in his *The Historical Anthropology of Early Modern Italy: Essays on Perception and Communication* (Cambridge, 1988), pp. 63–75; and Roger Chartier, 'Les élites et les gueux', *Revue d'histoire moderne et contemporaine*, vol. 21 (1974), 376–88.

direct impact on the lives of most French men and women as climatic changes or declining birthrates. Thus, the attempt here is to eschew the traditional court-centred approach in favour of one that takes into account what the wars meant to those who lived in the towns and in the countryside, not because it is more fashionable or more important, but because ordinary French men and women bore just as many of the hardships of the wars as courtiers and soldiers. One cannot ignore altogether the central actors, who after all made the decisions that mattered in waging war for half a century; but surely it is time someone attempted to grasp the nettle and tried to integrate the new research of the past twenty-five years with the traditional historical narrative of the civil wars into a digestible form suitable for student and teacher alike. Of course, this perspective is not the only way to view the religious wars, and I would urge interested readers to explore the many other useful and valid attempts to make sense of this complicated period. And I hardly need add that this is not a 'total history' of the civil wars, much less a comprehensive history of France from 1562 to 1629. It is simply one historian's 'attempt' at making sense of a complex problem that still plagues the world at the advent of the twenty-first century: religious wars.

1 Prologue: Gallicanism and reform in the sixteenth century

Ever since the Middle Ages French kings were both consecrated and crowned during the coronation ceremony that marked their ascension to the throne. And though French ceremonial shared much in common with English coronations across the Channel, by the sixteenth century it was clear that the constitutional aspects of the ceremony so emphasized in England took a backseat to the liturgical nature of the coronation so heavily accentuated in France. The ceremony itself was called a *sacre* in France, emphasizing consecration rather than coronation. Patterned after the first such ceremony, the crowning of Charlemagne by the pope in Rome in the year 800, French coronations traditionally took place in the cathedral church of Reims with the local archbishop officiating. With the ecclesiastical and lay peers of the realm, as well as the bishops of the French church and the royal princes of the blood assembled around him, the new king was required to make explicit his duties and responsibilities to the Christian church in his coronation oath. In the first part of the oath, called the ecclesiastical oath, the king swore: 'I shall protect the canonical privilege, due law, and justice, and I shall exercise defense of each bishop and of each church committed to him, as much as I am able – with God's help – just as a king ought properly to do in his kingdom.' Then in the concluding section, called the oath of the kingdom, the king further underscored his duty to defend the church as well as the kingdom. 'To this Christian populace subject to me, I promise in the name of Christ: First, that by our authority the whole Christian populace will preserve at all times true peace for the Church of God ... Also, that in good faith to all men I shall be diligent to expel from my land and also from the jurisdiction subject to me all heretics designated by the Church. I affirm by oath all this said above.' Then, each new king of France would be consecrated as the archbishop anointed him with the sacred oil of the holy ampulla, anointing his body and smearing the sign of the cross on his forehead as he uttered, 'I anoint you king with sanctified oil. In the name of the Father, and of the Son, and of the Holy Ghost. Amen.' This was the highlight of the entire ceremony, as the holy oil connected the new king to

God as well as to all his predecessors of the previous thousand years (since, according to legend, a dove had first delivered the holy ampulla upon the occasion of the baptism of Clovis and all French kings had been anointed with it ever since). Only after consecration was the new monarch addressed as king and presented with his crown, sceptre, and regal vestments. The coronation concluded with prayers, psalms, and the celebration of mass, where the sacerdotal nature of French kingship was underscored once again as the newly consecrated and crowned monarch partook of the eucharist in both kinds – the host and the communion cup – demonstrating that in this one moment at least he was more priest than ordinary layman.

This assemblage of language, symbols, and gestures was anything but coincidental. Though the coronation ceremony had clearly evolved and been amended to meet changing political needs over the centuries, by the sixteenth century one historical constant at least was clear: the enfolding together of the French monarchy and the Catholic church. The language and symbols of the French coronation went far beyond the usual ecclesiastical overtones surrounding other monarchs of western Christendom, all of whom paid homage to their Lord as the true dispenser of their authority and on whose behalf they acted as his secular sword on earth. For French kings as well as their subjects the anointing with the sanctified oil of the holy ampulla, the explicit promise to defend the church from heresy, and the public display of the celebration of mass in both kinds were all signifiers full of meaning, as well as evidence that in France there was a special relationship between church and state that was not duplicated elsewhere. As Jean Golein, a fourteenth-century commentator, had described it, when each new king removed his clothing for the consecration, 'that signifies that he relinquishes his previous worldly estate in order to assume that of the royal religion, and if he does that with the devotion with which he should, I think that he is washed of his sins just as much as whoever newly enters orthodox religion'. While the pope may have recognized and singled out other monarchs for their service to God with special appellations – Ferdinand and Isabella were called 'Catholic kings' and Henry VIII was 'defender of the faith' – French kings had earned a much older and more redoubtable title: *Rex christianissimus*, the 'most Christian king'. Thus, the *sacres* of the kings of France were more than culturally replete symbols of the sacred nature of French kingship denoting a special relationship with God. As the General Assembly of the Clergy declared in 1625, French kings were not only ordained by God, 'they themselves were gods'. And as the Wars of Religion were to demonstrate, the special powers of these god-kings were accompanied by explicit responsibilities, the foremost of which was combatting heresy.

In Protestant England, by contrast, although their kings were also perceived to be quasi-sacred and appointed by God, the coronation imagery
symbols were taken much less seriously. The holy oil with which English
kings were anointed was 'but a ceremony', as Thomas Cranmer declared
to Edward VI upon his coronation in 1547. The 'solemn rites of coronation' were nothing but 'good admonitions' to the king. That Cranmer was
making a very Protestant point in this instance only underscores the ties
between the French *sacre* and the traditional Catholic church.[1] (Map 1
shows France during the period under discussion here.)

Naturally, the sacerdotal and god-like powers bestowed on French
kings in their *sacres* necessarily required some sort of accommodation
with the ultimate temporal authority in matters spiritual, the papacy. And
it was this relationship between monarch and pope that had largely
shaped the king's ability to govern the Gallican church in France. The
term 'Gallican' itself was used by contemporaries to denote just such a
peculiar (or rather independent) relationship between the French church
and Rome; and the sacerdotal king of France stood as a prophylactic
barrier to protect the Gallican liberties from papal intervention. By the
sixteenth century, however, royal domination of the French church had
become so strong that the Parlement of Paris, the supreme sovereign
court in the realm, found itself faced with the prospect of protecting
and guaranteeing the Gallican liberties of the French church from the
grasp of royal rather than papal interference. 'By 1515', notes the historian R. J. Knecht, 'royal control of the ecclesiastical hierarchy was an
acknowledged fact'.[2]

This was nowhere more evident than in the Concordat of Bologna of
1516. Because of the changing dynastic situation of the early sixteenth
century, with the Valois at war against the Habsburgs in Italy over
disputed possessions in Milan and Naples, Francis I sorely needed
papal support for his military adventures in Italy. In return for support
from Pope Leo X, Francis virtually decimated the Pragmatic Sanction of
Bourges of 1438: an agreement whereby king and pope had agreed to let
cathedral chapters elect both bishops and abbots independent of royal
and papal control. The king not only assumed the right to nominate
directly candidates for vacant bishoprics and archbishoprics, but also
to fill vacancies in the principal abbeys and monasteries in the realm.

---

[1] For an analysis of the French coronation ceremony see Richard A. Jackson, *Vive le Roi!
A History of the French Coronation from Charles V to Charles X* (Chapel Hill, NC, 1984),
quotations from pp. 20, 57–8, 215, and 218. Cranmer's speech to Edward VI quoted in
Peter Burke, 'The Repudiation of Ritual in Early Modern Europe', in his *The Historical
Anthropology of Early Modern Italy* (Cambridge, 1987), p. 233.
[2] R. J. Knecht, *Francis I* (Cambridge, 1982), p. 53.

Map 1 France during the Wars of Religion

In return, Leo received the right to veto any of Francis's nominations if they were unqualified (bishops, for example, had to be twenty-seven years old and trained in theology or canon law) as well as the right to collect annates (one year's revenues) from all newly appointed holders of bene-fices. Though the papacy had clearly much to gain by the Concordat,

it was Francis who really benefitted from it most by winning almost unprecedented power of appointment in the Gallican church. And while the
remonstrances of the Parlement of Paris – which refused initially to
register the Concordat – were couched in anti-papal language, it was
evident that the court's concern was over Francis's decision to trample
upon the Pragmatic Sanction which guaranteed the church's Gallican
liberties and independence. The point of the entire episode, however, is
that when all the smoke had finally cleared the Parlement was forced to
recognize the power of appointment the king had won. Although it would
be a mistake to assume that Francis had won anywhere near the independence and total break with Rome effected by Thomas Cromwell and
Henry VIII in England just a couple of decades later, it is true to say
that the growth of royal power in the ecclesiastical realm in France in the
late fifteenth and early sixteenth centuries was such that interference from
Rome was never a serious issue in determining French reaction to
Protestantism. And while many doctors of the Sorbonne (the theology
school of the University of Paris) may have wished for a more ultramontane (that is, papal) look to French ecclesiastical policy, the symbol of
consecrated king as guardian of both church and state ultimately guaranteed that the French monarch rather than the pope was to oversee the
safekeeping of God's Gallican flock. Jean du Tillet, a historian and clerk
in the Parlement of Paris, made this clear in a tract he wrote in 1551 called
'On the liberties of the Gallican church':

> Malady has always been the result when the absolute power of the said Popes has
> been admitted and received in this kingdom. The means to good government in
> this kingdom is that the two jurisdictions, ecclesiastic and temporal, are both
> harmoniously administered together under and by the authority of the said
> kings ... When bishoprics have been vacant, it is well known ... that since the
> time of Charlemagne the kings have appointed them.

Du Tillet went on to point out that even if custom later dictated that 'the
clergy and the people' had come to elect these benefices, it was after all
only because Charlemagne 'had permitted the elections of the bishoprics
to the said clergy and people' in the first place.[3] Thus, the symbol of the
consecrated king acting as priest during his coronation was much more
than a meaningless gesture of tradition in the sixteenth century. It underscored to every Frenchman who witnessed it that one of the king's
principal tasks was to safeguard the church, as his coronation oath
made explicit. Moreover, Du Tillet's sentiments only reflected what

---

[3] Jean du Tillet, *Memoire & advis de M. Jean du Tillet, protenotaire et Secretaire du Roy tres-
Chrestien, Greffier de sa cour de Parlement. Faict en l'an 1551 sur les libertez de l'Eglise Gallicane*
(n.p., 1594 edn.), pp. 4–5 and 7.

was made clear in the *sacre* itself. Jean Jouvenal des Ursins was the archbishop of Reims, who, when consecrating Louis XI in 1461, summed up the king's power within the Gallican church very nicely: 'As far as you are concerned, my sovereign lord, you are not simply a layman but a spiritual personage, a prelate ... You may pass judgment on the liberties and freedoms of your church and erect them into a law, an ordinance, a pragmatic sanction, and you may take all due and proper measures to see that the law is kept and observed.'[4]

One of the unfortunate by-products of increased royal control of ecclesiastical patronage in the early sixteenth century, however, was the explicit growth of corruption and decline of spirituality among the episcopate as a whole within the Gallican church. In short, Francis I and his son Henry II used their unprecedented powers of appointment to fill the ranks of the episcopacy with their clients, relatives, and political allies. In Francis's reign (1515–47), for example, of the total of 129 bishops he appointed, 102 were either princes of the blood or members of the nobility of the sword, that is, members of the most powerful as well as oldest noble families in France. And the fact that so few of these bishops met the requirements of the Concordat of Bologna regarding theological training clearly indicates that their commitment was to the monarchy rather than to the church. In the reign of Henry II (1547–59), of the 80 bishops appointed by the king only 3 had theology degrees while 15 had studied canon law – a total of only 23 per cent – despite the requirements of the Concordat. Moreover, the fact that over one-fourth of Henry's appointments to vacant sees (21 out of 80) went to Italians, nearly all of them clients of the pope or other Italian allies of the French monarchy in the wars against the Habsburgs in Italy, indicates that political patronage rather than spirituality was the ultimate by-product of royal control of the Gallican church. The inevitable result was corruption and blatant absenteeism among the upper echelons of the church hierarchy. Of the 101 incumbent bishops in 1559, for example, it has been determined that only 19 resided in their dioceses regularly. And taking into account the fact that there were still many other vacancies and pluralities (that is, examples of one bishop holding two or more dioceses simultaneously), one can say that 65 per cent of all French bishops in 1559 did not live in or visit their dioceses on a regular basis. Examples of the most blatant offenders just underscore how chronic the problem was. François de Foix, bishop of Aire in Gascony, for example, never even set foot in his diocese in the twenty-four years he was its bishop. While in

---

[4] Quoted in J. H. Shennan, *Government and Society in France, 1461–1661* (London, 1969), p. 84.

1547 alone, the cardinals of Este, Armagnac, Lorraine, Tournon, Longwy, Du Bellay, and Louis and Charles of Bourbon all held at least three sees apiece. A number of bishops were neither ordained nor consecrated, further making a mockery of ecclesiastical appointment. Thus, while the state of the French church by the middle of the sixteenth century certainly warranted the many vocal outcries for reform that echoed throughout France at the advent of the Reformation, it was also symptomatic of the peculiar nature of the Gallican church where there was no separation of church and state. Both kings and prelates alike viewed service to the crown as service to the church, and vice versa, as the king's sworn duty to protect the church really rested on his ability to place his own men in positions of influence in the ecclesiastical hierarchy. As the threat of heresy from both Lutheranism and Calvinism began to loom large in the 1530s and 1540s, it is perhaps less surprising that Francis I and Henry II should want to make sure that those who administered the Gallican church were above all else loyal servants of the Most Christian King.[5]

Calls for reform were not just the result of the deplorable state of the French clergy in the early sixteenth century but were based on a tradition that went back well into the late Middle Ages. The secular tradition of the revival of antiquity which emerged in Renaissance Italy had become fused in northern Europe in the late fifteenth century with a distinctly religious revival. This movement had decidedly spiritual and mystical overtones, which took shape in the form of contemplation, prayer, and inner devotion. Earmarked by works such as Thomas à Kempis's *Imitation of Christ,* the ideas of this movement came to embody both the scholarly methodology of the Italian humanists as well as the inner spirituality of the *Devotio moderna,* or 'modern devotion', of northern Europe. As a result, throughout the intellectual centres of Europe in the early sixteenth century, and particularly in Paris, there emerged what one scholar has dubbed the 'pre-reform', or a movement of thinkers who not only sought to reform the obvious abuses within the church, but who also sought to establish a new and more scholarly platform upon which to question traditional religion. Although historians have traditionally called these thinkers 'Christian humanists', in an effort to underscore their hybrid intellectual ancestry from both Renaissance Italy and northern Europe, there were many different currents and debates within this 'pre-reform'. Men such as Erasmus of Rotterdam and Jacques Lefèvre d'Etaples, a Frenchman from Picardy, both of whom were in Paris in the 1490s and

---

[5] Much of this paragraph is based on Frederic J. Baumgartner, *Change and Continuity in the French Episcopate: The Bishops and the Wars of Religion, 1547–1610* (Durham, NC, 1986), pp. 110–13.

early 1500s, came to exemplify this 'pre-reform' movement in their quest to effect religious renewal. Though biblical scholarship and the ultimate goal of presenting scripture to the laity in the vernacular were foundations of both men's work, which made their ideas heterodox, it must be remembered that they were both scholars and spiritual writers rather than true reformers in the mold of Luther. Indeed, Erasmus and Lefèvre d'Etaples were both characteristic of the 'pre-reform' as a whole in their insistence in maintaining the unity of the Christian church despite their unorthodox ideas; thus, 'pre-reformers' were clearly not proto-Protestants.[6]

It is nevertheless true that many of the intellectual currents that emerged from the French 'pre-reform' shared much in common with explicitly Protestant ideas, particularly those of Martin Luther. This group had shifted from Paris to Meaux, just east of the capital along the Marne, after 1516 when Guillaume Briçonnet was appointed the new bishop there. Briçonnet, who was abbot of Saint-Germain-des-Prés in Paris prior to his bishopric in Meaux, had attempted reforms in his abbey along the lines of those suggested by Jacques Lefèvre d'Etaples, whom Briçonnet had in fact sheltered there. In Meaux this intellectual circle widened considerably to include not only clerics and scholars – Lefèvre d'Etaples was appointed Briçonnet's vicar general, for example – but a fair number of locals from the lower orders of society at large. Most visible of all were the new preachers hired by Briçonnet, each of whom was permanently assigned to one of thirty-two sub-divisions of the parishes in the city to further evangelism and religious renewal. Above all, men such as Gérard Roussel, François Vatable, Martial Mazurier, and Guillaume Farel among the most notable, began a regime of reading scripture to their parishioners during mass, particularly the gospels and St Paul's epistles. It was out of this biblical tradition that Lefèvre d'Etaples came to publish a vernacular French translation of the gospels in June 1523, a French translation of the entire New Testament later that same year, and by 1530 the whole of the holy scriptures in French. Lefèvre d'Etaples, it should be remembered, had a proven track record of biblical scholarship, having published his own critical Latin edition of the epistles based on Greek manuscripts in 1512, pointing out four years before Erasmus that the Latin Vulgate translation of St Jerome was not without error.

[6] For the 'pre-reform' in Paris see Augustin Renaudet, *Préréforme et humanisme à Paris pendant les premières guerres d'Italie, 1494–1517* (Paris, 2nd edn. 1953). For a brief summary of this work in English, see the same author's 'Paris from 1494 to 1517', in Werner L. Gundersheimer, ed., *French Humanism, 1470–1600* (London, 1969), pp. 65–89.

As heterodox as the Meaux circle's emphasis on vernacular scripture may have seemed at the time, however, it probably would have been viewed as just another revival of spirituality rather than as heresy had it not been for the widespread publicity and propagation in France of the ideas of the Saxon monk, Martin Luther. The role of the printing press in disseminating Luther's critiques of the special St Peter's indulgence contained in his 'Ninety-five theses' of 1517, and his emphasis on justification by faith, the priesthood of all believers, and the primacy of scripture in his three treatises of 1520 has long been a commonplace of the Lutheran Reformation. And it was ominous for the Meaux circle when the faculty of the Sorbonne censured and condemned Luther's writings as heretical in 1521: especially his rejection of free will and insistence on justification by faith rather than good works as the way to salvation, since these ideas were close to Lefèvre's own views. The issue of salvation, of course, was the principal sticking point between Luther and Rome, and the German monk's insistence that salvation depended entirely on God's grace and that man's efforts mattered not a whit could not easily be reconciled with the medieval church's emphasis on acts of charity and good works. Even though some of the younger and more radical members of the Meaux group were clearly leaning in this direction (most notably Guillaume Farel), the Sorbonne's misguided belief that Briçonnet and Lefèvre d'Etaples were organizing a Protestant and heretical sect in Meaux resembling Luther's flock in Saxony was erroneous. When first confronted with charges of heresy in 1523, Briçonnet responded by requiring all his preachers to make explicit in their sermons their fundamental belief in some of the traditionally Catholic doctrines that were attacked by Luther: the existence of purgatory, the efficacy of prayers to the Virgin Mary and the community of saints, etc. Briçonnet even withdrew licences to preach from a number of the most radical members of his circle, but the Sorbonne remained convinced that they were spreading heresy in Meaux. Things finally came to a head in 1525 when both the Sorbonne and the Parlement of Paris broke up the circle for good. Some like Briçonnet, simply recanted and abandoned all efforts at spiritual reform to return to the practices of the traditional church. Many others, however, like Lefèvre d'Etaples and Farel, fled into exile, most notably to the German-speaking city of Strasbourg. While a few like the very elderly Lefèvre d'Etaples remained technically Catholic for the rest of their lives despite their unorthodox views, many others emulated his pupil Farel, who not only publicly converted to Protestantism but ten years later would join another French exile, the young John Calvin, in Geneva. For the moment, however, that segment of the Gallican church which defined orthodox doctrine, the faculty of the Sorbonne, had beaten back the first French experiment in 'pre-reform'.[7]

But what was the reaction of the crown to all of this? Though one might expect the Most Christian King to remain as staunchly opposed to any form of heterodoxy as the doctors of the Sorbonne, Francis I was actively supportive of Christian humanist scholarship generally and the 'pre-reform' circle at Meaux in particular. To be sure, Francis was one of the first to denounce Lutheranism as heresy, but this was not necessarily inconsistent with his patronage of humanist scholarship. That a Guillaume Farel could flee Meaux in order to convert to Protestantism does indicate the fluid boundary between the evangelical spirituality of the Briçonnet circle and Lutheranism. But as already mentioned, 'pre-reformers' were not necessarily 'proto-Protestants', even though there were no clear-cut boundaries between them in the 1520s and 1530s, except in the eyes of the zealous theologians of the Sorbonne, where any deviation from its narrowly defined scholasticism was deemed heretical. Thus, Francis could quite easily reconcile his opposition to Protestantism with his support for humanist scholarship. After all, if his coronation oath required him to protect the Gallican church, this meant guarding it from ignorance as well as from heresy. Therefore, when Francis decided to found a college of higher learning devoted to classical scholarship in 1517, he invited the most renowned scholar in Europe – Erasmus of Rotterdam – to head what would become the Collège de France. Though the itinerant Erasmus politely declined, the king's choice was a clear sign of his intention to patronize Christian learning at the highest level. More to the point, when the Sorbonne tried to add the writings of both Erasmus and Lefèvre d'Etaples to their index of heretical works in 1523–24, their Greek and vernacular translations of the scripture in particular, Francis stepped in and forbade the doctors from discussing their works on the grounds that they were reputable scholars known all over Europe. It should also be pointed out that the king's sister, Marguerite of Angoulême (who would later become queen of Navarre when she married Henri d'Albret in 1527), was actually a humanist writer herself as well as a disciple of the Meaux circle, and carried on a very close correspondence with bishop Briçonnet during the early 1520s. When the Sorbonne and the Parlement of Paris finally dissolved that group despite royal patronage in 1525, Marguerite provided refuge and jobs to a

[7] Much of the preceding two paragraphs is based on the contemporary account compiled by the Protestant deputy to Calvin in Geneva, Theodore Beza, *Histoire ecclésiastique des églises réformées au royaume de France*, 3 vols. (Paris, 1883–89 edn.), I, 10–14; as well as Mark Greengrass, *The French Reformation* (London, 1987), pp. 14–20.

number of them, including the elderly Lefèvre d'Etaples who died at her court at Nérac in 1536. Though her major writings, *Mirror of the Sinful Soul* and *Heptaméron,* did share certain heterodox ideas with the works of her mentors, like them she never abandoned the Gallican church for Protestantism, which was still not clearly defined in any case. That both Francis and Marguerite could so easily distinguish humanist scholarship from what they viewed as heresy, in fact, was clearly underscored in their reaction to the famous 'Placards affair' of 1534.[8]

In the early hours of Sunday morning, 18 October 1534, a great number of small, printed broadsheets were posted in conspicuous places throughout Paris and a number of other cities throughout northern France. Organized by a band of French Protestant exiles in Switzerland, the placards were intended to be seen by French Catholics on their way to mass later that morning. The author of the four brief paragraphs printed on the placards was one Antoine Marcourt, a French Protestant pamphleteer who was then residing in the Swiss city of Neuchâtel. The bold headline of the placard, printed in large capital letters, made it very clear that this was an organized attack on the holy eucharist: 'TRUE ARTICLES ON THE HORRIBLE, GROSS AND INSUFFERABLE ABUSES OF THE PAPAL MASS, invented directly contrary to the Holy Supper of Jesus Christ'. The vitriolic and polemical text went on to say that 'I invoke heaven and earth as witnesses to the truth against this pompous and arrogant popish mass, by which the whole world (if God does not soon remedy it) will be completely ruined, cast down, lost, and desolated; and because our Lord is so outrageously blasphemed and the people seduced and blinded by it, it can no longer be allowed to endure.' The placard went on to spell out four specific arguments against the Catholic mass in turn: (1) that since Christ had already performed a perfect sacrifice on the Cross, it was both unnecessary and blasphemous to pretend to repeat this sacrifice at Holy Communion; (2) that although the Catholic church falsely claims that 'Jesus Christ is corporally, really, and in fact entirely and personally in the flesh contained and concealed in the species of bread and wine, as grand and perfect as if he were living in the present', scripture makes it very clear that his body is with God in Heaven and cannot be in any way present in the bread and wine; (3) that the Catholic doctrine of transubstantiation is thus 'the doctrine of devils against all truth and openly contrary to all scripture'; and (4) that Communion is thus just a symbol in reverence of the memory of Christ's perfect sacrifice, not a miracle of sorts all over

---

[8] Much of this paragraph is based on Knecht, *Francis I,* pp. 132–45.

again. The most excoriating rhetoric was reserved for the end of the last paragraph, however:

By this [mass] the poor people are like ewes or miserable sheep, kept and maintained by these bewitching wolves [Catholic priests], then eaten, gnawed, and devoured. Is there anyone who would not say or think that this is larceny and debauchery? By this mass they have seized, destroyed, and swallowed up everything; they have disinherited kings, princes, nobles, merchants, and everyone else imaginable either dead or alive. Because of it, they live without any duties or responsibility to anyone or anything, even to the need to study. What more do you want? Do not be amazed then that they defend it with such force. They kill, burn, destroy, and murder as brigands all those who contradict them, for now all they have left is force. Truth is lacking in them, but it menaces them, follows them, and chases them; and in the end truth will find them out. By it they shall be destroyed. Fiat. Fiat. Amen.

The polemic of the placard was so acerbic, in fact, that even Theodore Beza, Calvin's future deputy in Geneva, distanced himself from it when he compiled the official history of the French Protestant church a few decades later. 'Everything was shattered by the indiscreet zeal of a few', he wrote, 'who having drawn up and printed certain articles in a sharp and violent style against the mass in the form of a placard in the Swiss city of Neuchâtel, not only posted and disseminated them throughout the squares and thoroughfares of the city of Paris, against the advice of some wiser heads, but they even posted one on the door of the king's bedchamber, who was then at Blois.' Though Francis I was actually a few miles west of Blois at his château at Amboise, Beza realized well enough the mistake of imposing one of these placards upon the royal person himself.[9]

Yet what so shocked and outraged French men and women on their way to mass that Sunday morning, indeed what made the 'Affair of the placards' so revolutionary, was not so much the heterodox doctrine of the eucharist itself but rather its social implications. For lay French Catholics the mass was the principal focus of reconciliation and communal satisfaction. Before receiving the host the communicants were required to seek forgiveness of their sins and redress any grievances with their neighbours. Only then could they be enjoined together by the sacrifice and satisfaction of the priest with the entire community of Christ living and dead. Thus, the 'communion' of the entire ritual was not so much a symbol to underscore the bond between an individual and God as the bond between the communicants themselves. As both John Bossy (for Catholics) and

[9] The text of the placard is printed as an appendix in the best study of the entire affair, Gabrielle Berthoud, *Antoine Maracourt, réformateur et pamphlétaire: du 'Livres des marchands' aux placards de 1534* (Geneva, 1973), pp. 287–9. Theodore Beza's reflection is in his *Histoire ecclésiastique*, I, 28–9.

David Sabean (for Lutherans) have demonstrated in their respective work, sixteenth-century Christians on both sides of the confessional divide were well aware of the serious consequences that awaited them should they go to mass without first attempting to remedy whatever discord existed in their own community. 'Whoever, therefore, eats the bread or drinks the cup of the Lord in an unworthy manner', according to St Paul (I Corinthians 11:27), 'will be guilty of profaning the body and the blood of the Lord'. And the result was that parishioners who were unable to overcome any personal discord generally stayed at home during the celebration of mass. It was only in the celebration of Communion that 'hostility became impersonal and retired beyond the borders of the community, to lurk in a dark exterior cast into more frightful shadow by the visible brightness of heaven among them'.[10] Or as Virginia Reinburg has shown so convincingly, for lay Catholics the mass 'was less sacrifice and sacrament than a communal rite of greeting, sharing, giving, receiving, and making peace'.[11] Thus, for French men and women on their way to mass that Sunday morning in 1534 the savage attack on the eucharist as evidenced in the 'sacramentarian' placards was much more than just a doctrinal joust with their Gallican theology; it was perceived as a dagger stuck in the heart of the body social.

On a somewhat different level, the placards were also an affront and threat to the body politic. Certainly Francis I viewed with alarm the last paragraph of the placard, excoriating Catholic priests for disinheriting kings and princes, even had it not been nailed to the door of his own royal bedchamber. But more generally, as the Most Christian King any attack on the authority of priests and the Catholic religion threatened to undermine his authority as sovereign ruler of France as well. Moreover, the 'sacramentarian' denial of the real presence in the eucharistic elements was an assault on the co-existence of the temporal and the sacred. Yet the king himself embodied that very same fusion of human and divine as his consecration and coronation *sacre* made abundantly clear. He even received Communion himself immediately upon acquiring his sacred and temporal authority to illustrate that very fact. Thus, for all these reasons the Protestants who disseminated the placards in October 1534 were viewed very differently from evangelical humanists like Briçonnet and Lefèvre d'Etaples. Unlike the latter who never threatened the

---

[10] John Bossy, *Christianity in the West, 1400–1700* (Oxford, 1985), p. 69. Also see the same author's 'The Mass as a Social Institution, 1200–1700', *Past and Present*, no. 100 (1983), 29–61; and David Warren Sabean, 'Communion and Community: the Refusal to Attend the Lord's Supper in the Sixteenth Century', in his *Power in the Blood: Popular Culture and Village Discourse in Early Modern Germany* (Cambridge, 1984), pp. 37–60.

[11] Virginia Reinburg, 'Liturgy and Laity in Late Medieval and Reformation France', *Sixteenth Century Journal*, vol. 23 (Fall 1992), 532.

Catholic church or the Gallican monarchy, the perpetrators of 1534 were not just heretics, but rebels. It is thus no surprise that just a few years later Francis authorized the sovereign courts of the crown – Parlements as well as lower courts – to take over the prosecution of heresy from the inquisitional courts of the church. The edict which put this into effect noted specifically that prosecuting heresy was 'a question of a seditious crime and the agitation of the state and public tranquility', and that even harbouring heretics was 'in itself a crime of divine and temporal lèse-majesté, popular sedition, and a disturbance of our state and the public peace'.[12] This more than anything else explains why Francis reacted as he did to the 'Affair of the placards' with calls for justice and retribution against all 'Lutherans', the catch-all term most Frenchmen used for any Protestants.

In the immediate aftermath, however, a search for culprits began and at least six were rounded up and burned by the end of November. When Francis returned to Paris in December, moreover, he ordered a general religious procession through the city, the likes of which the capital had never witnessed. On 21 January 1535 this spectacular event took place, and the intermingling of the sacred and profane, the royal and divine, could not have been more calculated or more explicit. The corporate community of Paris was represented: the monarchy, the law courts, the University of Paris, the religious orders, magistrates of the city hall, and members of the various craft guilds. Significantly, a number of religious relics were also displayed in the procession, including the crown of thorns normally displayed in the Sainte-Chapelle, which caused some people's hair to stand on end when they sighted it according to one witness. The principal focus of the entire event, however, was the *Corpus Christi*, the holy sacrament itself, borne by the bishop of Paris, who himself was walking reverently under a royal canopy carried by four princes of the blood (Francis's three young sons and the duke of Vendôme). And behind the sacrament walked Francis himself, bareheaded and dressed in black. The co-existence of the royal and the sacred, the king and his royal offspring walking together with the very sacrament which had been profaned and desecrated by the 'sacramentarians' just three months earlier, could not have been more explicit. The day's events culminated with prayers, masses, and the execution of six more heretics just in case anyone had overlooked the point of the entire exercise. While recent historians are quite right to point out that the 'Affair of the placards' did not in itself turn Francis I from a monarch sympathetic to heterodoxy into a

---

[12] Isambert, *et al.*, *Recueil général des anciennes lois françaises, depuis l'an 420, jusqu'à la Révolution de 1789*, XIII (Paris, 1828), 679–80 (edict of 1 June 1540).

bloodthirsty persecutor of heretics, it was one of those signal events which did help to crystallize and underscore the difference between heterodoxy and heresy. And from 1534, most French Catholics forever perceived that Protestantism and rebellion went hand in hand.[13]

In the wave of persecutions that followed the 'Affair of the placards', one of the many who fled France into exile was twenty-five year old John Calvin (1509–64). Trained as a lawyer at the Universities of Orléans and Bourges, Calvin's legal background which immersed him deeply in Christian humanist scholarship would play a major role in shaping the thought and ideas of this would-be reformer. Unlike Luther, who was not a product of a Christian humanist education, Calvin was enamored with classical learning in the same way that Lefèvre d'Etaples was in Meaux. Calvin had written a humanist commentary on a treatise of Seneca in 1532, which had given him some small degree of notoriety among French humanists. And the reformer was even sheltered by Margaret of Angoulême at her court in Nérac in 1534, where he had the chance to meet and discuss his ideas with Lefèvre d'Etaples directly. By January 1535, however, when he arrived in Basel from France in the wake of the 'Affair of the placards', Calvin had already become infused with the evangelicism of a still undefined Protestantism. As he himself noted much later, 'So it came to pass that I was withdrawn from the study of arts and was transferred to the study of law. I endeavoured faithfully to apply myself to this, in obedience to my father's wishes. But God, by the secret hand of his providence, eventually pointed my life in a different direction.'[14] Moreover, his stay in Switzerland allowed him to come in contact with some of the leaders of his generation of Protestant reformers, above all, Guillaume Farel in Geneva and Martin Bucer in Strasbourg. Although Calvin had already broken with Rome when he published the first edition of his famous *Institution of the Christian Religion* in Basel early the next year in March 1536, it was his sojourn in Strasbourg from 1538 to 1541 which fundamentally forged and shaped his evangelical ideas, as later editions of the *Institution* would make clear.

After the wave of repression in France in 1534–35 and Calvin's own exile, it is ironic that the first edition of the *Institution* should be dedicated to none other than the French king Francis I. Although some historians have suggested that Calvin may have felt that Francis was still wavering

---

[13] A number of points in this and the preceding paragraph are based on Knecht, *Francis I*, pp. 248–52; and Donald R. Kelley, *The Beginning of Ideology: Consciousness and Society in the French Reformation* (Cambridge, 1981), esp. pp. 13–19, 199, and 324.

[14] From Calvin's introduction to his *Commentary upon the Book of Psalms* (1557), quoted in G. R. Potter and Mark Greengrass, eds., *John Calvin* (London, 1983), p. 10.

on whether to continue his persecution of Protestants and was thus hoping to influence the king to become more sympathetic to the movement, the bulk of the preface is concerned chiefly with trying to prove that French Protestants were not the seditious rebels and disturbers of the public peace they were perceived to be since the 'Affair of the placards'. Since the boundaries between orthodoxy and heterodoxy were still not as well defined as the Sorbonne pretended, Calvin certainly hoped to persuade the king to change his mind. The dedicatory preface to the *Institution* was thus really an apology for his countrymen's actions in France.

But I return to you, O King. May you be not at all moved by those vain accusations with which our adversaries are trying to inspire terror in you: that by this new gospel (for so they call it) men strive and seek only after the opportunity for seditions and impugnity for all crimes ... And we are unjustly charged, too, with intentions of ... contriving the overthrow of kingdoms – we, from whom not one seditious word was ever heard ... [and] who do not cease to pray for the full prosperity of yourself and your kingdom, although we are now fugitives from home!

Whether unjustly accused or not, the fact that Calvin was obliged to make such an apology for French evangelicals is an indication of just how widespread the perception of Protestants as rebels was among French Catholics. Though Calvin would never be able to convince Francis, or later his son Henry II, that his followers were not a threat to law and order in France, his *Institution of the Christian Religion* nevertheless became, after the Bible itself, the single most important influence on French Protestantism.

Despite the fact that it underwent numerous revisions, amendments, and reorganizations right through the final Latin edition published in 1559, the *Institution* did not really add to the corpus of Protestant theology in any significant way. That is to say, the principal Protestant doctrines of justification by faith, primacy of scripture, and the priesthood of all believers had all been enunciated in print by Luther as early as 1520. What Calvin did do, however, was offer a much fuller and more logical analysis of these doctrines than Luther – and doubtless his legalistic training was responsible – with the result that the *Institution* proved to be a much more effective handbook for educating and teaching than Luther's polemical treatises, particularly when a French translation of the original Latin was published in 1541. An example is Calvin's analysis of predestination, a doctrine closely tied to justification by faith and over which Luther and Erasmus had argued in print a decade earlier. Although just as fundamentally important to Lutheran doctrine as Calvin's, it was the exposition of this doctrine in book 3, chapters 21–25 of the *Institution* that made it a hallmark of Protestant reform. What Luther had mentioned only in passing, though he understood it to be central to the doctrine of justification by faith, Calvin devoted nearly a hundred pages to explain: 'eternal election, by which God has predestined some to salvation, others to destruction'.

The really significant departures from Luther, however, were not theological but social: specifically in the practice and enforcement of doctrine. It may seem ironic that someone who was so determined to separate human actions and works on earth from eternal salvation – and this is really the gist of the doctrine of justification, grace, and predestination – was so completely absorbed with re-ordering the temporal world. Indeed, as his most recent biographer has pointed out, Calvin himself was convinced that he was called by God 'to set the world right ... to bring the world to order'. 'Truly', Calvin noted, 'we ought to labour most for our own time and take it most into account. The future should not be overlooked, but what is present and urgent requires our attention more'.[15] Thus, one could say that the really distinguishing feature of Calvin – or rather, Calvinism – was the emphasis on social discipline.

Given the fact that Christianity itself was perceived by Protestants and Catholics alike as a community of believers rather than a body of beliefs, the attention to social discipline is hardly surprising. And it is clear from Calvin's writings in particular, that for him religion played the role of a 'bridle' in that community. God the creator naturally intended a certain order for His world, and it was Christianity which defined this order. Thus, for Calvin there was a real concern for the ordering of the temporal world which mankind could still affect, as opposed to the heavenly world, which God had already pre-ordained. In this context, a primary function of religion was to bridle the mind, the spirit, the will, the emotions, and above all the flesh. 'Each of us should watch himself closely', he argued, 'lest we be carried away by violent feeling'. Above all, we must 'bridle our affections before they become ungovernable'.[16] The Christian life was thus characterized by discipline and moderation: 'The life of the godly ought to be tempered with frugality and sobriety [so] that throughout its course a sort of perpetual fasting may appear'.[17] Thus, while Luther had emphasized the 'freedom of a Christian' (the title of one of his three 1520

---

[15] Quoted in William J. Bouwsma, *John Calvin: A Sixteenth-Century Portrait* (Oxford, 1988), p. 191, a book to which I owe much for the paragraphs that follow (particularly chap. 5).

[16] Quoted in ibid., p. 88.

[17] John Calvin, *Institutes of the Christian Religion*, ed. John T. McNeill, 2 vols. (Philadelphia, 1960), I, 611 (book 3, chap 3, para. 17).

treatises), Calvin's emphasis was much more focused on the servitude and moral repression of a Christian.

But how was Calvin able to achieve this social discipline in Geneva, where he established his godly rule after 1541? Ironically, it was Calvin's subtle fusion of church and state – similar in principle to that of the pope in Rome and the monarchy in France, though very different in practice – that was to provide for the enforcement of social discipline in a godly community. Like nearly all sixteenth-century political thinkers Calvin was content to accept that the authority of the state (princes, magistrates, republics, etc.) came from God precisely to maintain God's order on earth. And he certainly did not

disapprove of princes interposing their authority in ecclesiastical matters, provided it was done to preserve the order of the church, not to disrupt it; and to establish discipline, not to dissolve it. For since the church does not have the power to coerce, and ought not to seek it (I am speaking of civil coercion), it is the duty of godly kings and princes to sustain religion by laws, edicts, and judgments.[18]

For Calvin, then, the state not only had the right to intervene in spiritual matters, but it was its *duty* to do so.

Civil government has as its appointed end, so long as we live among men, to cherish and protect the outward worship of God, to defend sound doctrine of piety and the position of the church, to adjust our life to the society of men, to form our social behaviour to civil righteousness, to reconcile us with one another, and to promote general peace and tranquility.[19]

And exactly how the state was supposed to carry out this responsibility was spelled out by Calvin when he drew up the charter of the Genevan church in September and October 1541, the so-called 'Draft ecclesiastical ordinances'.

Social discipline in Geneva after 1541 was thus effectively regulated by a group of a dozen elders, who according to the ordinances were to be selected by the three Genevan city councils who governed the city. The 'Little Council', the Council of Sixty, and Council of Two Hundred had only recently assumed civil authority of the city from the local Catholic bishop, and it was Calvin's success in convincing these magistrates of the benefits of their protection and participation in his church that enabled it to succeed. The main function of the elders, who were all appointed by the civil magistrates rather than the church, was 'to have oversight of the life of everyone, to admonish amicably those whom they see to be erring

---

[18] Ibid., II, 1228–19 (book 4, chap. 12, para. 16). Also see Bouwsma, *John Calvin*, pp. 204–13.

[19] Calvin, *Institutes*, II, 1487 (book 4, chap. 20, para. 2).

or to be living a disordered life, and, where it is required, to enjoin fraternal corrections'. The elders were to be selected from every quarter of the city and were supposed 'to keep an eye on everybody'.[20] The elders reported every week to the company of pastors of the church, and meeting as a consistory these representatives of church and state would interview each and every backslider, sinner, fornicator, adulterer, or law-breaker called before it to mete out the respective punishment. With the power to admonish and even excommunicate, the consistory acted as an effective policing agent in Geneva, to ensure that the bridle of religion was executing its function of social control. If certain repeat offenders required more serious punishment, the consistory could recommend that the secular magistrates impose fines, community service, bodily punishment, or ultimately even death. It was in Strasbourg during his stay there in the late 1530s that Calvin first learned of the effectiveness of the consistory from his friend Martin Bucer. And one historian has even called Bucer's *On the Kingdom of Christ*, rather than Calvin's *Institution*, 'the ur-text of Reformation *disciplina*'.[21] Though many of its critics considered the elders no more than 'peeping toms', the consistory did more than anything else to make Calvin's Geneva a very different place from Luther's Saxony. While both reformers had a very similar theology and even a similar vision of a more godly community, Calvin used the consistory to enforce social discipline in Geneva in a much more effective and regulated manner than elsewhere. The power of excommunication, not enjoyed in similar bodies in Strasbourg and Zurich, was inevitably what gave the consistory such power. And for all its critics, it was the success with which the consistory was able to enforce social order and discipline in Geneva, as much as its theology, that made this new religion so attractive to many.[22]

The point of this entire discussion of Calvin's ideas (and Calvinism in practice) is precisely that this particular form of Protestantism shared a vision of church and state that was entirely incompatible with that of most politically-minded French men and women. In France, the fusion of church and state was in the person of the monarch, who was bound by his office to protect the Catholic church. Indeed, because the Gallican king of France was the *Rex christianissimus*, his power and authority were defined and clarified by the very theology – particularly the powers of the

[20] 'Draft Ecclesiastical Ordinances, September and October 1541' printed in John Dillenberger, ed., *John Calvin: Selections from his Writings* (Missoula, MT, 1975), p. 235.

[21] Bossy, *Christianity in the West*, p. 180.

[22] A useful analysis of the consistory is in E. William Monter, *Calvin's Geneva* (New York, 1967) pp. 136–9.

priest in regard to the laity – that Protestantism so sharply criticized. In France the amalgamation of church and state thus had the effect of using the former to legitimate the latter, whereas in Geneva the effect was rather the opposite. Thus, for most Frenchmen one of the essential theological cornerstones of Calvinism appeared to jeopardize or at least to threaten the authority of the king of France. In the short run this meant that Calvinism became politicized when pastors were first dispatched into France in the 1550s as part of Calvin's evangelical campaign to spread the word. At least eighty-eight of them (and more likely many more) who had been trained in Geneva made efforts to organize Calvinist congregations in France from 1555 to 1562 alone. In the long run, however, it meant that either the Gallican monarchy or the reformed religion from Geneva would have to modify its essential make-up significantly if either was to accommodate the other. Despite its ready acceptance in other parts of Europe, the success of Calvinism in France would ultimately hinge on this basic fact.

The death of Francis I in 1547 and the succession of his son Henry II did not fundamentally alter the pattern of suppression of Protestants by the crown that had more or less existed since the 'Affair of the placards'. Nevertheless, the crown's position vis-à-vis the French Protestants became much more complex, while relations between the French monarchy and the papacy became more strained. The latter deteriorating relationship was largely the result of Pope Paul III's convocation of the Council of Trent in the final years of the reign of Francis I. The council, which was to meet off and on for the next eighteen years, was the high-water mark of the Catholic church in its efforts at first to try to resolve its differences with the Protestants in order to restore the unity of Christendom, and then eventually to reject outright all Protestant doctrine as heresy. Both Francis and Henry had suspected that the Holy See's sympathies toward the French in the Habsburg–Valois dispute in Italy had significantly shifted since the days of the Concordat of Bologna. And the selection of Trent, an imperial city, as the site of the council only confirmed their suspicions. Moreover, the king of France had no desire to participate in the amelioration of the religious troubles in Germany that were plaguing the emperor Charles V, as any distraction to the emperor, including heresy, worked to favour the French in their war against the Habsburgs. Thus, France had reacted coolly to the Council of Trent from the beginning when it opened in 1545. When Julius III succeeded Paul III as pope in 1549, however, French fears of a pro-Habsburg papacy became even more acute. The bull convening the first session of the council under the new pope in November 1550 was met with much more than indifference in France, as Henry II ordered all his bishops to remain in their dioceses rather than journey to Trent and to begin making preparations for a French national council of the Gallican church, over which the king himself would preside. Moreover, Henry cut off the flow of annates to Rome, revenue the papacy had been entitled to ever since the Concordat of Bologna. When Julius III responded in kind by threatening to excommunicate and depose the king of France and replace him with the emperor's son, Prince Philip of Spain, relations between France and Rome reached a nadir and resembled the conflict between Philip the Fair and Boniface VIII two hundred and fifty years earlier. That dispute, of course, had fundamentally weakened ecclesiastical authority throughout Europe when the king of France, under a similar threat of excommunication, not only refused to back down but sent a French army to Italy in 1303 to kidnap Pope Boniface. It was in the midst of this 'Gallican crisis' in 1551 that anti-papal, pro-Gallican rhetoric reached its apex, including Jean du Tillet's 'On the liberties of the Gallican church' cited at the beginning of this chapter. With the recent defection of England, where the succession of Edward VI in 1547 only further undermined the Catholic church by formally adopting Protestant doctrine and a state church, further division could only weaken Catholic efforts to combat a growing Protestant menace throughout Christendom. And it was this argument that eventually forced a compromise with Rome, as both Henry and Julius backed down from their previous polemic. Henry agreed to postpone any meeting of a Gallican council, while the pope temporarily agreed to allow the king to continue collecting annates in France. Although a new schism was avoided, the 'Gallican crisis' of 1551 only further underscored the seriousness with which the king took his duties to defend the church in France, and that included protection from outside interference from Rome.[23]

But what were Henry's attitudes towards Protestantism in France? The creation immediately upon his succession of the *chambre ardente*, the special 'burning chamber' in the Parlement of Paris devoted exclusively to the prosecution of heresy, is clear evidence that he was a zealous pursuer of heretics. An analysis of the surviving records of this chamber, however, reveals a more complex situation. From May 1548 to March 1550, the only period for which records of this court have survived, the magistrates prosecuted a total of 323 persons for heresy. Of that number thirty-seven (11.5 per cent) were executed, with six of the thirty-seven

---

[23] For further analysis of this episode see Lucien Romier, *Les origines politiques des guerres de religion*, 2 vols. (Paris, 1913–14), I, 220–92; and Marc Venard, 'Une réforme gallicane? Le projet de concile national de 1551', *Revue d'histoire de l'église de France*, vol. 67 (1981), 201–21.

being burned as unrepentant heretics, and the other thirty-one receiving the less painful death by hanging for admitting and confessing their errors prior to execution. The other 286 individuals received punishments ranging from banishment and confiscation of property (6.5 per cent), beating (6.2 per cent), public penance (20.7 per cent), chastisement (9.6 per cent), fines (0.9 per cent), or were held over for further consideration (32.5 per cent) or actually acquitted and released without any punishment (12.1 per cent). The 11.5 per cent execution rate – or actually 17 per cent of those cases that received a final judgment – do mark a dramatic rise in executions from the six months immediately preceding the introduction of the *chambre ardente* in October 1547, when the Parlement of Paris executed only two of fifty-seven persons it prosecuted for heresy (3.5 per cent). This should not necessarily be interpreted solely as the result of the renewed zeal of Henry II, however repressive the new court might be. A special chamber of judges established only to hear heresy cases was always more likely to find and prosecute Protestants than the general criminal chamber called the *tournelle*, which had to deal with criminal cases of all types as well as heresy. This becomes clear in comparing the Parlement of Paris with the provincial courts. In the late 1540s, for example, the Parlement of Paris tried more than six times the number of heresy cases than the Parlement of Toulouse and meted out more than six times the number of death sentences for heresy.[24] Moreover, the growth of Protestantism in France since the days of the 'Affair of the placards' rather than the growth of the crown's zeal to prosecute them could also partly explain the rise in the number of cases in the early years of Henry II.

What the records of the *chambre ardente* show most clearly, however, is that Henry II associated the problem of heresy with the Catholic clergy. The occupations of 160 of the 323 defendants who were tried are recorded, and the pattern is a significant one. Artisans and small shopkeepers made up the largest number (37.5 per cent), followed by clergymen both regular and secular (34.4 per cent), merchants (10 per cent), royal officers (8.8 per cent), barristers and solicitors (5.6 per cent), and nobles (3.8 per cent).[25] At first glance it might appear that Henry's concern was primarily a social one to focus on the lower classes. But the artisans were significantly under-represented among the victims

[24] William Monter, *Judging the French Reformation: Heresy Trials by Sixteenth-Century Parlements* (Cambridge, MA, 1999), p. 136.
[25] Quoted in Jonathan Dewald, 'The "Perfect Magistrate": Parlementaires and Crime in Sixteenth-century Rouen', *Archiv für Reformationsgeschichte*, vol. 67 (1976), 298. Much of the preceding paragraphs is based on Frederic J. Baumgartner, *Henry II: King of France, 1547–1559* (Durham, NC, 1988), pp. 114–32.

compared to their proportion in the population at large, and no peasants were executed at all. On the other hand, the percentages of merchants, officers, and nobles executed compares favourably to their proportion in the population at large. The real victims of the *Chambre ardente* were the clergy, who made up fewer than five per cent of the population but more than a third of the total victims of Henry's repression. This does not take away from the king's general perception that heresy and rebellion went hand in hand, but it does suggest that Henry was not just focusing on heresy among the lower orders.

In the infamous edict of Châteaubriant of June 1551, where Henry enunciated a more comprehensive and legalistic ban on Protestantism with increased efforts to enforce it, the intention was to eradicate sedition and rebellion as much as heterodox opinion. To be sure, the edict did proscribe the printing, sale, and even possession of Protestant opinions, as well as outline in much greater detail the powers of censorship of the courts (articles 2–22). More significantly, however, the edict was concerned with illicit assemblies of heretics and spelled out incentives for would-be informers (articles 27–33). Any informer would receive one-third of the confiscated property of anyone he or she turned in. Moreover, any Protestant who attended an illicit assembly would be pardoned from similar offences if he or she became an informer. The edict not only prohibited anyone from harbouring or sheltering heretics, as had been the case since 1534, but magistrates were now given the power to seek them out, including the right to search private homes. With further clauses aimed at preventing Protestants from holding any public office but especially those in the sovereign courts (articles 23–24), or teaching in any school, academy, or university (articles 34–35), the emphasis on public order was clear. The king even required the Parlement of Paris to hold a special *mercuriale* every three months, so-called because it met on Wednesdays, in order to examine the magistrates themselves to see if any of them had fallen prey to heretical ideas (article 25). The main thrust of the edict was clearly spelled out in article 1, however, where the magistrates were commissioned to seek out those of 'the Lutheran heresy' as they were still incorrectly called, and 'to punish them as fomenters of sedition, schismatics, disturbers of public harmony and tranquility, rebels, and disobedient evaders of our ordinances and commandments'.[26] Under Henry II more than ever, Protestants were

---

[26] The edict is printed in Eugène and Emile Haag, *La France protestante*, 10 vols. (Paris, 1846–59), X, 17–29 (quote from article 1 on p. 19). A good summary of the edict, on which my own discussion is based, is N. M. Sutherland, *The Huguenot Struggle for Recognition* (New Haven, 1980), pp. 44–7.

perceived as dangerous threats to the social order, as fractious rebels who fomented sedition among the lower classes of society.

But were French Protestants on the eve of the Wars of Religion really from the lower classes as Henry II and other contemporaries believed? Many historians have thought so. The sociology and social geography of French Protestantism – Who were they? How many of them were there? And where did they live? – have always been important questions and the answers are by no means clear. Mark Greengrass has recently estimated that in the decade 1560–70, surely the high water-mark of their success, there were roughly 1,200 Protestant churches in France. Even allowing for a generous 1,500 communicating members for each congregation, and some were much larger than this, of course, at most Protestant strength would have reached about 1,800,000 members – or roughly 10 per cent of the total population of the kingdom.[27] And as Map 2 shows, these Protestants were by no means evenly distributed throughout the kingdom. While there were a number of Protestant churches north of the Loire, particularly in the province of Normandy, the bulk of them were located in the south in an arc-like distribution from La Rochelle on the Atlantic coast, down to Bordeaux and Toulouse, then over to Montpellier, and up to Lyon. This crescent of strength in Guyenne, Languedoc, Provence, and Dauphiné – that region usually called the Midi – played a significant role in the history of the Huguenots, as French Protestants came to be called in the religious wars. Moreover, it is equally clear from the map that there were also areas of France where Protestantism was peculiarly absent, particularly the border provinces of Burgundy, Champagne, Picardy, and Brittany. How is the historian to explain this 'fertile crescent' of Protestant strength in the Midi, as well as its relative absence else-where? Surely proximity to Geneva is not especially relevant, as Burgundy would have been among the first areas to be proselytized and Guyenne among the last. Nor does the cultural division between the *langue d'oc* (Occitan, where *oc* is the word for 'yes') in the south and the *langue d'oeuil* (French, where *oui* is the word for 'yes') in the north offer any better explanation, as Protestantism appealed mainly to those in the Midi who spoke French rather than Occitan. As historians have recently pointed out, hardly any effort was made to translate the scriptures or any of the Protestant liturgy into Occitan during this period, nor is there any evidence of preaching in the local dialect. The language and culture of Calvinism in France was clearly

---

[27] Greengrass, *French Reformation*, p. 43. Much of the discussion that follows is based on pp. 42–62 of this useful study.

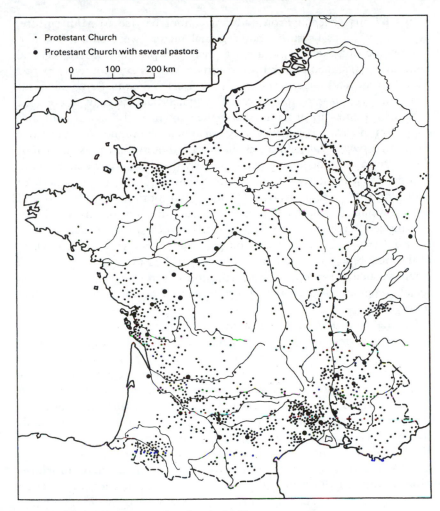

Map 2 Protestant churches in 1562

French.[28] Nor was Protestantism especially attracted to those towns where there were printing presses. Lyon is one notable exception, of course, but for the most part the printing industry was located mainly in northern France rather than in the south. How, then, is the social geography of Protestantism in France to be explained?

[28] See Emmanuel Le Roy Ladurie, *Les paysans de Languedoc*, 2 vols. (Paris, 1966), I, 333–6; and Greengrass, *French Reformation*, p. 45.

Just because French Protestantism cannot be tied to Midi culture, does not necessarily mean that regional factors were entirely absent. Languedoc, for example, is a good case of a province where regional institutions managed to link Protestantism with its autonomous struggle with the crown for lower taxes and fewer fiscal demands. Languedoc was one of the *pays d'états*, those provinces which had the right to convoke provincial estates in order to assist the crown in the assessment and collection of royal taxes (Burgundy, Brittany, Dauphiné, and Provence were other *pays d'états*). And it is significant that in the 1550s and 1560s the estates of Languedoc – and particularly the third estate composed of bourgeois representatives from the towns, many of them sympathetic to Protestantism – made overt attempts to expropriate church land and clerical wealth to help meet their fiscal demands from the crown. Thus, in Languedoc regional autonomy and the Protestant Reformation came to be linked together when local bourgeois saw their own survival and that of the new religion going hand in hand. And as the Midi was an area where particularism and regional autonomy were especially strong, the social geography of French Protestantism becomes somewhat less murky.[29]

On the other hand, in Burgundy, another *pays d'état*, precisely the opposite occurred. In that province the provincial estates, the Parlement of Dijon, and the city councils of the major towns (Dijon, Beaune, Auxonne, among others) all came to perceive their regional identity as well as their future as tied to the traditional church rather than to Protestantism. Partly this was because the duchy of Burgundy had only recently been incorporated into the French crown in the late fifteenth century, and when the province promised its allegiance in 1479 to Louis XI after the assassination of Charles the Bold, it was upon the condition that the king would guard and protect the Catholic religion in the province. More importantly, a significant sector of the Burgundian economy was tied to the wine industry. Already in the sixteenth century the Côte-d'Or had a reputation for producing the best red wine in Europe. 'The wine of Beaune, reigns all alone', noted one authority.[30] And significantly, much of the land occupied by the vineyards either was owned or had ties to local

---

[29] Le Roy Ladurie, *Paysans de Languedoc*, I, 359–62; and for the background to this issue, see James E. Brink, 'Les états de Languedoc de 1515 à 1560: une autonomie en question', *Annales du Midi*, vol. 88 (1976), 287–305. The Reformation in the town of Montauban is a good case study of this process in action. See Philip Conner, *Huguenot Heartland: Montauban and Southern French Calvinism during the Wars of Religion* (Aldershot, 2002).

[30] Barthélemy de Chasseneux, *Catalogus gloriae mundi* (Lyon, 1546), p. 315: '*Vinum belnense, super omnia recense.*'

cathedrals, abbeys, and monasteries. Moreover, the winegrowers who pruned the vines tended to remain culturally tied to the Catholic church almost to a person because of the bonds of community, commensality, and sociability of their occupation. 'I am the vine and my Father is the wine-grower', stated Jesus in the gospels, 'I am the vine and you are the branches'.[31] That the fruit of their labour alone had been chosen by God to become Christ's blood, and then had become further elevated by being consumed only by priests during communion in the late Middle Ages, proved to be too great a cultural hurdle for Protestantism to overcome in Burgundy. Thus unlike in Languedoc, regional identity and autonomy came to be linked to traditional Christianity in Burgundy.[32] The cases demonstrated by these two provinces seem to suggest, moreover, that the social geography of French Protestantism hinged more on local factors and traditions than on any mono-causal determinant like language, literacy, or proximity to Geneva. This is not to suggest that these factors were not relevant. Clearly, a religion that stressed the Word was more likely to succeed where that Word could be both read and disseminated in print and heard by Geneva-trained pastors. The local context, however, espe-cially how the local elites perceived the church in relation to their own situation, may ultimately have played a crucial role in determining the success or failure of Protestantism in any given region or province.

If the social geography of French Protestantism is problematical, the sociology of the movement is even more so. Though the new religion attracted converts from virtually all walks of life, countless historians have tried to link the success of French Protestantism with one particular social group or another. The fact remains that with 90 per cent of the population as a whole rejecting the new religion, a clear majority of *all* social groups remained Catholic. Nevertheless, ever since Karl Marx and Max Weber sparked off the debate nearly a century ago, historians have argued that the advent of Protestantism in the sixteenth century initiated a social as well as a religious reformation. Given the explicit fusion of 'religion and society' in the sixteenth century (see Introduction), this is hardly surpris-ing. Henri Hauser was one of the first to take up the mantle of the social reformation at the turn of the twentieth century when he tied the cause of French Calvinism to the coat tails of the urban artisans and working classes: 'It was not solely against doctrinal corruptions and against eccle-siastical abuses, but also against misery and iniquity that the lower classes rebelled', he argued. 'They sought in the Bible not only for the doctrine of

[31] John 15: 1, 5.
[32] Mack P. Holt, 'Wine, Community and Reformation in Sixteenth-century Burgundy', *Past and Present*, no. 138 (February 1993), 58–93.

salvation by grace, but for proofs of the primitive equality of all men.'[33] A similar argument was taken up some thirty years later by Lucien Febvre between the two world wars. More subtle and persuasive than Hauser, Febvre argued for a rethinking of the French Reformation altogether and urged his colleagues to abandon traditional approaches which focused on specificity (whether the French Reformation was unique), dating (whether it pre-dated Luther), and nationality (whether French Protestantism was a nationalist movement). More important, he argued, were the social forces of Protestantism, and specifically the question of which social groups were most attracted to it. Febvre looked beyond Hauser's urban artisans and higher up the social ladder to embrace merchants, the magistracy, and officers of the crown, in short, the *bourgeoisie*, social groups which turned to Protestantism as a result of their search for 'a religion more suited to their new needs, more in agreement with their changed conditions of their social life'. In a *tour de force* of historical argument, Febvre went on to analyse why these middle classes found Calvinism so attractive:

The whole of the merchant bourgeoisie, which untiringly engaged in trade over the highways and vast seas of the world ... that bourgeoisie composed of lawyers and officers of the Crown ... in short, all those who in exercising precise trades and minute techniques developed within themselves a temperament inclined to seek practical solutions ... all had equal need of a clear, reasonably human and gently fraternal religion which would serve as their light support.

Thus Febvre's social foundation of the Reformation was a far cry from Hauser's urban proletariat composed of 'mechanics'. His view was that in a period of economic change and social flux such as the sixteenth century, it was only 'the best, noblest and liveliest minds who endeavoured to make the tremendous effort required to fashion for themselves a faith adapted to their needs'.[34]

During the past three decades, however, historians interested in the social history of the Reformation have managed to go far beyond these older approaches of Hauser and Febvre. A more sophisticated quantitative approach to the subject based on unpublished material in local archives has allowed Emmanuel Le Roy Ladurie, Natalie Davis, Philip

---

[33] Henri Hauser, 'The French Reformation and the French People in the Sixteenth Century', *American Historical Review*, vol. 4 (1899), 217–27; and in French as 'La Réforme et les classes populaires en France au XVIe siècle', in his *Etudes sur la Réforme française* (Paris, 1909), pp. 83–103.

[34] Lucien Febvre, 'The Origins of the French Reformation: A Badly-put Question', in his *A New Kind of History and other Essays*, ed. Peter Burke (New York, 1973), pp. 44–107; original French edition, 'Une question mal posée: les origines de la Réforme française', *Revue historique*, vol. 161 (1929), 1–73.

Benedict, and David Rosenberg among others, to replace the rather impressionistic explanations of Hauser and Febvre with analyses supported by precise statistical data of the social make-up of the Huguenot movement and how it compared to society as a whole. And though local and regional variations must be weighed carefully, we simply now know a great deal more about why Protestantism was so successful in France in the mid-sixteenth century, who was attracted to it, and why. It is clear, for example, that in its initial stages French Protestantism was largely an urban movement composed of adherents who, for the most part, were literate. It is no coincidence that in Montpellier, for example, on a list of Huguenots in 1560 nearly 85 per cent of those whose professions were recorded were either artisans or learned professionals, while fewer than 5 per cent were peasants, day-labourers, or farmers. In the same city illiteracy was low among artisans (26 per cent) and high among peasants (72 per cent). In a religion that put so much emphasis on the primacy of scripture it is hardly surprising that it would draw its initial strength from among those best able to interpret the printed gospel.[35]

Moreover, certain trades and professions seemed to provide a disproportionate number of converts to the new religion. These included not only those trades in which literacy was an essential skill and which were also important for the propagation of the new religion (printers, booksellers, etc.), but also a number of vocations which were both highly skilled and in which there was some novelty. Natalie Davis has described the sociology of Protestantism in Lyon, where trades involving new technology (printers), new claims for prestige (painters, jewelers, goldsmiths), and recent establishment in the city (manufacturers and finishers of silk cloth) were all overrepresented in the Lyonnais Protestant movement in the 1560s. Members from virtually all social and economic levels within those particular vocations were attracted to the new religion, while very few members of any status of older and less skilled trades (such as butchers, bakers, vintners, etc.) became Protestants. Philip Benedict's data from Rouen tend to support Davis's findings in Lyon: well-educated and high status artisans were overrepresented in the Protestant movement of that city, while more traditional and lower status trades – the food and drink trades and textile trades, particularly weavers – tended to be underrepresented compared to their proportions in Rouen as a whole. Apart from the very wealthiest and most destitute, every social rank in the city was represented in the Protestant movement; but as in Lyon, they were generally drawn from those professions where 'the degree of literacy,

---

[35] Le Roy Ladurie, *Paysans de Languedoc*, I, 343–5.

self-confidence, and personal independence needed to reject the tutelage of the clergy and embrace the idea of a priesthood of all believers' was already important. Thus, with a far greater degree of sophistication and persuasion, recent social historians have echoed the view of Lucien Febvre that French Protestantism was initially at least a movement of 'the literate and self-assertive'.[36]

The problem of local and regional variation is significant, however, because historians of other parts of France have argued that Protestantism in Montpellier, Lyon, and Rouen is not necessarily representative of the movement as a whole. Indeed, in various cities throughout the kingdom, especially Amiens, it has been argued that Protestantism was hardly a movement of the independent, self-assertive, and literate middle classes, but a movement of the frustrated, exploited, and economically oppressed. David Rosenberg has demonstrated that in Amiens the bedrock of Protestantism was the city's textile workers, especially the woolcombers and weavers, 'a relatively disadvantaged section of the population from an economic standpoint'. These textile workers were not especially literate compared to other artisans in the city and were certainly neither independent nor self-assertive, with the power of the cloth merchants virtually controlling their livelihood. Above all, the precariousness of their economic position was nothing like the more prosperous printworkers in Lyon or merchants and artisans of Rouen. Concerning the Protestant weavers of Amiens, 'one is left with the impression not only of poverty, but of a precarious kind of poverty, which a small reversal of fortune might quickly convert into destitution'. With a quantitative sophistication that is entirely convincing, Rosenberg has thus turned the Protestantism of Le Roy Ladurie, Davis, Benedict, and ultimately Febvre on its head, and has produced a movement that more clearly resembles the proletarian mechanics of Henri Hauser.[37]

---

[36] Natalie Davis, 'Strikes and Salvation at Lyon', in her *Society and Culture in Early Modern France* (Stanford, 1975), pp. 1–16; and Philip Benedict, *Rouen during the Wars of Religion* (Cambridge, 1981), pp. 71–94. Also see Timothy Watson, 'Preaching, Printing, Psalm Singing: The Making and Unmaking of the Reformed Church in Lyon, 1550–1572', in Raymond A. Mentzer and Andrew Spicer, eds., *Society and Culture in the Huguenot World, 1559–1685* (Cambridge, 2002), pp. 10–28.

[37] David L. Rosenberg, 'Social Experience and Religious Choice, a Case Study: The Protestant Weavers and Woolcombers of Amiens in the Sixteenth Century', unpublished PhD thesis, Yale University, 1978, chap. 2, esp. pp. 74–5. A more recent study based on research in seven provincial cities, though one without the quantitative sophistication of Rosenberg's work, has echoed his main argument that the French Reformation was a reaction by the journeymen and poorer craftsmen to a decline in living standards, economic difficulty, and fiscal oppression. See Henry Heller, *The Conquest of Poverty: The Calvinist Revolt in Sixteenth-century France* (Leiden, 1986), esp. p. 234.

What are we to make of all this? Simply that local social and cultural variables could produce a variety of different contexts which were conducive to the growth of Protestantism? For one thing, sixteenth-century Amiens was a very different place from Lyon and Rouen, the former being a textile centre where the clear bulk of *all* artisans worked in the textile trades. Both absolutely and proportionately, the numbers of printers, goldsmiths, tanners, and booksellers in Amiens was significantly smaller than in either Lyon or Rouen, the two largest cities in France outside Paris. On the other hand, the textile industry was relatively new to Amiens, only becoming fully established in the late fifteenth century. And as a result, most of the woolcombers and weavers who turned to Protestantism there – perhaps as many as 90 per cent – were first generation textile workers, plying their skills in a different trade from their fathers. In this respect, they had more in common with the more prosperous printers and silkworkers in Lyon than is at first apparent. It was the particular social context in which the Amiens textile workers existed that is at the root of their overwhelming support of the new religion. Due to the size and importance of their profession to the local economy, local authorities did not allow them to follow the normal path of corporate organization and control practised by other craftsmen in the city. The textile workers thus did not enjoy the autonomy to regulate themselves or the same corporate identity common to other artisans in Amiens, and as a result, sought for such an identity and means of hegemony in the reformed religion.[38] The point to be underscored here is that though there may be some social and cultural determinants concerning confessional choice among the various Protestant communities throughout France in the 1550s and 1560s, each of the social environments in which it succeeded needs to be analysed carefully. Dijon, for example, the capital of the province of Burgundy, had a large, prosperous, and literate artisanate. It was close to Geneva, as well as being in the traffic and communication routes between Paris and Lyon. It also had a large group of merchants, lawyers, and royal officers. In short, it was just the sort of town like Lyon and Rouen where Protestantism might be expected to thrive.[39] As already indicated, however, the reform movement failed to take hold in Burgundy because of the region's winegrowers and the orientation of the province's elites. Thus, each social context must be examined in detail before one can assess why the Reformation succeeded

---

[38] Rosenberg, 'Social Experience and Religious Choice', pp. 66–7, 156–63, and 189–202.
[39] On the religious and social make-up of Dijon, see James R. Farr, *Hands of Honor: Artisans and their World in Dijon, 1550–1650* (Ithaca, NY, 1988).

or failed. And recent historians have demonstrated how this approach can be far more illuminating than economic reductionism.

Although the earliest converts and even the bulk of the Huguenots may have been made up of journeymen artisans, master craftsmen, merchants, lawyers, and royal officials in some combination in every Protestant community in France, the movement as a whole would doubtless never have survived the crown's attempt to root out heresy during the reign of Henry II without the support of a significant number of elites: primarily members of the nobility, and particularly those with the ability to offer protection. The period from 1555 until the outbreak of the Wars of Religion in 1562 witnessed the recruitment of a number of nobles to the cause that proved to be a godsend for the future of the movement. This was no accident, as Calvin's evangelical ministry in France began in 1555 with the aim of attracting aristocratic support. Of those ministers sent into France from Geneva between 1555 and 1562 whose social status can be identified, nearly one-third were themselves noble. And foremost among the many nobles who joined the Protestant movement in that period, despite the serious consequences of opposing the policy of the king, were several influential members of the Bourbon family, who were themselves of royal blood and directly related to the ruling Valois dynasty. Antoine de Bourbon, king of Navarre, had extensive seigneurial holdings in and around Béarn in southwest France, and it is hardly a coincidence that the southwest – Béarn, Gascony, and Guyenne – was an area where Calvin enjoyed his clearest success in establishing Protestant congregations. Sixteen of the first eighty-eight ministers Calvin dispatched to France (nearly one-fifth) were sent to this area. Calvin made an especially explicit attempt to befriend the king of Navarre, in light of his importance, and began a lengthy correspondence with him in 1557 to that effect. 'If men of low condition', Calvin wrote him in December 1557, 'can sacrifice themselves so that God may be purely worshiped, the great should do all the more. God, who has pulled you from the shadows of superstition . . . and illumined your understanding of the Gospel, which is not given to all, does not want this light hidden, but rather wishes you to be a burning lamp to lighten the way of great and small.' Although Navarre was forever to remain a waverer, sympathetic but never firmly and publicly committed to the new religion, his wife Jeanne proved to be the 'burning lamp' that Calvin had in mind. As the daughter of Francis I's sister Marguerite of Angoulême by her second husband, Jeanne d'Albret was queen of Navarre. She had been reared at her mother's court when Lefèvre d'Etaples, Roussel, Farel, and others from the Meaux circle were being sheltered there. And although many historians have assumed that it was Antoine de Bourbon who converted his wife to Protestantism,

Nancy Roelker has convincingly proved that it most likely was the other way round. Even though she did not formally announce her conversion until Christmas Day 1560, it is clear that she favoured reform long before her husband displayed any sympathies for it. In a letter written from Pau in December 1555, these Protestant feelings were self-evident:

I well remember how long ago, the late King [of Navarre], my most honored father ... surprised the said Queen [Marguerite of Angoulême] when she was praying in her rooms with the ministers Roussel and Farel, and how with great annoyance he slapped her right cheek and forbade her sharply to meddle in matters of doctrine. He shook a stick at me which cost me many bitter tears and has kept me fearful and compliant until after they had both died. Now that I am freed by the death of my said father two months ago ... a reform seems so right and so necessary that, for my part, I consider that it would be disloyalty and cowardice to God, to my conscience and to my people to remain any longer in a state of suspense and indecision.

Jeanne d'Albret, queen of Navarre would come to play a pivotal role in the future of the Protestant movement in France in the ensuing decade and a half of her life. What Calvin ultimately lost in her wavering husband, he more than made up for in the unqualified support of this French noble-woman. She and other noblewomen like her, moreover, were unusually active in the movement and helped to sustain it during this crisis period of persecution on the eve of the religious wars.[40]

Among other noble converts in this period was Louis de Bourbon, prince of Condé, Antoine's younger brother. In October 1555 on his return from a military campaign in Italy, he visited Geneva where he attended Calvinist sermons and asked to be shown around the city. Although there is no surviving evidence that he saw Calvin or any other Genevan pastor during this short visit, Condé's ardor for the new faith dated from this period and stood him in marked contrast with the king of Navarre's more distant commitment to the religion. The younger Bourbon not only promised 'mountains and marvels' in the way of princely protection and patronage of the Huguenots in France, but he requested the services of a Calvinist pastor as early as 1558 in order to underscore his public and formal commitment to the reformed religion. Moreover, when Navarre died at the outset of the religious wars, it was Condé who assumed the mantle of military leadership of the Huguenots in their struggle for recognition by the crown. It was he to whom Calvin

[40] Nancy L. Roelker, *Queen of Navarre: Jeanne d'Albret, 1528–1572* (Cambridge, MA, 1968), letter from Calvin to Navarre quoted on p. 130, letter from Jeanne quoted on p. 127. Also see Roelker's 'The Role of Noblewomen in the French Reformation', *Archiv für Reformationsgeschichte*, vol. 63 (1972), 168–94.

and all French Protestants would look for leadership in the 1560s.[41] Other prominent noble converts included the three Châtillon brothers, nephews of the Constable of France, Anne de Montmorency. Constable Montmorency was *de facto* head of the French military and a loyal and well-rewarded client of Henry II. Although he remained Catholic, his three nephews converted to Calvinism early on with a helping hand from a pastor from Geneva. Gaspard de Coligny had won the office of admiral as the result of his uncle's position at court and also had extensive land holdings in Normandy. Thus, as was the case in Béarn and Navarre in the southwest, Normandy became a stronghold of Protestantism because of the degree of aristocratic protection. The other two brothers, François d'Andelot and Odet de Châtillon, though perhaps ultimately less significant in the Protestant movement, displayed no less zeal. In any case, the Bourbons and the Châtillons were only the tip of the iceberg of noble converts who provided French Protestantism with both legitimacy and protection in the period 1555–62. Moreover, these nobles enabled the movement to spread to the countryside in areas of Normandy and the southwest where it could be protected and guarded from royal prosecution. It was thus no longer exclusively an urban movement of artisans and merchants. It is true that some of these nobles were attracted to Calvinism for political or personal gain rather than for its theology; but that was also true for the masses as well. And for every Antoine de Bourbon there was a Gaspard de Coligny, whose sympathies for the new religion were genuine. Above all, with a significant number of nobles among their numbers including some influential at court, the French Protestant movement was able to survive whatever the motives of its aristocratic leadership.

Moreover, there was one small but worrisome faction of elites who were converting to the new religion that clearly posed a threat to the social and political order: the judges in the sovereign courts of the parlements. As Henry II had already made a concerted effort to increase the powers of the royal courts to prosecute heresy among the masses, that effort was jeopardized if some of the judges themselves were tainted with heresy and less than fully committed to the eradication of Protestantism. The king's fears were not without foundation, as there was a small minority of Protestant sympathizers among the magistrates in the Parlement of Paris as well as in most of the provincial parlements. The most notorious was Anne du Bourg, a vocal Protestant magistrate who in June 1559 had the temerity to insult Henry II when the king made a personal visit to the Parlement of Paris. He and six of his colleagues were arrested and charged

[41] Robert M. Kingdon, *Geneva and the Coming of the Wars of Religon in France, 1555–1563* (Geneva, 1956), p. 59; and Sutherland, *Huguenot Struggle*, p. 71

with heresy. The other six soon recanted and were eventually released, but Du Bourg stood firm and remained in prison. He sealed his own fate when from prison he wrote a treasonous pamphlet which suggested that no French subject was required to recognize the legitimacy of a monarch who contravened the will of God. Even Calvin had refrained from going that far, and it was no surprise to most Parisians when Du Bourg was soon thereafter burned at the stake not just for heresy but, significantly, for sedition and *lèse-majesté*. Though Anne du Bourg became a martyr to the Protestant cause, his execution was intended as an example for his colleagues on the court. How many other Protestant sympathizers were there within the Parlement of Paris? It is impossible to say with any precision, but it is revealing that when every member of the court was required to make a public profession of faith as a Catholic in June 1562, 31 of the 143 members of the court (6 presidents and 137 counselors) absented themselves: more than a fifth of the court's membership.[42] Not all of the absentees were bonafide Protestants, to be sure; several were out of town, some even on the crown's business. Nevertheless, even though the Parlement of Paris was quick to root out heresy from its own ranks, the ceremonial of the profession of faith demonstrated that there was hardly unanimity among the king's own magistrates on how that should be achieved. While the clear majority of all judges in the parlements were loyal Catholics and as anxious as the king to purify the kingdom of the pollution of heresy and rebellion, the spectre of more Anne du Bourgs continued to haunt the last years of the reign of Henry II.[43]

The king's reign was cut short in July 1559, however, when he died of a head wound suffered in a jousting accident. The tragedy occurred during the celebration of the recently concluded peace treaty of Cateau-Cambrésis ending the Habsburg–Valois wars in Italy and the accompanying marriage alliance between Spain and France (with Henry II's daughter Elisabeth marrying Philip II of Spain). Henry had inherited both the war against the Habsburgs in Italy and the domestic struggle against Protestantism from his father. And while military defeat and financial exigency had forced him into a compromise peace with Philip II in April 1559, the war against the Huguenots had only escalated during his reign. Despite the increased suppression of the new religion in France since the Edict of Châteaubriant in 1551, Protestant strength had

---

[42] Linda C. Taber, 'Royal Policy and Religious Dissent within the Parlement of Paris, 1559–1563', unpublished PhD thesis, Stanford University, 1982, esp. pp. 265–71.

[43] For an example of the overwhelming Catholic sympathies of most magistrates in the parlements, as well as an indication of their zeal to extirpate Protestantism, see Jonathan Powis, 'Order, Religion, and the Magistrates of a Provincial Parlement in Sixteenth-century France', *Archiv für Reformationsgeschichte*, vol. 71 (1980), 180–96.

increased during the latter years of Henry's reign because of the stepped-up evangelical effort from Geneva. With the king's life cut so tragically short in the summer of 1559, the religious situation was exacerbated by the power struggle at court that ensued among the various noble factions struggling to dominate Henry's eldest son, the fifteen year-old Francis II. Moreover, the Huguenots had little reason to think that the crown's policy of persecution under his father and grandfather would be any better under Francis II, as the young king had only recently been married to Mary Stuart, Queen of Scots, a niece of the most militantly Catholic family in France: the Guise family from Lorraine. Mary's mother was a sister of Francis, duke of Guise, and Charles, cardinal of Lorraine. The former was not only a powerful noble in his own right but also one of the most ardent defenders of the Catholic faith and persecutors of heresy in all of France; while the latter was probably the wealthiest and most influential cleric in the entire realm. As the Guises managed to take over control of the governmental administration within days of Henry II's death – including the royal *cachet*, the church, the military, the diplomatic corps, as well as the royal treasury – the accidental death of Henry II was an ominous portent for the continuation of the suppression and persecution of Protestantism in the summer of 1559.

The domination of the young king by his uncles, the Guises, did not go unchallenged, as there were many who sought to contest their authority. There was the king's own mother and Henry II's widow for one, Catherine de Medici. While her own Catholicism was never in doubt, she was left to rear four young sons alone and only wanted what was best for them, especially for the eldest, Francis II. And in her view, the domination of the crown by the Guises was hardly conducive to a strong and independent reign. The Queen Mother (as the widowed Catherine de Medici came to be called after her husband's death) was a pragmatic woman; and though she had many faults, looking after the best interests of her children was not among them. Unfortunately, she quickly discovered that Francis seemed to take his uncles' advice much more seriously than her own, and she found herself at a loss over how to weaken the influence of the Guises over her eldest son.

Other opponents of the Guises naturally included Antoine de Bourbon, king of Navarre, and Louis de Bourbon, prince of Condé. As Protestants their interests could hardly have been more jeopardized by the rise to power at court of the Guises. Because of the influence of the duke of Guise in the military and the cardinal of Lorraine in the Gallican church, it appeared that the royal policy of the suppression of Protestantism would only continue. Some Protestants even suggested that because Francis II was not yet twenty-one years of age that he was technically a minor and that a regent should be appointed to govern until he reached his age of majority. Naturally, they looked to the king of Navarre as first prince of the blood to fulfill that role. This was only a Protestant view, however. Though this issue was not explicitly spelled out in fundamental law, most politically minded Frenchmen had traditionally assumed the age of majority to begin in a king's fourteenth year (i.e., on his thirteenth birthday). Moreover, even if a regency government was required, there was no custom or tradition that required the first prince of the blood to become regent. The last time there had been a need for such a regency government after the death of Louis XI in 1483, the first prince of the blood was bypassed altogether in favour of someone else. Thus, most French men and women readily accepted the new king as legitimate and of age, fully capable of administering his kingdom and appointing his advisors according to his pleasure.[44] Jean de la Vacquerie, a doctor of the Sorbonne, represented the views of many when he cautioned the new king to take seriously the oath to safeguard the Catholic church that he had recently sworn in his coronation *sacre*:

Other than God we could not choose a more competent or better judge than the Most Christian King for the defence and propagation of the Christian faith and religion. Since he is the Most Christian King, he has the zeal to guard God's honour; and since he is a virtuous and powerful king, he will not allow the Catholic church in his kingdom to be wrongly oppressed and afflicted. From the very day of his coronation and the possession of his kingdom, he swore and promised God that he would faithfully protect the Christian faith.[45]

As it happened, Antoine de Bourbon, king of Navarre, was neither ready nor willing to assume the mantle of Protestant leadership in order to challenge the authority of the Guises at court, and he remained secluded in Guyenne during the months following Henry II's death. His younger brother, the prince of Condé, however, was much less ambivalent about the religious and political situation and very soon decided to force the issue of the Guise domination of the new king. The politicization of French Calvinism had thus become complete, as the religious issue became thoroughly immersed in the political struggle at court between the Guises on the one hand and the Bourbons and the Châtillons on the other.

---

[44] See the sentiments in the anonymously written pamphlet, *Pour la majorite du Roy treschrestien contre les escrites des rebelles* (Paris: Guillaume Morel, 1560), unpaginated, fol. Clv.

[45] Jean de la Vacquerie, *Catholique remonstrance aux Roys et princes Chrestiens, a tous magistrats & gouverneurs de repub [liques] touchant l'abolition des heresies, troubles & scismes qui regnant auiourd'huy en la Chrestienté* (Paris: Claude Fremy, 1560), p. 5r.

What became called the 'conspiracy of Amboise' in March 1560 was an overt Protestant attempt to liberate the young Francis II from Guise influence as the court wintered at the royal château at Amboise along the Loire. With the backing of several hundred armed nobles from the provinces, the organizer of the plot, Jean du Barry, seigneur de la Renaudie, hoped to kidnap the king in order to free him from Guise influence. La Renaudie had been in contact with both Condé and Geneva, and while the Bourbon prince clearly endorsed the plot, Calvin had more prudently kept his distance and urged the conspirators not to confront the king physically. Plans of the impending attack on the court somehow leaked, moreover, and the plot backfired. As the conspirators began to assemble near Amboise in early March 1560, they were surprised by royal troops under orders of the duke of Guise, and several hundred of those Protestants captured were summarily executed as rebels and traitors and hanged from the walls of the château. The failed conspiracy not only put paid to whatever plans the Huguenots may have had of ending the Guise domination of the crown, but it only further reinforced Catholic perceptions that they were primarily seditious rebels who aimed to overthrow the state. The same Jean de la Vacquerie of the Sorbonne exhorted that 'heresy is a crime, the most dangerous and stinking crime there is in a city or commonwealth'. He insisted that 'religion is the primary and principal foundation of all order, and the bourgeois and citizens are more bound together and united by it than by their trade in merchandise, the communication of laws, or anything else in a civil society ... and that there is never more trouble or a greater tempest in a commonwealth than when there is some schism or dissension concerning the issue of religion there'. La Vacquerie spelled out his fears of the consequences of sedition very clearly. The Huguenots 'have always been the mortal enemies of kings and great nobles ... and by their false doctrines they have often incited their subjects to rebel against them, and to forsake the obedience, the recognition, and even the respect they owe to their masters and seigneurs'. His message was clear: these seditious rebels must be rooted out before all of France became infested with rebellion and revolution.[46] And though this might be just the sort of rhetoric to be expected from a doctor of the Sorbonne, somewhat similar sentiments were evident from more moderate voices. Jacques de Silly, seigneur de Rochefort, was a gentleman of the king's bedchamber and less militantly Catholic than

---

[46] Ibid., pp. 23r–v and 30r.

La Vacquerie. His published harangue of the following year also spelled out the same exhortation for public order:

The three things that kings ought to desire most are religion for the clarity of their consciences, the nobility to defend them with arms, and justice for the conservation of their subjects. So, if we employ them together, each according to the purpose for which God has ordained it ... we shall strengthen this body of France and we shall see it flourish more than ever, provided that by your [i.e., the king's] rule you remove the causes of sedition from us.

'Peace and public tranquility are the strongest walls in the world', he concluded, 'they are the sinews of the prince'.[47]

And in order to make a public demonstration that they were keeping the peace, the Guises not only had several hundred of the conspirators executed, but they also ordered the arrest of the prince of Condé, who although absent from Amboise was clearly implicated in the plot. His own martyrdom would have quickly followed, in fact, had not the young Francis II suddenly died from an ear abscess in December 1560 while Condé was awaiting execution. Just as suddenly as they had been elevated to power in July 1559 with one royal death, so the Guises found themselves dismissed with another only eighteen months later when Francis was succeeded by his younger brother Charles IX. Because the new king was only eleven years old, a regency government was required after all. Seizing the initiative herself this time, Catherine de Medici declared herself the regent for her son Charles, dismissed the Guises from power at court, released Condé from prison, and ultimately hoped to steer an independent course for the new king, free from domination by all factions. Was this possible, however, in light of the escalating religious tensions in France? Above all, could this be achieved in light of the crisis of authority at court, now exacerbated by an under-age king on the throne?

It became immediately clear that the Queen Mother's policy would be one of moderation in light of the extremist positions of Protestants and Catholics alike in recent months. She had little time for either the Guises or the conspirators at Amboise, and ultimately she hoped to restore order and eradicate violence on both sides. She did hope this could be achieved without damaging the unity of the Gallican church, to be sure, but peace and the future of her son's kingdom were what ultimately mattered most. Her regime's new direction, so distinct from the Guise-dominated reign of Francis II, was evident by her appointment of the king of Navarre as the

---

[47] Jacques de Silly, seigneur de Rochefort, *La Harangue de par la Noblesse de toute la France au Roy tres-chrestien* (Paris: Charles Perier, 1561), p. 13v.

lieutenant-general of the realm, recognizing his position as first prince of the blood. After the constable, Anne de Montmorency, Navarre was thus second in command of the royal army as lieutenant-general. No further sign of the fall from grace of the Guises was necessary after the appointment of Navarre. Moreover, Catherine found other moderates on the royal council more to her liking and began listening to them for advice on policy. Foremost among them was the chancellor, Michel de l'Hôpital, a moderate voice who urged that all sides put down their arms in order to decide the religious question peacefully. L'Hôpital was a former councillor in the Parlement of Paris and a man of law by background. As chancellor he was the king's advocate in the Parlement and carried some weight in that conservative body. Also more prominent on the royal council under the Queen Mother's regency was Gaspard de Coligny, a moderate Protestant who had condemned the plot at Amboise and had wisely distanced himself from it from the start. Thus, for the first time since the persecution began following the 'Affair of the placards' more than twenty-five years earlier, French Protestants had some reason to believe that the crown itself might at last be wavering in its suppression of the new religion. Although two separate meetings of the Estates-General at Orléans in December 1560 and Pontoise in August 1561 had failed to resolve the religious dispute, Catherine soldiered on. (The Estates-General were meetings of selected representatives from all over France from the traditional three estates of the realm – the clergy, nobility, and bourgeois elites from the towns – convoked by the crown in times of crisis or emergency, such as during the minority of a king.)

The result was an attempt to mediate the religious dispute by discussion and compromise when Catherine de Medici invited leaders from both sides (she even extended invitations to Calvin and Beza to come from Geneva) to come to Poissy in September 1561 to see if there was any way possible to re-unite all Frenchmen together under the Gallican church. The resulting colloquy of Poissy ultimately failed, as neither side was willing to compromise with the other. On both theological, and social and political issues, each side's perception of the other had become too hardened over the preceding years to compromise. The real legacy of the colloquy of Poissy, however, was not the Queen Mother's failure to bring about reconciliation, but rather the heightened fear among militant Catholics that she might be willing to compromise with the Huguenots. Each passing month since the death of Francis II had only underscored that fear, and many began to wonder if a Catholic plot to liberate the new king from his 'captors' was now required. When Francis, duke of Guise, along with the constable, Anne de Montmorency, and an army marshall, the sieur de St-André, formed a military 'triumvirate' in late 1561 to seek aid from Philip II of Spain in order to drive out all Protestants from France, a Catholic conspiracy of Amboise was a distinct possibility. And that the triumvirs threatened civil war was clearly stated in their published goals: not only 'to extirpate all those of the new religion', but also 'to obliterate completely the name of the family and race of the Bourbons'.[48]

The Guises' worst fears came to pass in January 1562 when Catherine issued the Edict of Saint-Germain proclaiming the limited but legal recognition of the Huguenots. Usually referred to as the 'Edict of January' or the 'edict of toleration', this edict was the first public and formal recognition that the French crown had ever given the Huguenots to practise their religion without interference. As a result, it marked a watershed in the crown's position on religion and was decidedly the result of Catherine de Medici's attempts to mediate a religious settlement without civil war. The preamble of the edict made it very clear that her purpose was 'to appease the troubles and seditions over the issue of religion'. It was a very narrow and limited recognition of the Protestants' right to exist, however, forbidding them to practise or worship inside all towns, to assemble anywhere at night, and to raise arms. But for the first time in their short history in France, they were now allowed to preach openly in the countryside by day as long as they did so peacefully. Moreover, unlike the restrictions placed on townspeople, the edict allowed Protestant nobles to organize and protect Calvinist congregations on their own rural estates. Catherine made it clear that all mobilization of arms and sedition would be dealt with harshly, but the Huguenots could now at last meet openly and peacefully.[49] This was a *volte-face* that most Catholics found difficult to swallow. Even though Charles IX was still a minor and had not yet taken his solemn and sacred oath to safeguard the Catholic church, it was clearly understood that the edict of Saint-Germain was a radical departure from the past.

Among the first to react against the edict were the conservative magistrates of the Parlement of Paris, who at first refused to register it as they were required by law to do. They issued a formal remonstrance to the Queen Mother, hoping she would withdraw the edict or at least alter it so that the crown could not be accused of harbouring heretics in the kingdom. Their theme was clear from the title page of the published

---

[48] *Sommaire des choses premièrement accordées entre les ducs de Montmorency connestable, et de Guyse grand maistre, pairs de France, et le mareschal Sainct André, pour la conspiration du triumvirat ...* [1561], printed in N. M. Sutherland, *The Massacre of St Bartholomew and the European Conflict, 1559–1572* (London, 1973), pp. 347–50 (quote on p. 349).

[49] The edict is printed in Haag and Haag, *La France protestante*, X, 48–52, and is ably summarized in Sutherland, *Huguenot Struggle*, pp. 354–5.

remonstrance sent to her, with St. Matthew 12:25 printed beneath the title: 'Every kingdom divided against itself goes to ruin.' The judges underscored their perception of the Huguenots as a threat to the social and political order, calling them 'indigents collected from all parts, mixed together with criminals, thieves, and trouble-makers ... who live and pillage under the pretext of religion'. The king's responsibility to the Catholic church was their principal theme. The young Charles IX, 'just like all his predecessors in his *sacre* and coronation', would soon make his solemn oath to drive heresy out of his kingdom, 'which obligates him to God and his subjects who owe him obedience. For Him and for them, keeping the oaths made in his *sacre* is his reciprocal duty. And to allow or tolerate diverse religions in this kingdom is clearly a far cry from his promise to exterminate heresy altogether.' The magistrates further complained of the edict's explicit departure from tradition. 'The king has more occasion than any other Christian prince to maintain the traditional religion in which his predecessors have prospered from king Clovis up until the present, which is more than a thousand years.' They concluded by appealing to the law, and especially to the patriarchal hierarchy which protected religious unity. With clear allusions to Catherine's sex and the minority of the king, they implied that the edict itself was perhaps illegal as well as divisive for recognizing the Protestant religion:

Laws both sacred and profane insist that the woman is in holy bond to her husband and children in holy bond to their father, which is to say that the entire family [and by implication, the family of Henry II] is of the same religion as the father of the family. And not without good reason, as this is the firmest bond of union, friendship, and obedience owed; which if lacking, produces nothing but contention, rancor, and division, and one could not say that God resides there.[50]

Only after receiving two formal letters of *jussion* (royal commands to the court to register legislation without further delay) did the Parlement of Paris reluctantly register the 'Edict of January' on 6 March 1562. Even then, they did so with the explicit amendment that they were doing so against their will and only at the king's command. But they already knew it would be impossible to enforce, as the Catholic reaction to the edict had already erupted in violence. Just a few days earlier on 1 March, in fact, Catherine's edict that was supposed to bring peace ultimately led to the civil war she had so desperately wanted to avoid. The first shots were fired by troops of the duke of Guise, as he encountered a group of unarmed Protestants worshipping inside the town of Vassy. The resulting

[50] *Remonstrances faictes au Roy par messieurs de la cour de Parlement de Paris, sur la publication de l'Edict du moys de Ianvier* [1562] (Paris: Nicolas Lombard, 1566 edn.), unpaginated, fols. Aiiii, Biii–iiii, and Cii.

'massacre', as the Huguenots would henceforth call it, marked the beginning of three generations of armed struggle over the issue of religion. The Protestant churches of France held a national synod the following month at Orléans and requested that Louis de Bourbon, prince of Condé, raise troops to protect them from further persecution. When Condé issued a manifesto calling on Protestants to raise arms to oppose Guise and the Triumvirate, the kingdom of France was divided against itself.

2 'The beginning of a tragedy': the early wars of religion, 1562–1570

When the Parisian lawyer and historian Etienne Pasquier heard the news of the massacre at Vassy, his reaction was typical of many among the upper classes. 'All one talks about now is war ... [and] there is nothing to be more feared in a state than civil war ... particularly when a king, due to his minority, does not have the power to command absolutely ... If it was permitted to me to assess these events, I would tell you that it was the beginning of a tragedy.'[1] What must have particularly worried elites such as Pasquier was the likely prospect that religious division would exacerbate the social tensions inherent in the hierarchical society of the Old Regime. And this seemed a well-founded fear when in the aftermath of the incident at Vassy a number of powerful nobles seized the leadership of the Huguenot movement. Military figures such as Condé and Coligny naturally assumed the military command of the Huguenot army in an effort to defend what they saw as an organized attempt by French Catholics to eliminate them by force. But there were also large numbers of noble converts to the new religion in the provinces, especially in the south. While these converts provided much needed political and military protection, as well as the safety and security of places of worship on their rural estates, they further exacerbated existing social tensions.

Only a few months earlier in Agen in the southwest the intersection of religious and social tensions had already reared its head. The Catholic baron François de Fumel, whose estates included a small Huguenot congregation, forbade his Calvinist peasants from worshipping according to the new religion. They eventually took up arms in protest and were joined by several hundred Catholic peasants in an attempt to seize Fumel's château, making it very clear that religion was not the foundation of the revolt. When Fumel was eventually murdered in his bed and beheaded with his wife looking on, it was obvious that religious tensions had been overtaken by longstanding social and economic complaints. The episode

---

[1] Etienne Pasquier, *Lettres historiques pour les années 1556–1594*, ed. Dorothy Thickett (Geneva, 1966), pp. 98, 100, letter of Pasquier to monsieur de Fonssomme, spring 1562.

shows above all how difficult it is to divide sixteenth-century French men and women into neat communities of Protestants and Catholics along doctrinal or even cultural lines. The Wars of Religion erupted in a society long divided by social hierarchy and deference, and those older social tensions were not obliterated by religious division at the time of the Reformation. Perhaps the principal point of the assassination of Fumel, however, is that both the ultra-Catholic Parlement of Bordeaux and the Calvinist synod that met at Nîmes in 1562 overlooked the participation of several hundred Catholic peasants in the uprising and assumed it was a Calvinist revolt. As a result, both groups considered the Protestant perpetrators of the murder as 'seditious disturbers of the public order' and 'totally perverse people only superficially instructed in religion [who] think the gospel promises them agrarian freedom and enfranchisement'.[2] Thus, the stereotype of Protestants as seditious rebels continued to be propagated.

When a significant segment of the rural nobility seized the leadership of the Huguenot movement away from Calvinist pastors at the start of the religious wars, the new religion also became further politicized. This politicization was already apparent as many leading nobles relied on their vast clientage networks to recruit troops to the Protestant cause. While it is incorrect to view these noble conversions as primarily materially or politically motivated, it is striking that many of Condé's clients in Picardy, Coligny's clients in Normandy, La Rochefoucauld's clients in Poitou, and Rohan's clients in Brittany emulated their respective patrons by adopting the new religion.[3] Clearly all their clients did not adopt the new religion, nor did the nobles in question have the power to make them do so. Indeed, kinship relations and clientage networks tell us more about the pattern of transmission of Calvinism than about the intentions and beliefs of these noble converts, who in any case had many other overlapping bonds with their patrons besides religion.[4] The result was a growing powerbase of rural nobles (estimated to be as many as one-third of all the lower nobility in the

---

[2] Quoted in Emmanuel Le Roy Ladurie, *Les paysans de Languedoc*, 2 vols. (Paris, 1966), I, p. 393, for the Calvinist view. For the view of the Catholic Bordeaux magistrates see Jonathan Powis, 'Order, Religion, and the Magistrates of a Provincial Parlement in Sixteenth-Century France', *Archiv für Reformationsgeschichte*, vol. 71 (1980), 193. The best brief accounts of the Fumel incident are in Janine Garrisson-Estèbe, *Protestants du Midi, 1559–1598* (Toulouse, 1980), pp. 166–7; and Denis Crouzet, *Les guerriers de Dieu: La violence au temps des troubles de religion, vers 1525–vers 1610*, 2 vols. (Seyssel, France, 1990), I, pp. 515–23.

[3] J. H. M. Salmon, *Society in Crisis: France in the Sixteenth Century* (London and New York, 1975), p. 124.

[4] As is argued by Kristin B. Neuschel, *Word of Honor: Interpreting Noble Culture in Sixteenth-century France* (Ithaca, 1989), pp. 30–3.

provinces[5]), who, whatever their motivation, responded to the vocal appeals from the Calvinist churches for protection.

It was the specific need for protection and organization that was the foundation of the Calvinist assemblies. Representatives from each Calvinist congregation met together in local colloquies; deputies from the colloquies formed provincial synods; while deputies from these bodies met from time to time in national synods in order to discuss religious issues. The first such national synod met secretly in Paris in May 1559 just prior to the death of Henry II, while a second met in Poitiers in March 1561. Both these meetings were dominated by issues of social discipline and theological purity, as the deputies left political decisions to Protestant nobles in separate political assemblies. When the third national synod met at Orléans in April 1562 just after the outbreak of the first civil war, however, politics became forever entangled in Huguenot affairs. At Orléans Louis, prince of Condé was not only proclaimed to be the protector of all the Calvinist churches in the kingdom, but was designated 'protector and defender of the house and crown of France' as well. Most of the leading nobles in the Huguenot movement subscribed to this arrangement, with the result that the French Huguenot movement became dominated by the nobility for the duration of the first civil war. These nobles were not only independent of Geneva, but they clearly had superseded the local ministers and pastors who had formed the groundswell for the church in the 1550s. And in April 1562 these same nobles, led by Condé, were now calling for armed resistance to the duke of Guise and the body of Catholic forces he was marshalling in Paris.[6]

The court, in Fontainebleau for the spring of 1562, was in an uproar. The minority of the eleven-year-old king, Charles IX, meant that nobles from both sides were able to take advantage of the power vacuum at the top of the government. The beleaguered regent, Catherine de Medici, who had long sought to prevent the outbreak of warfare was now powerless to prevent it. She was forced to watch helplessly as the crisis escalated, as both Catholic and Huguenot armies began to mobilize. Although the duke of Guise was ordered to come to court after the massacre at Vassy, he opted instead to go to the capital of Paris where he was treated as a hero by the overwhelmingly Catholic populace. Not only did he begin to raise even more troops along with the other two triumvirs – Anne de Montmorency and the marshal St-André – but Guise managed to persuade the vacillating king of Navarre, Antoine de Bourbon, to abandon the Protestant movement to support the Catholic triumvirate. When a

[5] Salmon, *Society in Crisis*, p. 124.   [6] Ibid., pp. 142–3.

large Catholic force suddenly appeared at the court at Fontainebleau claiming to 'protect' the king, a Guise-led equivalent to the 'conspiracy of Amboise' was afoot. With the king of Navarre now firmly in the Catholic camp, the Queen Mother had no alternative but to treat seriously the prince of Condé's claim to be 'protector and defender of the house and crown of France', as he was a prince of the blood and her only option to thwart the Guise-dominated triumvirate. Rather than coming to court as Catherine de Medici requested him to do, however, Condé, fearing the ambitions of the triumvirate, remained in Orléans with the Huguenot nobility and the national synod and issued a call to arms.[7]

Having taken over the city of Orléans as the Protestant base of operations, Condé and the other nobles had already decided on a strategy of seizing the towns along the main waterways, bridgeheads, and land routes of the kingdom. Orléans itself proved useful in policing the Loire, and when Rouen on the Seine and Lyon at the confluence of the Saône and Rhone fell to the Huguenots immediately thereafter, Condé's plan became clear. In response to orders sent out via the church network, the trickle of towns that sided with the Protestant cause turned, especially in the Midi, into a flood. Within three months of the start of the first civil war Orléans, Rouen, and Lyon had been joined by Tours, Blois, Sens, Angers, and Beaugency on the Loire; Poitiers and Bourges in central France; Le Havre on the Channel coast at the mouth of the Seine; Grenoble, Die, Vienne, and Gap in Dauphiné in the Rhone valley; and Nîmes, Montpellier, Orange, Béziers, Beaucaire, Saint-Gilles, Montauban, Castres, Millau, Puylaurens, Rabastens, Gaillac, and Saint-Antonin in Languedoc. Blaise de Monluc, a zealously Catholic supporter of the crown, remarked that in April 1562 'all of Guyenne save Toulouse and Bordeaux is lost' to the new religion.[8] Although many of these towns came into the Protestant fold via military conquest, many others were won over by conversion of the leading municipal magistrates, who then were in a position to seize power from within and enforce the recognition and protection of a town's Protestant citizens even if they were not in a majority. The example of Rouen is a good case in point.

On the night of 15 April 1562 a group of armed Huguenots seized the convent of the Celestines, the town hall, and the château occupied by the pro-Guise bailiff of Rouen, Villebon d'Estouteville. Catching the

---

[7] Lucien Romier, *Catholiques et Huguenots à la cour de Charles IX* (Paris, 1924), pp. 318–51; and James Westphall Thompson, *The Wars of Religion in France, 1559–1576: The Huguenots, Catherine de Medici, Philip II* (New York, 1958 edn.), pp. 131–40.

[8] Quoted in Garrisson-Estèbe, *Protestants du Midi*, p. 168. A list of the towns that went over to the Protestant cause is in ibid., pp. 168–9; and in Salmon, *Society in Crisis*, pp. 146–7.

Catholics completely by surprise, the Protestants cemented the coup by quickly taking over all the gates of the city as well as the night watch. They soon expelled Villebon and made themselves the political and military masters of Rouen. On 3 and 4 May the Huguenot victory was consolidated with a wave of iconoclasm, as armed Protestants systematically vandalized the city's churches. They smashed and destroyed altars, idols, baptismal fonts, pews, coffers, and any holy objects they could prise loose. Catholic citizens throughout Rouen began to flee in large numbers, fearing for their safety. On 10 May even the judges in the Parlement of Rouen, one of eight such sovereign courts in the kingdom, felt they could no longer safely reside in town and departed. By the end of May very few Catholics remained in Rouen and Catholic services had disappeared.[9] This was clearly a coup from within, as no Huguenot army had forced the new religion upon the city. Three of the six municipal magistrates who governed on the city council were Protestants, and, in league with the Huguenot pastors in Rouen, they formed the nucleus of this Protestant coup. When the three Catholic magistrates fled the city along with the parlement, the Huguenots were left in complete control of Rouen's political machinery. It was successes such as this in Lyon and elsewhere – particularly in the Midi – that demonstrated Protestant strength at the start of the civil wars. They were not triumphant everywhere, as coups were thwarted in Dijon, Toulouse, Aix-en-Provence, and Bordeaux. Nevertheless, the winning over of a significant number of towns and cities in the early stages of the first civil war proved that the new religion was more than a flash in the pan.

Catherine de Medici now had no option but to turn to the Catholic triumvirate to put down the Huguenot insurrections. Thus, the pacifist Queen Mother now found herself reluctantly forced to support a war. Orchestrated by the duke of Guise, royalist forces were dispatched to lay siege to the Protestant towns in the north, with the aim of breaking the Protestant grip on the Loire and cutting communications with Condé in Orléans. Claude, duke of Aumale, Guise's brother, headed the army that surrounded Rouen over the summer, while other Catholic forces laid siege to Bourge, Blois, and Tours. With Huguenot garrisons now firmly dug in, winning back these Protestant towns proved to be a difficult task. Superiority in numbers did eventually prove decisive for the triumvirate, but it was not until late summer of 1562 before any real gains were achieved. Blois and Tours were the first Huguenot towns to be recaptured, and Poitiers and Angoulême quickly followed under the command of the

---

[9] This episode is discussed in Philip Benedict, *Rouen during the Wars of Religion* (Cambridge, 1981), pp. 96–8.

triumvir St-André. Bourges fell in September, and the duke of Aumale finally forced the surrender of Rouen in October. When Antoine de Bourbon, king of Navarre, was fatally wounded during the siege of Rouen, the Catholics lost a valuable leader. This loss was compounded in December 1562 when, in the only major open battle between the two armies in the first civil war, the marshal St-André was killed at the battle of Dreux. Although the duke of Guise won the day at Dreux, his victory was short-lived. The constable Montmorency was captured by the Huguenots, though this was offset by the capture of Condé by Catholic forces. The bulk of the Protestant army managed to escape to the safety of Orléans, however, led by the young admiral Coligny, Montmorency's nephew. The first civil war thus came to a climax when Guise himself was fatally wounded during the siege of Orléans two months later in February 1563. With three of the four principal Catholic military leaders dead, and the bulk of Protestant communities in the south virtually untouched, an outright victory over the Calvinists proved impossible. Anxious to mediate peace between the two sides, Catherine de Medici arranged the release of Montmorency and Condé and the three of them drew up a compromise peace settlement at Amboise in March 1563.[10]

Although it was modelled on the Edict of January 1562, the Edict of Amboise of March 1563 had several significant differences. Above all, it reflected the domination by the nobility of the Huguenot movement that emerged during the first civil war. Catherine de Medici, who had tried in vain to mediate between the sides in order to bring peace to her son's kingdom, understandably sought a compromise peace to end all hostilities. Given the fact that neither side was able to defeat the other militarily, some kind of compromise was inevitable. The terms of the edict, like the earlier edict of 1562, allowed the legal practice of Calvinism, though it was now restricted to the suburbs of one town in each *bailliage* or *sénéchaussée* (the smallest administrative units of the kingdom) rather than anywhere outside any town in the kingdom. Exceptions were granted to Protestant nobles, who could continue to exercise the new religion at home and on their estates. As the edict did not allow for the establishment of any new Huguenot churches, this gave Protestant nobles a decided advantage over ministers and townspeople in maintaining their leadership of the movement. Thus, the toleration clauses of the edict were heavily weighted toward the nobility,

[10] Details of the first civil war are in N. M. Sutherland, *The Huguenot Struggle for Recognition* (New Haven, 1980), pp. 137–40; idem, 'The Assassination of François Duc de Guise, February 1563', *The Historical Journal*, vol. 24 (1981), 279–95; Salmon, *Society in Crisis*, pp. 146–7; and most completely in Thompson, *The Wars of Religion in France*, pp. 131–97.

while the really militant tensions – not to mention the bulk of the Calvinist population in France – lay in the towns.[11] Thus, the first civil war that ended with the edict of Amboise on 19 March 1563 set a pattern that would be repeated seven times over the next four decades: a military campaign in which neither side could defeat the other comprehensively, followed by a compromise peace that the crown could neither administer nor enforce. The inevitable result was the continuation of the civil wars.

Another aspect of the first civil war that became symptomatic of the entire series of conflicts was that both sides sought foreign aid to their respective causes. Guise had made specific overtures to the papacy as well as to Philip II of Spain through the papal nuncio and Spanish ambassador in Paris, while Condé and Coligny had sought out aid from the Protestant princes (both Calvinist and Lutheran) of the Holy Roman Empire as well as England's Queen Elizabeth. Both sides harvested some substantial gains from these overtures, though neither got enough foreign support to alter the outcome significantly. The triumvirs received funds to hire companies of Swiss and German mercenaries as well as 2,500 men supplied by Pope Pius IV, while Philip II provided troops to fight in Guyenne. On the Protestant side Coligny's brother, François d'Andelot, commanded 4,000 German reiters (cavalry of paid mercenaries) that proved decisive in Orléans in holding off the siege by the forces of Aumale, and Elizabeth provided both money and troops in return for the English occupation of Le Havre and Dieppe. She demanded these ports as guarantees against the eventual return of Calais, which England had maintained after the end of the Hundred Years' War but had subsequently lost to France; and Condé promised Calais would be returned to England after a Huguenot victory. Even though English troops did occupy the two channel ports in October, Elizabeth refused to release them to help relieve the siege of Rouen, which fell to Guise only a few weeks later. So, although the foreign support both sides received in the first civil war was not enough to produce an outright victory, it set a pattern that would be repeated in each successive phase of the conflict. The French Wars of Religion quickly became an international conflict, as a number of European states became involved either to support the Protestant cause or to oppose it, which in turn further politicized the entire conflict.[12]

---

[11] The edict itself is printed in André Stegmann, ed., *Edits des guerres de religion* (Paris, 1979), pp. 32–6; while a very good summary of it is in Sutherland, *The Huguenot Struggle for Recognition*, pp. 142–4 and 356–7.

[12] On foreign involvement in the first war, see Salmon, *Society in Crisis*, p. 147; N. M. Sutherland, *The Massacre of St Bartholomew and the European Conflict, 1559–1572* (London, 1973), pp. 10–23; and Bernard Vogler, 'Le rôle des électeurs palatins dans les guerres de religion en France (1559–1592)', *Cahiers d'histoire*, vol. 10 (1965), 51–85.

The immediate problem for Catherine de Medici and the young Charles IX in administering the Edict of Amboise was that the Parlement of Paris as well as the provincial parlements opposed the toleration articles and refused to register it. Not only were the eight parlements the highest courts of appeal for all criminal and civil cases in France (each had its own jurisdiction with the Parlement of Paris's being the largest, most of northern France), they also bore the special responsibility of registering all royal edicts. No royal edict could be enforced, in fact, without such registration. Moreover, the judges could record their opposition to any edict in the form of a remonstrance, but they were required to register all royal edicts in a prompt fashion as a charge of their office. Thus, opposition to the Edict of Amboise was a serious offence. One need only recall the fate of Anne du Bourg to remember how quickly the judges in the parlements rooted out heresy among their own ranks in the 1550s, and their opposition to the new religion was longstanding. Just as they had opposed the 'edict of toleration', they opposed the peace edict of March 1563 for legally recognizing the right of Calvinism to exist in France. In the capital the Parlement of Paris did eventually register the edict, as they were required to do, on 27 March, but only after attaching remonstrances registering their opposition as well as a proviso that limited the authority of the edict until the king reached his age of majority, when a national (and presumably Gallican) council could resolve the religious dispute. This provisional registration was a clear constitutional slap at the edict as well as at the authority of the crown in a period of minority kingship. Moreover, the footdragging in the provincial parlements followed the lead from Paris. The Parlement of Dijon delayed in registering the edict three full months in an attempt to get Burgundy removed from the edict's jurisdiction. When this failed, the judges grudgingly registered it in June with a recalcitrant remonstrance to the effect that 'the consequence of the said edict of pacification was so great that it could lead to the destruction of the Christian and Roman religion, division among the population, and civil war'. And in the Parlement of Bordeaux, where the first president (the highest presiding judge) Jacques-Benoît Lagebâton managed to get the edict registered despite the resistance of a majority of his fellow magistrates, the court eventually hounded him out of office.[13]

[13] For the Parlement of Paris see Sarah Hanley, *The Lit de Justice of the Kings of France: Constitutional Ideology in Legend, Ritual, and Discourse* (Princeton, 1983), p. 154; for the Parlement of Dijon see Bibliothèque Nationale, Paris (hereafter B. N.), Fonds français 22304, fo. 14, 19 June 1563 (copies of the registers of the Parlement of Dijon); and for the Parlement of Bordeaux see Jonathan Powis, 'Order, Religion, and the Magistrates of a Provincial Parlement', pp. 194–5.

The Queen Mother seized the initiative and countered all this constitutional opposition by staging a formal declaration of Charles IX's majority (that is, the beginning of his fourteenth year) in the Parlement of Rouen in August 1563 in the form of a *lit de justice*. This was not required of the young king, but by holding the royal ceremonial in the provincial court in Rouen, Catherine seized the opportunity to humiliate the senior Parlement of Paris for its provisional registration of the peace edict. Moreover, it was an opportunity to excoriate all the parlementaires, including those in Rouen, for not registering the edict promptly and without provision as the king had commanded. Called a *lit de justice* – literally the 'bed of justice' where the king sat whenever he visited a parlement expressly to enforce the registration of a declaration, law, or edict – the ceremony symbolized the king as the living law of the French constitution. Whenever the king visited parlement in person, his will became law and the judges were powerless to oppose it, as they themselves recognized. These visits were relatively rare, since usually *lettres de jussion* (letters expressing the king's will and ordering the registration of a particular piece of legislation) or the threat of a personal visit were enough to achieve registration. In any case, no *lit de justice* had ever taken place outside the Parlement of Paris, and the Queen Mother correctly recognized that the snubbing of the senior court on this occasion would further undermine the privileges of the Parlement of Paris. Thus, the young king's declaration of majority in the form of a *lit de justice* in the Parlement of Rouen in August 1563 had constitutional as well as religious overtones.[14]

As powerful as the king's presence was in Rouen on that occasion, it is his actions and words that merit closer attention. For the young Charles IX demanded the immediate and unconditional registration of the Edict of Amboise, as well as the loyalty of the magistrates in enforcing it. To do otherwise, as they had clearly done, was an affront to royal authority. His speech chastizing the judges on this point was so hostile and vitriolic that numerous contemporaries made note of it:

I have wanted to come to this town to thank God, who has never deserted me or my kingdom, and also to make you understand that having reached my age of majority as I have at present, that I do not intend to endure any longer the disobedience that many have shown me ever since these troubles began ... FIRSTLY ... we intend, desire, and command very explicitly, on pain of imprisonment and confiscation of property, that all our subjects observe and maintain completely and perfectly the declaration we made last March concerning the pacification of the said troubles, in all its points and

---

[14] The constitutional issues are fully examined in Hanley, *The Lit de Justice*, pp. 160–208; for the religious issues see Mack P. Holt, 'The King in Parlement: The Problem of the *Lit de justice* in Sixteenth-Century France', *The Historical Journal*, vol. 31 (1988), 507–23.

articles ... You have heard my will ... and I want to tell you that to this end you ought no longer to behave as you have been accustomed during my minority ... From this hour I am in my majority ... And when I command you [to do] something, if you find any difficulty or do not understand something, I will always be open to any remonstrances you might make to me. But after having made them, having heard my will, you are to obey me without any further fuss.[15]

Charles IX had clearly put the parlementaires in their place, or rather the Queen Mother, who had orchestrated the entire affair for her young son, had done so. The fact remained that the judges in the parlements represented a significant number of French Catholics who viewed the legal recognition of the Huguenots by the crown as a severe breach of the king's prerogative, whose declaration of majority only underscored the oath of office he took upon his *sacre* to defend the kingdom from heresy.

The prudent Catherine de Medici recognized this and immediately put in motion a campaign of royal propaganda. Her goals in announcing a long royal progress of the French court throughout the provinces in the spring of 1564 were twofold. First, she intended for the king and his chancellor, Michel de l'Hôpital, to visit each of the provincial parlements that had also opposed the edict of Amboise in order to repeat the scene enacted at Rouen. And second, she hoped that by presenting the young king personally to as many of the provincial nobles as possible she might win over a moderate block of nobles who could serve as a bulwark against the Guise and Bourbon factions that dominated the first civil war. Thus, what the Queen Mother called *'le grand voyage de France'* was a royal tour of the provinces that would last two years. Its design was clearly political: to attract support to the new king. And though such tours were hardly a novelty, it was also a sign of Catherine's desperation to win back the initiative for her young son. Virtually ignored by the warring noble factions during the first civil war, Charles and his mother were anxious to avoid being dominated by either side. Above all else, Catherine hoped to maintain peace in her son's kingdom. As the latest historians of the royal tour have remarked, the voyage that lasted from March 1564 to March 1566 was 'a strategy in response to a political crisis'.[16]

---

[15] *La Declaration faicte par le Roy de sa maiorité, tenant son lict de justice en sa cour de Parlement de Roüen, et ordonnance par luy faicte pour le bien et repos public de son Royaume: et ce qu'il dict en ladicte cour avant la publication de ladicte ordonnance* (Paris, 1563), pp. Aii and Dii–Diii. Numerous contemporaries commented on this speech, including the Parisian lawyer, Etienne Pasquier. See Etienne Pasquier, *Ecrits politiques*, ed. Dorothy Thickett (Geneva, 1966), p. 293.

[16] Easily the best of several accounts of the royal voyage is that by Jean Boutier, Alain Dewerpe, and Daniel Nordman, *Un tour de France royal: Le voyage de Charles IX, 1564–1566* (Paris, 1984), quote on p. 169.

Departing the royal château at Fontainebleau in March 1564, the court headed eastward to Sens, Troyes, Châlons, and Bar-le-Duc, before turning southward down the eastern frontier of the kingdom (see Map 3). The Burgundian capital of Dijon was reached in May, when the scene at Rouen was repeated in the Parlement of Dijon in another *lit de justice*. There on 24 May 1564, in the Parlement of Toulouse on 5 February 1565, and in the Parlement of Bordeaux on 12 April 1565, the king and the chancellor scolded the parlementaires for disobeying the king by refusing to register the Edict of Amboise unconditionally and for deliberately not enforcing it. The same speeches and royal ceremonial used in Rouen were reenacted in *lits de justice* in these three provincial parlements (one was planned for the Parlement of Aix-en-Provence in October 1564 but was cancelled at the last minute). Chancellor l'Hôpital made explicit the king's and the Queen Mother's anger if the parlementaires were in any doubt after Charles's own speech:

The king has not come to this region simply to see the world, as rumour has it, but to supervise his family like any good father … He has discovered a number of faults in this parlement … and the principal shortcoming is the disobedience that you demonstrate toward your king. You ought to require and encourage the publication of the king's edicts and ordinances [rather than resist them] … He has achieved a lasting peace [with the Protestants] but is still at war with the parlement.

And it was this war with the parlements that the Queen Mother hoped to win conclusively on the royal tour. The speeches of the king and l'Hôpital were generally met by embarrassed and stony silence, as the provincial courts had gone to great trouble and expense to prepare for the royal visits, their first *lits de justice* as at Rouen. And while the episodes did nothing to counteract the opposition of the magistrates to the edict of pacification, the king's presence did guarantee the edict's unconditional registration.[17] Wintering in Languedoc the first winter and at Moulins the second, the peripatetic court did not return to Fontainebleau until the spring of 1566. While much of the Queen Mother's political strategy had been achieved by the long voyage, so many petitions were presented to her and the king en route that it became increasingly clear that both Protestants and Catholics alike were failing to uphold the various articles of the edict throughout the realm. Many Catholics complained bitterly that Protestant services

[17] Ibid., pp. 241–7. The primary sources also show that the *lit de justice* at Rouen was repeated with very few alterations at Dijon, Toulouse, and Bordeaux. For Toulouse and Bordeaux, see Théodore Godefroy, *Le Cérémonial francoys*, 2 vols. (Paris, 1649 edn.), II, 580–1 and 590; and for Dijon see B. N., Fonds français 22302, fos. 1–10 (copies of the registers of the Parlement of Dijon).

Map 3 Royal Tour of the Provinces, 1564–66

were held in many more places than those explicitly allowed in the edict. This was especially true in the south where in many towns Protestant services went on undisturbed as before the war. Likewise, Huguenots protested that many Catholics were not enforcing or recognizing the toleration clauses allowing them to worship in specific places. Or more generally, many Catholics were finding all kinds of pretexts to disrupt the lives of French Protestants. It was thus very clear to Catherine that agitators on both sides had initiated violence of various sorts.

Typical of these complaints was a remonstrance from Protestant noblemen in the county of Maine, presented to the king when the court passed through that region on the royal progress. It catalogued 56 printed pages of anecdotal episodes of Catholic violence against Huguenot nobles, of which the following was fairly representative:

Marguerite de Hurtelon, widow of the sieur de la Guynandière ... was the twenty-fourth of last October [1563] massacred in her house in the parish of St-Georges; along with Charles her son, aged eleven or twelve; Faith, Juliette, and Hope her daughters, the oldest of whom was not yet eighteen years old; and two chambermaids. Almighty God, how can you allow and suffer to happen such bloody butchery of so many innocent people? How can you watch this horrible tragedy with your own eyes without it moving your spirit? Did not you observe with fright and astonishment these execrable executioners when they slit the throat of this mother, then shot her five times in her breasts with a pistol, and then burned the hands and feet of Faith, her eldest daughter, in order to make her tell them where her mother had hidden some money she had recently received? And after the massacre was completed and the house was ransacked, did not you see them lead the pigs into the house and enclose them there, in order to make them eat all those poor dead corpses?[18]

Even if these lurid details were entirely accurate and without exaggeration, there appear to be forces other than religion at work here. Although it is implied that the murderers killed this Huguenot widow and her children and servants on account of religion, all the internal evidence indicates that theft, robbery, and the chance to display their sexual power over women was what motivated them. The perpetrators' own religious motives are neither mentioned nor analysed. Nevertheless, it is also clear from the sheer number of such complaints, whether exaggerated or not, that Catholics in many parts of France made little effort to treat the lives and property of Protestants with the respect and recognition that the Edict of Amboise required. To many Catholics, Huguenots were still perceived as an impurity to be purged, a blemish to be excised, or indeed, nothing but garbage to be fed to pigs. 'Which house of those of the [reformed] religion have they [French Catholics] approached', asked

---

[18] *Remonstrance envoyee au Roy par la noblesse de la religion reformee du païs & Comté du Maine, sur les assassinats, pilleries, saccagements de maisons, seditions, violements de femmes et autres exces horribles commis depuis la publication de l'Edit de pacification dedans ledit Comté: et presentee à Sa Maiesté à Rossillon le x.iour d'Aoust, 1564* (n.p., 1564), pp. 16–17.

these same Protestant nobles, 'that they have not pillaged, tainted with blood, and polluted with garbage and debauchery?'[19]

Despite the assassination of the duke of Guise and the deaths of the king of Navarre and the marshal St-André during the first civil war, the Catholic faction at court remained dominant under Guise leadership, principally the two brothers of the slain duke of Guise: Claude, duke of Aumale and Charles, cardinal of Lorraine. The latter especially took up the mantle of his elder brother and came to dominate the council of the young Charles IX by the end of the royal tour of the provinces. As one of the wealthiest members of the episcopate, he had represented France at the closing sessions of the Council of Trent and developed close ties with Rome and Madrid in the process. By the end of the royal tour in 1566 the cardinal of Lorraine had not only come to wield great influence on the royal council, but he had become its de facto leader: this is exactly what Catherine de Medici had been hoping to avoid. And the Guise domination of the council was all the more alarming to her because Condé and Coligny had stopped attending council meetings, and because the king's heir and younger brother – Henry, duke of Anjou – had come under the spell of the cardinal. The result was that Lorraine pressed for two complementary policies: a continuation of the war against the Huguenots, and for the crown to recognize the Guise vendetta against admiral Coligny, whom they believed had masterminded the assassination of Francis, duke of Guise at the siege of Orléans in 1563. Both these goals were clearly counter-productive to the peace aims of the Queen Mother.[20]

Catherine de Medici had even less control of the international situation. The summer of 1566 witnessed a wave of iconoclastic riots in the major towns of the provinces of the southern Netherlands, part of the former Burgundian empire on France's northern frontier administered by Philip II of Spain. Organized by a small number of Calvinist preachers, these rioters unleashed a wave of destruction against all sacred images in the Catholic churches (Calvin himself had denounced such images), resulting in Philip's sending a Spanish army to the Netherlands to put down this 'iconoclastic fury' and to restore law and order.[21] What made this situation so alarming for both Protestants and Catholics in France was that this Spanish army, led by the duke of Alva, travelled overland

[19] Ibid., pp. 5–6: 'Quelle maison de ceux de la Religion [reformée] ont-ils approché, qu'ils nayent pillee, teincte de sang, & souillee d'ordure & de paillardise?'
[20] Sutherland, *The Massacre of Saint Bartholomew*, pp. 47–56.
[21] See Phyllis Mack Crew, *Calvinist Preaching and Iconoclasm in the Netherlands, 1544–1569* (Cambridge, 1978), especially ch. 6; and Geoffrey Parker, *The Dutch Revolt* (London, 1977), ch. 2.

along France's eastern frontier to get to the Netherlands. The presence of so many foreign troops along this 'Spanish road' was always likely to worsen an already volatile religious situation in France, and it was the march of Alva's Spanish army along the French frontier in June and July 1567 that led directly to the outbreak of civil war once again.[22]

With the Guises dominating the royal council and the young Charles IX having contracted for 6,000 Swiss mercenaries to supplement his personal guard, many Huguenots not unreasonably feared that there might be some secret agenda afoot to divert Alva's army into France en route to the Netherlands in order to defeat the Protestants militarily once and for all. That Catherine de Medici had briefly met with the duke of Alva in Bayonne when the French court passed close to the Spanish border during the royal tour of the provinces in the spring just two years before only intensified their suspicions, even though we now know that the Queen Mother had no such ideas of conspiracy against the Huguenots in mind. Thus, fearing something sinister Condé and Coligny organized yet another plot in September 1567 to liberate the king from the Guise-dominated court. Planning to surprise the court at Meaux, the Huguenot leaders hoped to avoid the mistakes of the earlier planned coup that backfired at Amboise in March 1560. Like that attempt, this conspiracy also failed, but not before a number of risings planned to coincide with the coup had been carried out. Even though they were unable to capture the king, the Protestants did seize a number of fortified towns: Orléans, Nîmes, Valence, Auxerre, Mâcon, and Montpellier among the most important. The result of all these events was the beginning of the second civil war in September 1567. And the possibility that Alva's troops might intervene was now real, as an alarmed Catherine de Medici was unable to prevent the cardinal of Lorraine from dispatching an agent to Alva to invite him to intervene.[23]

Militarily, the second civil war was virtually a repeat of the first. The supplement of the 6,000 Swiss guards ultimately prevented the conspiracy at Meaux from succeeding, as they escorted the king and Queen Mother safely back to Paris. Condé and Coligny were unwilling to concede defeat and mounted a siege of the capital even though their own troops were far outnumbered by the royal troops and Swiss guards within. The result of this Protestant strategy – another attempt at kidnapping the king and a siege of the capital with Charles and his court captive within – only intensified many

[22] For a description and analysis of the strategic importance of this route along the French frontier, see Geoffrey Parker, *The Army of Flanders and the Spanish Road, 1567–1659* (Cambridge, 1972).
[23] Sutherland, *The Massacre of Saint Bartholomew*, pp. 58–62; and Salmon, *Society in Crisis*, pp. 168–70.

Catholic fears that Protestantism and rebellion went hand in hand. This might not have mattered if the Huguenots could have defeated the king's forces militarily, but they could not, even with large reinforcements of German troops led by John Casimir, the son of the Calvinist Frederick III, count and elector of the Palatinate. The only major confrontation of troops occurred at Saint-Denis just north of Paris in November 1567. In the fracas the constable, Anne de Montmorency, repelled the Protestant army of Condé, who was forced to flee southward to try to rendezvous with the German reinforcements led by Casimir. But the royal victory was a costly one, as Anne de Montmorency died from wounds suffered in battle. The death of the last of the original triumvirs – and the only really experienced Catholic military commander not in league with the Guises – resulted in another stalemate. Though Condé, Coligny, and Casimir continued to besiege several towns along the Loire, they were powerless to defeat the king's army militarily wthout a massive amount of additional foreign support, which additional overtures to Elizabeth and further agents dispatched to other German princes failed to procure. Thus, compromise and a return to the status quo of the peace of Amboise proved to be the best result for both sides. After only six months of fighting a negotiated peace settlement was reached at Longjumeau in March 1568.[24]

The Edict of Longjumeau essentially restored the Edict of Amboise of March 1563. Protestantism was legally recognized by the crown and its worship was allowed in the suburbs of one town in each *bailliage* and *sénéchausée* in the kingdom, as well as on noble estates outside the towns. The only significant addition was that this time the edict was sent directly to the royal governors in the provinces for publication and implementation, rather than awaiting registration by the parlements. Catherine de Medici was not about to stand for the footdragging of the parlements after the Edict of Amboise, and the Edict of Longjumeau explicitly ordered the courts to register the peace settlement forthwith (it was registered in the Parlement of Paris on 27 March 1568, just three days after it was first published). But given that it was Catholic opposition to the terms of the Edict of Amboise that was the principal cause of the renewal of the Wars of Religion, it seemed clear to all that this peace settlement was destined to be a temporary one. Above all, the cardinal of Lorraine, with support from both Madrid and Rome, was determined to overturn it.[25]

[24] For details of the second civil war, see Thompson, *The Wars of Religion in France*, pp. 326–48; Sutherland, *The Massacre of Saint Bartholomew*, pp. 57–62; and Salmon, *Society in Crisis*, pp. 168–72.

[25] The text of the Edict of Longjumeau is printed in Stegmann, ed., *Edits des guerres de religion*, pp. 53–8; while there is a good summary in English in Sutherland, *The Huguenot Struggle for Recognition*, pp. 156–8 and 358.

A conspiracy designed by the cardinal of Lorraine almost immediately led to a renewal of the civil wars. Within weeks of the publication of the Edict of Longjumeau the cardinal had convinced those members of the council opposed to any reconciliation with the Protestants that it was necessary to seize the initiative. A plot was hatched that had as its goals not only the seizure of the Protestant towns of Orléans, Soissons, La Rochelle, and Auxerre, but also the capture of the Huguenot leaders Condé and Coligny. Because Lorraine so dominated the council, it was not long before moderates such as l'Hôpital, who had advocated toleration of the Huguenots and the enforcement of the peace edicts, found themselves in a distinct minority. Neither the weak Charles IX nor his worried mother were able to undermine the Guise domination of the council, a grip that was strengthened by the apparent winning of the confidence of Charles's younger brother, Henry, duke of Anjou. Anjou had been appointed as lieutenant-general of the royal army, making him in effect the commander-in-chief of Charles's forces since the death of the constable in November 1567. With a royal prince of the blood – and the heir to the throne – now backing him, the cardinal of Lorraine was able to overturn the recent peace agreement in the council. When in August 1568 the council voted to revoke the peace of Longjumeau and to arrest Condé and the admiral, they effectively declared war on the Huguenots. As with all the previous coup attempts, however, this one failed miserably. Condé and Coligny managed to make their escape to La Rochelle in September where they raised Protestant forces for the third civil war.[26]

The outbreak of the third civil war in September 1568 was much more closely tied to the international scene than either of the previous two struggles. Events in France were being closely followed all over Europe as the third civil war was entwined with events both in the Netherlands and in England. In the Netherlands the arrival of the duke of Alva the previous year had resulted in a policy of terror, whereby Alva was seeking to arrest and execute those members of the Netherlands nobility who had been involved in the revolt. This policy reached a climax in June 1568 when sixty Netherlands nobles (including Coligny's cousin, the count of Horne) were put to death on the Grand Place in Brussels. William of Orange managed to escape to Germany, where he had undertaken the task of raising a foreign army to lead back to the Netherlands in hopes of driving out Alva's Spanish forces. Although he sought out principally German Protestant princes for their support, it was only natural that Orange should also turn in his time of need to the French Protestant

[26] Sutherland, *The Huguenot Struggle for Recognition*, pp. 158–70; and Salmon, *Society in Crisis*, pp. 173–4.

leaders to see if they could help. In August Orange signed a formal treaty of mutual support with Condé and Coligny, in which each side agreed to help the other defeat the 'evil councillors' who were misleading their respective sovereigns to destroy the new religion as well as the nobility. While neither side was in a strong enough position to offer much sustained aid to the other, both Orange and the Huguenots recognized the need for an alliance in order to survive. And since Philip II of Spain, who had encouraged and supported the efforts of the cardinal of Lorraine to renew the war against the Protestants in France, was a common enemy, it was a union that made a lot of sense. The ultimate result was, moreover, that the revolt in the Netherlands and the French Wars of Religion would remain firmly linked for the next sixteen years.[27]

Events in England had also become closely connected with the religious wars in France through the diplomacy of the cardinal of Lorraine. The Catholic Mary Stuart, queen of Scotland was Lorraine's niece (Mary's mother, Mary of Guise, was the cardinal's sister), and in May 1568 she had fled from Scotland into England as a large number of Scottish noblemen converted to Calvinism and turned against her. What made Mary such a dangerous exile was the fact that she was next in line to the Tudor crown in England as long as Elizabeth remained childless. Thus, Lorraine saw in Mary's exile an opportunity to try to undermine English Protestantism as well as a chance to widen his own influence in English affairs. Elizabeth had Mary promptly imprisoned, and Lorraine made no secret of his wish to liberate his niece and place her on the English throne in place of the heretic Elizabeth. He even went so far as to advocate that Mary might then marry the duke of Anjou, thus eventually uniting the two Catholic crowns. His various machinations to do so led to his being perceived as the 'arch-priest of the papacy' and 'the minister of mischief'. And while his involvement in several plots against Elizabeth never achieved his desired aims, it meant that the advent of war in France was being watched with great interest from both England and the Netherlands, as Lorraine had clearly established himself as a champion of the anti-Protestant cause.[28] It was precisely because of these international ties that the third civil war was destined to be a longer and more protracted affair than the previous two. Foreign support from various Protestant states enabled the Huguenots to withstand the royal army much more effectively than in the earlier wars, and for this reason the third civil war lasted nearly two years.

What further fuelled the flames of civil war again in 1568 was less international politics than the same cultural clash between Protestants

---

[27] Sutherland, *The Massacre of St Bartholomew*, pp. 74–5.   [28] Ibid., pp. 68–74.

and Catholics that had spawned religious violence for over a decade.
The most visible sign of the growing uneasiness many lay Catholics felt
about royal accommodation of the new religion was the burgeoning
number of lay confraternities that emerged in the towns throughout the
kingdom. In theory they existed to demonstrate piety and devotion before
God in a time of religious strife, but in many instances these confraternities were designed to provide arms and men for the church militant in
a holy crusade against French Protestantism. One such example was
the Confraternity of the Holy Ghost formed in 1567 in Dijon by the
lieutenant-general of the province, Gaspard de Saulx, seigneur de Tavannes.
The oath sworn upon admission into this group required all its members
to be willing to take up arms and follow its leader – Tavannes – in
defending the faith. Under the banner of the cross, the Confraternity of
the Holy Ghost stressed the eucharistic community of the faithful, as the
Mass was God's means for 'men of good will to serve with him and each
other, such that they were made from the bones of his bones, the flesh of
his flesh, and the members of his members'.[29] In essence, the confraternity
was a crusade against the infidel Protestants, with the kingdom of France
being the new Jerusalem infiltrated by God's enemies. Tavannes's
influence in Burgundy resulted in similar confraternities being founded
in Autun, Beaune, Chalon-sur-Saône, Tournus, and Mâcon within a year.
And their popularity was hardly limited to the ultra-Catholic province of
Burgundy, as by September 1568 Catholic confraternities of the Holy
Ghost appeared in Bourges, Troyes, Beauvais, Maine, Anjou, and
Languedoc. All these groups stressed Catholic community and solidarity
against the rising tide of heresy, or as Tavannes explained to the Dijon
magistrates, 'justice is painted holding a pair of scales: seeing one side full
of sedition, heresy, and rebellion, and on the other the honour of God and
the service of the king'.[30] Thus, the image of another holy crusade against
Protestantism to drive the infidel out of God's kingdom was at the heart of
the popularity of these confraternities. Although they were ineffective in
some areas, they proved very successful in stemming the spread of
Calvinism in others. In Dijon, for example, these shock troops of the
church militant were largely responsible for the hundreds of abjurations
of the new religion between 1567 and 1570, as Huguenots were evicted
from their homes and threatened with loss of property if they did not
abjure. The Confraternity of the Holy Ghost, like many other similar

[29] The text of the oath is printed in Edmond Belle, *La Réforme à Dijon des origines à la fin de la lieutenance-générale de Gaspard de Saulx-Tavanes, 1530–1570* (Dijon, 1911), pp. 215–19 (quotes on pp. 215 and 217).
[30] Quoted in ibid., p. 112.

groups throughout the kingdom, was a sure sign of the popular discontent many Catholics felt over the crown's inability or unwillingness to extirpate the new religion from the realm of the Most Catholic King. And these confraternities were further evidence that the civil wars, while fought with many foreign troops and occupying the centre stage of international politics, were still fundamentally based on a deep-seated conflict of two conflicting godly cultures.[31]

The protracted fighting during the third civil war lasted from the autumn of 1568 to the summer of 1570. Instead of their previous strategy of trying to hold towns along the Loire, Condé and Coligny opted for a defence of the southwest by placing garrisons in fortified towns such as Cognac, Angoulême, Castres, and Montpellier. Moreover, the Huguenots had the advantage of foreign support in the form of troops from the Netherlands led by William of Orange and his brother, Louis of Nassau in December 1568, as well as a mercenary army from Germany led by the duke of Zweibrücken in June 1569. Even with these reinforcements, however, the first two major confrontations of the third civil war proved disastrous for the Huguenots. In March 1569 a royal army nominally under the command of the king's younger brother, Henry, duke of Anjou – the seigneur de Tavannes was actually in charge – soundly defeated the Protestant forces at Jarnac near Angoulême. The Huguenots suffered more than just a military defeat, however, as the many casualties included the long-suffering Protestant commander, Louis, prince of Condé, leaving Coligny in charge advised only by Jeanne d'Albret, her young son Henry of Navarre, and Condé's fifteen-year-old heir. Even with the reinforcements of Zweibrücken's German mercenaries in June, Coligny's troops proved no match for the superior royal forces. When in October 1569, Anjou – supported by his own German and Swiss mercenaries – handed a second major defeat to the Huguenots at Moncontour near Poitiers, Coligny and the remnants of his army were forced to retreat to the southeast towards Languedoc in order to regroup. Anjou was determined to break the Protestants' hold on the southwest once and for all, and instead of going after Coligny he mounted a long and very costly siege on the Huguenot stronghold of St-Jean-d' Angély

---

[31] On the confraternities in general, see Thompson, *The Wars of Religion in France*, pp. 352–4; Robert R. Harding, 'The Mobilization of Confraternities against the Reformation in France', *Sixteenth-Century Journal*, vol. 11 (1980), 85–107; Andrew E. Barnes, 'Religious Anxiety and Devotional Change in Sixteenth-century French Penitential Confraternities', *Sixteenth Century Journal*, vol. 19 (1988), 389–405; and Crouzet, *Les guerriers de Dieu*, I, pp. 383–91. On the Confraternity of the Holy Ghost in Dijon see Belle, *La Réforme à Dijon*, pp. 109–21, and pp. 201–8 for lists of Protestants imprisoned and those who abjured.

Map 4 The Third Civil War, 1568–70

near Saintes (see Map 4). Anjou's army suffered heavy losses during this long and unsuccessful siege, and he eventually was forced to abandon it altogether. Meanwhile, Coligny regrouped his forces in the south and was joined by 4,000 troops recruited by several Protestant viscounts in Languedoc. Following the Rhône northwards to Burgundy, the

Huguenot army met and defeated the royal army at Arnay-le-Duc in June 1570, giving Coligny a much stronger bargaining position with the crown. But with neither side able to inflict a permanent defeat on the other, the admiral and Catherine de Medici agreed to another peace settlement. Signed in August 1570, the Edict of St-Germain ended the third civil war with yet another compromise peace settlement that left both sides anxious and suspicious. And ironically, that same month the cardinal of Lorraine, who had precipitated the third civil war with his ambitious plans to exterminate heresy at home and abroad, was disgraced and forced off the king's council.[32] The peace edict signed at St-Germain on 8 August 1570 reflected the revived Huguenot strength at the end of the third civil war. It was a settlement that was far more favourable to the Protestants than the Edicts of Amboise or Longjumeau, and it provided the legal framework for the reintegration of the Huguenots into French Catholic society, from which they had been explicitly ostracized for nearly a decade. Besides repeating the religious privileges for the nobility that were included in the two earlier edicts, this edict allowed the open worship of Protestantism inside two towns in each of the twelve *gouvernements* (the largest administrative districts of the kingdom), granting the open worship of Protestantism inside towns for the first time. But unlike the earlier edicts, the Edict of St-Germain spelled out exactly which towns these were, making non-compliance much more difficult for Catholics. Another Protestant gain was the right to occupy four fortified towns for a period of two years: La Rochelle, Cognac, and Montauban, which cemented the Huguenot hold on the southwest, and La Charité, which gave them a bridgehead on the Loire. These towns not only provided a much-needed place of refuge for all Huguenots under persecution, but they allowed the Protestants to continue to arm and maintain garrisons of troops. Moreover, the port of La Rochelle – which would soon become the Huguenot capital – allowed further contacts with both England and the Netherlands. Finally, the edict made an effort to reintegrate the two cultures of Protestants and Catholics, or at least provided the framework to do so by requiring the recognition of a number of basic civil rights that Huguenots had been repeatedly denied: equality in taxation, the right to hold offices, in short, equality before the law. Moreover, all property and offices seized from Protestants since the outbreak of the civil wars, which was considerable in many parts of France, was to be restored. This was hardly complete toleration of the Protestant faith, which is what they had

---

[32] For the various military campaigns of the third civil war, see Thompson, *The Wars of Religion in France*, pp. 349–421; Sutherland, *The Huguenot Struggle for Recognition*, pp. 158–77; and Salmon, *Society in Crisis*, pp. 173–6.

been fighting for, but it was much closer to that than any previous settlement the Huguenots had agreed to. Yet despite all these gains, the Edict of St-Germain was decidedly not a Protestant victory; the same longstanding problem remained: how to enforce the peace settlement amidst a clear majority of Catholics who were pursuing a new Jerusalem devoid of all infidel.[33]

Three civil wars had been fought in less than a decade, and one obvious question is why the crown – with clearly superior manpower and resources – was so explicitly unable to defeat the undermanned and outmatched Huguenots. Why were the royal forces so utterly unable to mount a convincing victory on the battlefield? A number of factors were responsible, but in each war a similar set of problems were encountered that prevented a total victory: (1) a lack of preparedness, (2) difficulties of mobilization, (3) the large-scale nature of the conflict, (4) an inability to maintain armies in the field for long periods, and (5) structural problems involved in demobilization.[34] The unpreparedness of the royal forces was most clearly manifest in the way they were garrisoned. The heart and soul of an early modern army consisted of the *gendarmerie*, that is, the heavy cavalry. And the *gendarmes* of the royal army at the outbreak of the Wars of Religion were widely scattered across the kingdom with concentrations along the northeastern frontier. Of the 91 different companies in 1564 – a company was upwards of 200 men – 13 were garrisoned in Picardy, 15 in Champagne, and the other 63 companies scattered across 19 different provinces from Normandy to Provence. Thus, the widespread dispersal of these forces in peacetime made it virtually impossible for the crown to assemble the concentration of forces necessary for a strategic strike. Secondly, once war broke out, the difficulties involved in mobilizing these troops presented other problems. With the bulk of the *gendarmes* garrisoned on the frontier, it took time to mobilize them to Huguenot strongholds along the Loire and in the southwest. Moreover, the crown relied heavily on foreign mercenaries and they took even longer to raise and mobilize from abroad. During the second civil war for example, which lasted only six months from September 1567 to March 1568, Charles IX employed 429 companies of infantry, *gendarmes*, and light cavalry. Of the total of just over 72,000 men, fully one-third were mercenaries hired from abroad, largely Swiss, Germans, and Italians.

[33] The edict is printed in Stegmann, ed., *Edits des guerres de religion*, pp. 69–81; and a good summary in English is in Sutherland, *The Huguenot Struggle for Recognition*, pp. 176–7 and 358–60.
[34] This paragraph is heavily dependent on James B. Wood, *The King's Army: Warfare, Soldiers, and Society during the Wars of Religion in France, 1562–1576* (Cambridge, 1996).

Many of these only arrived months after they were promised, and some did not arrive until after the peace of Longjumeau had been concluded. The royal commanders were simply never able to amass this large force at any one time. A third problem they faced was the vast scale on which the civil wars were fought. France was an immense country and the Huguenots had seized numerous towns throughout the kingdom. For this reason the fighting was never concentrated in any one region. To defeat a Huguenot army on the field did not significantly affect the numerous fortified cities the Protestants held, particularly along the Loire and in the southwest. In the first civil war, the Huguenots were forced to abandon several towns along the Seine and Loire after lengthy sieges, but their numerical strength in the south was not threatened. A further problem was the difficulty of maintaining an army in the field for any protracted period of time. Troops had to be paid whether they were contracted or conscripted, and they also had to be fed. Thus, a perennial lack of funds was a continual hurdle. During the 1560s the crown spent an average of 4.6 million *livres tournois* per year to maintain its army. With an annual revenue of only about 10 million *livres*, this amounted to a military expenditure of forty per cent of total revenues. The fiscal picture was not nearly so rosy, however, as the royal debt – a legacy of the Habsburg–Valois Wars – stood at 60 million *livres* in 1560 and rose every year once the civil wars broke out in 1562. Companies invariably deserted, mutinied, or both, as wages built up in arrears, and the civilian population always paid the price for the break-up of the army. Finally, once all these factors forced a peace settlement on the crown, the king was anxious to demobilize his army as quickly as possible, to return them to their peacetime garrisons along the frontier, and initiate the cycle of unpreparedness all over again. So, even though the Huguenots made up less than 10 per cent of the French population, a variety of factors that were institutionalized in early modern warfare prevented a military victory over them in anything like short order. To be sure, Condé and Coligny were prudent enough to take advantage of this situation and the result was the new concessions won at St-Germain in August 1570.

The other side of the coin was that because of its size the Protestant minority did not have the same structural problems in fighting as did the royal forces. They were defending fortified towns, bunched primarily along the Loire and in the southwest, and did not have to garrison troops along a long frontier. Moreover, the Huguenot military organization took great advantage of the close ties and communication in the hierarchical structure of the Huguenot church itself, better to ensure the payment of troops as well as to coordinate its forces better. Finally, one has to take some account of the strategy and tactics provided by the Huguenot nobility, especially Condé and Coligny, in maintaining their struggle with the crown. In short, the Huguenots benefitted militarily from the structural weaknesses of the royal army, and this partly explains their revival at the end of the third civil war.

It was also clear to contemporaries that the third civil war had marked a new stage in the conflict. Whereas the first two civil wars had both been dominated by siege warfare in a few towns north of the Loire, the third war involved the mobilization of large numbers of troops over large distances throughout the centre and south of the kingdom, exposing the rural population to costs of war they had not previously known. While exact numbers of casualties – both military and civilian – are impossible to establish, it is evident that many more civilians suffered in the third civil war than in the previous two. In terms of murder, billeting of troops, sacking of homes, theft of property and livestock, disruption of agricultural production, and the flight of many defenceless peasants in the rural countryside to the protection of fortified towns, the third civil war brought the Wars of Religion to the civilian population of the kingdom as a whole with an immediacy that was lacking in the earlier wars. Because of this, the religious zeal and piety of the masses began to display itself more openly, not just in the form of confraternities but also in occasional violence. While Montaigne remarked that 'if anyone should sift out of the army, even the average loyalist army, those who march in it from the pure zeal of affection for religion ... he could not make up one complete company of men-at-arms out of them', this was not true of the populace at large.[35]

The crusade of popular piety and the zeal to extirpate the infidel Huguenots from the kingdom that earmarked so many of the confraternities in the late 1560s was accompanied by more open outbreaks of popular violence. Filled with a sense of mission and divine prophecy, many French Catholics took to heart the message to drive the infidel out of the kingdom spelled out explicitly in print and from the pulpit. One pamphlet published in 1568 called them 'to spill your blood for God, even to the last drop'.[36] The public display of the symbols or rituals of Protestant or Catholic culture seemed to invite a response from their opponents that often led to violence. In Amiens on the first Sunday after Easter 1568 violence erupted and more than a hundred people were killed after an artisan roofer spoke out against the mass and insulted a priest in the market place. A riot occurred in Rouen on 5 September

[35] Michel de Montaigne, 'Apology for Raymond Sebond' in *The Complete Essays of Montaigne*, ed. Donald M. Frame (Stanford, 1965 edn.), p. 323.
[36] Quoted in Crouzet, *Les guerriers de Dieu*, I, p. 377.

1568 after mass was celebrated in the church of the Cordeliers. Another uprising took place in Metz on 4 April 1569 when Protestants disrupted a Catholic procession honouring God for the defeat of the Huguenots and the death of Condé at Jarnac. And similar violence occurred in the Catholic stronghold of Dijon in May 1570 when a Protestant baptized his dog in a public fountain and forced the poor beast to drag a statue of St Anthony through the streets, 'in contempt of the holy sacrament of baptism and the veneration of the saints' as the Dijon magistrates remarked.[37] Even if Montaigne was correct about the relative lack of religious zeal of the soldiers on either side during the early civil wars, the French people were clearly becoming more attuned to the pamphlets and sermons urging them to heed God's will to eliminate the infidel threat within the kingdom. If political decisions at court, the mobilization of troops from abroad, international politics, and the leadership of the nobility determined the outcome of the first three civil wars, the growing religious zeal of the masses continued to bubble ever closer to the surface. This religious tension between Protestant and Catholic cultures finally exploded in an extended fury of popular violence in the fourth civil war, when all the political decision-making of the court nobility receded into the background as Catholics across the kingdom made a concerted effort to spill Protestant blood, 'even to the last drop'.

[37] The incidents at Amiens, Rouen, and Metz are recounted in ibid. The incident at Dijon is in Archives municipales de Dijon, B 206, fol. 164r, 9 May 1570.

3   Popular disorder and religious tensions: the making of a massacre, 1570–1574

The Peace of St-Germain that concluded the third civil war in August 1570 promised much in the way of establishing a genuine and lasting peace. With legal provisions for enforcing the reintegration of the Huguenots back into the mainstream of French society introduced by the peace edict, with the Protestant queen of England seeking to strengthen ties with France with a possible marriage to one of the king's younger brothers, and with Catherine de Medici herself seeking to strengthen the bonds between the crown and the Huguenots by trying to arrange a marriage between her daughter Marguerite and the Protestant Henry of Navarre, the period following the conclusion of the third civil war offered hope that the calamities and horrors of war of the previous decade might be excised. Nevertheless, the diplomatic efforts of the political leadership to engender harmony with the Huguenots only heightened the fears of those Catholics throughout the kingdom, who had been raising the stakes of religious violence in the late 1560s. Thus, diplomatic efforts at court to create a lasting peace and restore order masked the further polarization of the Protestant and Catholic communities among the popular classes. At the same time, many Catholic nobles at court were becoming alarmed at the increasingly radical – and sometimes revolutionary – rhetoric of much Huguenot political polemic published since 1567. Overt suggestions that kings contracted their authority from 'the people' struck at the heart of the sacral foundations of the French monarchy and went a long way toward alienating many Catholic nobles further from any lasting peace. Although it took a single event of great magnitude in the capital to spark off the violence – a bungled assassination attempt on the Protestant leader, Admiral Coligny – the popular religious tensions that had been building up over the course of several years would explode in a wave of massacres in a dozen towns throughout France. Thousands of Huguenots would be slain in a bloodbath of violence lasting over a month, and most of the Protestant blood which flowed from these massacres was spilled by the hands of civilians rather than soldiers. How diplomatic overtures for peace by the aristocratic leadership at court turned into a 'season' of popular religious violence throughout the kingdom from late August to early October 1572 is the initial focus of this chapter.[1] It concludes with the by now familiar pattern of both sides rearming to renew the civil wars. The St Bartholomew's massacres of 1572 did more than spark off the fourth civil war, however: these massacres radically transformed the nature of the conflict and seriously weakened the Protestant movement in France.

The situation in France in August 1570 was vastly different from the peace following the first two civil wars. The Edict of St-Germain had left the Huguenots not as a defeated minority, but as a strong military and political community in possession of four vital fortified towns: La Rochelle on the Atlantic coast, La Charité on the Loire, Cognac on the Charente, and Montauban on the Tarn. With legal and judicial safe-guards and guarantees built into the enforcement of the peace edict, most of the problems of Catholic non-compliance of the first two peace edicts had been circumvented. Moreover, the Huguenots' greatest opponents at court – the Guises – had fallen out of favour, leaving a more moderate coalition of Catholic nobles at court seemingly ready to implement Catherine de Medici's desire for peace.

Meanwhile, one of the Queen Mother's marriage projects collapsed under its own weight. Henry, duke of Anjou suddenly announced in January 1571 that he had no desire to marry the Protestant queen of England. He had long been a protégé of the Guises, and both the duke and the cardinal of Guise used members of Anjou's household to keep them informed of affairs at court. The Guise faction, along with the Spanish ambassador and papal nuncio at court, had all put serious pressure on Anjou to recognize his duty to the true faith and to renounce the heretic Elizabeth. They were more inclined to pursue an Anjou match with the Catholic Mary Stuart of Scotland, Elizabeth's prisoner, a scenario that the Ridolphi plot, uncovered in England a few months later, proved was no mere fantasy. In the short run, however, Anjou's dramatic announcement ruined the plans of his embarrassed mother, who was then forced to offer Elizabeth her youngest son, François, duke of Alençon, as a replacement. Although Catherine continued to proceed with marriage plans for Anjou for nearly another year, she began pushing Alençon's candidacy in earnest in February 1571. Already squeamish on account of Anjou's young age and his ties to the ultra-Catholics in France, Elizabeth found little comfort in the prospect of an even younger French suitor,

[1] I have borrowed the term from Janine [Garrisson-]Estèbe, *Tocsin pour un massacre: la saison des Saint-Barthélemy* (Paris, 1968).

especially one reputed to be disfigured from smallpox.[2] Thus, one of the marriage alliances the Queen Mother had hoped to arrange was definitely a non-starter by 1572. Catherine would have to be content with a marriage between her daughter Marguerite and the Huguenot king of Navarre. What was making her job of arranging a Protestant–Catholic alliance so difficult, however, was the escalating tensions between Huguenots and French Catholics by 1572.

One factor behind this rising tension was that Huguenot political rhetoric had acquired a decidedly anti-royalist tone during the second and third civil wars. While Calvin's *Institution of the Christian Religion* seemed to suggest that private citizens owed their obedience even to an ungodly king – only lesser magistrates could legally oppose the authority of a wicked king – his biblical commentaries published late in his life offered more intriguing possibilities. In his *Readings on the Prophet Daniel* first published in 1561, Calvin argued that when Daniel refused to obey King Darius, 'he committed no sin', since whenever rulers disobeyed God, 'they automatically abdicate their worldly power'. Calvin went even further in his *Sermons on the Last Eight Chapters of the Book of Daniel* published posthumously in 1565. Describing the same biblical incident, Calvin argued that when kings defy God, 'they are no longer worthy to be counted as princes ... [And] when they raise themselves up against God ... it is necessary that they should in turn be laid low'.[3]

The implications for French Huguenots were all too clear in the context of the religious wars, and a number of Protestant writers propagated anti-monarchical ideas as early as 1564. The anonymously written *Redoubtable Sentence of God's Judgment upon Encountering the Impiety of Tyrants* was published in Lyon in 1564 and circulated widely throughout the larger French cities. The author's principal attack was on the notion of Gallican monarchy itself.

I certainly confess that kings and princes are sovereigns set above men and that it is their right to have power over their sons and daughters and over the lands and goods of their subjects. But when they lose the love that they [their subjects] owe to them and when they abuse their authority, Aristotle said that they are no longer kings but tyrants.

The author's point was clear: kings only held their authority as kings so long as their subjects loved them. Here was an early advocate of a form of

---

[2] N. M. Sutherland, *The Massacre of St. Bartholomew and the European Conflict, 1559–1572* (London, 1973), pp. 153–6; and Mack P. Holt, *The Duke of Anjou and the Politique Struggle during the Wars of Religion* (Cambridge, 1986), pp. 21–2.

[3] Quoted in Quentin Skinner, *The Foundations of Modern Political Thought*, 2 vols. (Cambridge, 1978), II, 220.

popular sovereignty, a notion that threatened to undermine the sacral monarchy of the French crown. 'For just as the people are obligated to the king in one sense, the king is also obligated to the people in another.' The author even went on to describe how the ancient Tartars used to choose their kings 'by election'.[4]

A pamphlet of 1568 further distanced the Huguenots from the concept of sacral monarchy by declaring that 'the people' existed long before the institution of monarchy. The *Declaration and Protestation of those of the Reformed Religion in La Rochelle* thus argued that kings had no right to command the consciences of their subjects. The Huguenots' struggle against the French crown was just like the Hebrews' struggle against the Egyptian pharaoh. Kings ruled with divine authority only as long as they followed God's will. 'When they attack and turn themselves against God and his church, they are no longer true kings, but private persons whom it is not necessary to obey.'[5] Sentiments like these published in Huguenot centres of strength such as Lyon and La Rochelle could only alienate most French Catholics, for whom the sacral monarchy was the very foundation of social and political order. Moreover, they show clearly that theories of popular sovereignty were circulating long before the St Bartholomew's massacres of 1572 turned the Huguenots against the crown once and for all.

Catholic reaction to this rising Protestant tide against the sacral monarchy was evident in pamphlet and sermon alike. The Parisian preacher Simon Vigor was especially efficacious in arousing Catholic opposition to these radical Protestant views.[6] The situation in the capital was particularly volatile on account of an incident involving a traditional Catholic symbol: the cross. When Philippe de Gastines and his son Richard were arrested for holding illicit assemblies as well as a Protestant Lord's Supper in their house on the rue St-Denis in January 1569, religious tensions quickly surfaced. The two were hanged in the Place de Grève in July of that year for their offences and their property was confiscated. Parisian Catholics, anxious both to symbolize their victory over heresy as well as to purify the site where the Catholic mass had been profaned by the Protestant supper, tore down the Gastines' house and erected a Catholic monument in its place: a stone pyramid mounted with a large wooden cross. The Peace of St-Germain which ended the third civil war in August 1570 threatened this Catholic symbol, however, as it required

---

[4] Quoted in Denis Crouzet, *Les guerriers de Dieu: la violence au temps des troubles de religion (vers 1525–vers 1610)*, 2 vols. (Seyssel, 1990), II, 33–4.
[5] Quoted in ibid, II, 40–1.
[6] Barbara B. Diefendorf, *Beneath the Cross: Catholics and Huguenots in Sixteenth-century Paris* (New York and Oxford, 1991), pp. 152–8.

all property seized from the Huguenots to be returned as well as all monuments dedicated to the persecution of the Protestants to be torn down. City magistrates and eventually the king ordered the Gastines cross to be removed in accord with the peace edict, but Parisian Catholics refused to allow their sacred symbol to be disturbed. Under pressure from the crown, the city magistrates eventually were forced to remove the cross in the dead of night under heavy guard in December 1571, but even then the symbol was not destroyed. Out of fear of Catholic reprisal, the cross was simply transferred to the cemetery of the Holy Innocents. This did not placate the Catholic populace, however, as they sacked two houses on the Pont Notre-Dame, known as the Golden Hammer and the Pearl and believed to be inhabited by relatives of the Gastines and Protestant sympathizers, and burned their belongings in the street. A third house on the rue St-Denis, belonging to other relatives of the Gastines family, was even burned to the ground. This violence was accompanied with outbreaks of rioting between Protestants and Catholics, with as many as fifty people believed to have been killed. In short, popular religious tensions were at a fever pitch in the capital at the beginning of 1572. They were further exacerbated by the attempts of the authorities to round up the ringleaders of the riots, attempts that proved spectacularly unsuccessful. Moreover, the inhabitants of the Golden Hammer and the Pearl continued to be harrassed throughout the spring of 1572, as their homes were symbolically pelted with mud and garbage. It would not take much to spark off this tinderbox of sectarian hostility into a roaring bonfire of violence.[7]

Paris was hardly alone in seething with religious tension. A variety of urban centres where significant Huguenot minorities resided cheek by jowl with a Catholic populace were plagued with the same tensions. In Rouen, for example, where Protestants had actually seized control of the city temporarily during the first civil war, there were similar signs of trouble following the Edict of St-Germain. And once again, a traditional Catholic symbol was involved. On a Sunday in March 1571 during Lent a group of several hundred armed Calvinists on their way to Sunday services in the suburbs outside the city wall encountered a small Catholic procession with a cleric carrying the Host. When a number of Catholics in the vicinity knelt in honour of the Corpus Christi and ordered the Huguenots to do likewise, the latter began to mock the Host and violence broke out. Rocks were thrown and threats issued by the armed

---

[7] This entire incident is recounted in ibid., pp. 83–8. For the background to it, see Diefendorf's article, 'Prologue to a Massacre: Popular Unrest in Paris, 1557–1572', *American Historical Review*, vol. 90 (1985), 1067–91.

Protestants, but miraculously no one was killed. Later in the day, however, still smouldering from the confrontation earlier that morning, a group of Catholics armed themselves and assembled in order to attack the Huguenot community. The resulting 'massacre', as the Calvinists referred to it, ended with over forty Protestant deaths. As in Paris, attempts by the authorities to punish the leaders of the attack only exacerbated rather than diffused the religious tensions. When a commission eventually condemned 66 rioters for their role in the clash, threats against the officials designated to arrest the condemned proved so hostile that most of those convicted managed to escape. In Rouen as in Paris – and in nearly a dozen other towns as later events would show – tensions between Protestants and Catholics had escalated among the popular classes to such a degree that deadly violence could erupt at the slightest provocation. These tensions were seriously threatening the efficacy of all attempts by the authorities to maintain the social and political order.[8]

It is in the context of this rising tide of popular religious tension that the traditional political events leading to the St Bartholomew's massacres must be viewed. When Admiral Coligny was given a generous pension by the king and readmitted to the king's council in September 1571, Catholics all over France took note, especially in the capital. Coligny had long been perceived by them as a Huguenot rebel to the crown, and in the fall of 1571 he appeared to be restored to a position of royal influence. Because Coligny was one of the most vocal opponents of the Gastines cross in the capital, it was widely assumed that the Admiral had won over the king himself when the cross was finally removed in December. The announcement early in 1572 that a royal wedding was planned between the king's sister Marguerite and the Protestant Henry of Navarre only confirmed Catholic fears that Charles IX himself had fallen under the spell of the charismatic Coligny. And the final blow was the announcement in May 1572 that a French Huguenot army under the command of Louis of Nassau had secretly crossed into the Netherlands province of Hainaut and had seized the Catholic strongholds of Valenciennes and Mons. To many Catholics in France it appeared that the Huguenots had clearly seized the initiative at court and had convinced the king to support the Dutch rebels in their struggle against the Catholic Philip II of Spain. While all these rumours proved to be false – Coligny was only at court for five weeks between September 1571 and August 1572 and had little influence on the king's council, and he had serious reservations against supporting the Dutch rebels – these events only further heightened

---

[8] For the incidents in Rouen, see Philip Benedict, *Rouen during the Wars of Religion* (Cambridge, 1981), pp. 121–2.

Catholic fears and escalated religious tensions right through the summer of 1572. It was the royal wedding itself between the Catholic Marguerite de Valois and the Protestant Henry of Navarre that took place on 18 August in the capital that ultimately served as the backdrop to the greatest explosion of popular violence yet witnessed in the French Wars of Religion. Parisian preachers immediately informed their Catholic parishioners that 'God would surely be avenged for the impiety of this perverse union'.[9]

The series of events collectively known to history as the St Bartholomew's Day massacres was actually four separate but interconnected events that played out over the course of nearly six weeks after the royal wedding: (1) the attempted assassination of Gaspard de Coligny on 22 August; (2) the coordinated murder of several dozen Huguenot leaders sometime in the early morning hours of Sunday 24 August, St Bartholomew's Day; (3) the wave of popular killings that broke out in the capital of Paris during the next three days; and finally (4) the wave of provincial massacres that were spawned by the violence in the capital during late August, September, and early October 1572. As nearly every historian of the Wars of Religion has tried to determine who was responsible for the massacres and why – resulting in much controversy and misinformation – it cannot be emphasized enough that these separate incidents need to be analyzed individually before trying to ascertain who was responsible for the massacres. And as all the surviving evidence is either incomplete or tainted – all of the principals had reason to lie to protect themselves afterward – it is unlikely that the full story of the massacres will ever emerge.

The principal incident that sparked off the religious violence in the capital in August 1572 was the abortive attempt on the life of Coligny on Friday morning, 22 August. The admiral was still in the capital along with most of the Huguenot leaders after the royal wedding in order to present a list of violations of the Edict of St-Germain to the king. It was while returning from a meeting with Charles IX in the Louvre, in fact, that Coligny was shot in the arm and hand from an upper-story window. His would-be assassin, a sieur de Maurevert, managed to escape in all the confusion. What is significant about the attempt on Coligny's life is that it failed. Had Maurevert's aim been more accurate, the other Huguenot

---

[9] Diefendorf, *Beneath the Cross*, p. 91. Professor N. M. Sutherland was the first to attack the view that Coligny had the king's ear in 1572 and had talked him into a war against Spain. See her *Massacre of St. Bartholomew*, pp. 312–16 and also her *The Huguenot Struggle for Recognition* (New Haven, 1980), pp. 178–207. For a contrary view, see Marc Venard, 'Arrêtez le massacre!', *Revue d'histoire moderne et contemporaine*, vol. 39 (1992), 645–61.

leaders would almost certainly have fled the capital, seething as it was with religious tension, and probably tried to mobilize forces for the expected renewal of the civil wars. In that case, there would have been no massacre in Paris following the royal wedding. Coligny insisted, however, on remaining in Paris, and most of his fellow Huguenots remained with him. The admiral petitioned the king to investigate the shooting, and late on the day of 22 August Charles promised to find and arrest all those involved. Against the advice of many of his followers, who feared the assassins would likely return to finish the job, Coligny made the fatal decision to remain in the capital. Moreover, many of his Huguenot supporters were angry enough to talk rashly of revenge.[10]

Who was responsible for the attempted assassination? Generations of historians have long argued that Catherine de Medici was the principal villain, with the Guises as co-conspirators. Arguing that the Queen Mother was insanely jealous of Coligny's influence over Charles, these historians have traditionally insisted that she organized the murder attempt in order to prevent a French invasion of the Netherlands and an inevitable war with Spain.[11] Professor N. M. Sutherland was the first historian to try to rescue the Queen Mother's reputation, arguing that it would have been illogical for Catherine to jeopardize her efforts at establishing peace by trying to murder the Huguenot leader in Paris just after the royal wedding. Moreover, she claimed that the bulk of the evidence implicating Catherine – contemporary memoirs and foreign ambassadors' reports – was either confusing, prejudiced, or both.[12] She went on to imply that more likely candidates were the Guises, who had long been convinced that Coligny was implicated in the death of Francis, duke of Guise, at the siege of Orléans in February 1563. This vendetta against Coligny had been simmering for nearly a decade and provides a convincing justification for Guise involvement. Moreover, the house from which Maurevert fired his shots at Coligny was owned by the Guise family, which implicates them further. Other historians have recently joined the fray, some taking issue with Professor Sutherland's revisionist views to support the traditional interpretation, others corroborating her in order to suggest

---

[10] The fullest account of the massacres in English is Diefendorf, *Beneath the Cross*, pp. 93–106, and I have generally followed her analysis. Also see, however, Sutherland, *Huguenot Struggle for Recognition*, pp. 206–10.

[11] For just a few of many historians who have argued this line, see J. E. Neale, *The Age of Catherine de Medici* (London, 2nd edn 1957), pp. 76–7; J. H. Mariéjol, *La Réforme, la Ligue, l'Edit de Nantes (1559–1598)*, vol. VI, part i of *Histoire de France des origines à la Révolution* (Paris, 1983 edn, orig edn 1904), pp. 144–5; and [Garrisson-]Estèbe, *Tocsin pour un massacre*, p. 182.

[12] N. M. Sutherland, *Massacre of St. Bartholomew*, esp. pp. 312–46.

still more culprits (the oddest suggestion being that the leaders in the Parlement of Paris orchestrated the attempted murder of Coligny).[13] Thus, historical controversy still surrounds the first stage of the massacres. One fact emerges clearly from the documentation, however: whoever was implicated in the assassination plot, and the Queen Mother and the Guises are the most likely suspects, it was doubtless a plot to kill just one man – the admiral – and not the first stage of something far more sinister. If a general massacre of those Huguenot nobles still in Paris after the wedding had been contemplated, it would have made no sense at all to alert them to the danger by singling out Coligny first.

But more violence is just what followed during the night of 23–24 August. Again, the surviving evidence does not tell the full story, but sometime on Saturday 23 August, a council meeting was called to discuss the escalating tensions after Coligny's escape from death. During that meeting a number of proposals were discussed, largely concerning what to do about a genuine fear of Huguenot reprisal. Coligny's brother-in-law Teligny had 4,000 Huguenot troops stationed just outside the capital and many on the council feared that a Huguenot strike against the Guises, the Catholic populace of Paris, or even the king was a genuine possibility. Rumours to this effect – that a Protestant massacre of Catholics in the capital was imminent – certainly circulated after the assassination attempt on the admiral. And despite the fact that these rumours were unfounded – no such Huguenot attack was being organized – a consensus emerged in the council meeting to make a pre-emptive strike against the Huguenot leadership still in the capital.

But who first proposed this plan? Catherine? Guise? Charles IX? Anjou? All of them and even a few others have been blamed for instigating the larger plot, but there can be no doubt that, whoever came up with the idea, the king and Queen Mother supported it. This brooding mother, who had fought so long to keep the peace, and her weak second son, who

---

[13] J-L. Bourgeon has come to Sutherland's defence, and the Queen Mother's, but instead of suggesting that the Guises were behind the plot he claims that the leaders of the Parlement of Paris were the real culprits (though he offers no convincing evidence for this claim). See his book *L'assassinat de Coligny* (Geneva, 1992) as well as two articles: 'Les légendes ont la vie dure: à propos de la Saint-Barthélemy et de quelques livres récents', *Revue d'histoire moderne et contemporaine*, vol. 34 (1987), 102–16, and 'Pour une histoire, enfin, de la Saint-Barthélemy', *Revue historique*, vol. 282 (1989), 83–142. Both these historians have been attacked by Marc Venard, who provides reasons for accepting the traditional interpretation implicating Catherine and the Guises: 'Arrêtez le massacre!' Finally, Denis Crouzet has written most recently that all these historians have been too polemical and too sure of themselves in light of the lack of a 'smoking gun' in the archives. He also argues convincingly that the more significant question is not who wanted Coligny killed, but why? See Denis Crouzet, *La nuit de la Saint-Barthélemy: un rêve perdu de la Renaissance* (Paris, 1994).

as king stood forever in the shadows of others at court, are largely to blame for the escalation of violence in the capital. Their gross miscalculation of the situation at court – based on their fear of Huguenot reprisals for the attempt on Coligny's life – led them to order a quick strike against the Huguenot leadership still in Paris after the royal wedding, between two and three dozen noblemen. The traditional view that the Queen Mother acted alone or even browbeat the young king into agreeing to such a grisly order is not supported by the evidence, as there was a clear consensus on the royal council supporting Catherine and Charles. Indeed, there is no evidence of any dissent on the council to the decision made on 23 August. Fully expecting that Paris was about to be invaded by a Protestant army, the young king was ultimately convinced that a preemptive strike on the Huguenots was the only option left open to him. To be sure, Charles IX may also have sought out a remedy to win back the authority at court he never really had as sovereign. His mother governed for him in his early reign, but he had been overshadowed at court by a variety of others since he came of age, including his own younger brother Anjou after the victories at Jarnac and Moncontour in 1569, and his sister in recent days. Thus, Charles may have had other motives in mind when he gave the final orders that night. Still, what was proposed was a specific strike against a few dozen Huguenot noblemen – above all Admiral Coligny – and not a general massacre of all Protestants in the city. And there is no convincing evidence that the plot was either premeditated or organized in advance of 23 August.

The king's own Swiss guards as well as the personal bodyguards of the duke of Anjou were designated for the deed, which was to be carried out sometime that night after midnight, that is, in the early hours of Sunday morning, 24 August. This troop of at most about 100 men was to be led by Henry, duke of Guise. Moreover, the king ordered the city militia out to guard the streets while the murders were being enacted, further lending weight to the view that a Huguenot reprisal was feared. Between three and four in the morning this series of murders was duly carried out, as Coligny was among the first killed, slain by the duke of Guise himself. The cold-blooded deaths of several dozen other Huguenots slain in their beds did not end the affair, however.

The religious anxiety of the entire weekend exploded as a result of the noise and commotion of the murder of these Huguenot nobles, as a wave of popular violence was unleashed throughout the capital. This phase of the massacres was clearly the result of the popular tensions that had been rising ever since the Edict of St-Germain was issued two years before. And while it is problematic to assign blame for such spontaneous, popular violence, surely Barbara Diefendorf is right to excoriate both Catherine de Medici and Charles IX for yet another and far graver miscalculation. In that tinderbox of religious tension which was the capital city of Paris in August of 1572, any thoughtful person should have realized that the slightest provocation was liable to spark off an explosion of popular violence.[14]

The general massacre of Protestants that began on Sunday morning, 24 August, and lasted for three days, was aided and abetted by several of the most militant and radical members of the city militia. For the most part, however, the bulk of the deaths in the St Bartholomew's massacre in Paris were committed by civilians. That this general massacre was clearly fomented by popular religious tensions rather than any political decision by the elites at court is clear from the non-noble Huguenot victims targeted by Parisian Catholics. Among the first Huguenots killed after the noble leadership had been murdered were some family members of the Gastines, as well as the other inhabitants of the Golden Hammer and the Pearl, whom Catholics had always believed had supported the removal of the Gastines cross eight months earlier. The widow of Richard de Gastines, for example, was one of the first murdered on St Bartholomew's night. Her two young sons, according to a contemporary, cried 'until the blood came out of their noses and mouths' as they witnessed the horrible crime. The youngest Gastines brother, Jacques, had married into the Le Mercier family, and it was his in-laws, Nicolas Le Mercier and his wife, who still resided in the Golden Hammer on the Pont Notre-Dame. The two Le Merciers were also among the very first killed in the popular massacre, after which their youngest daughter Agnes was immersed 'stark naked in the blood of her massacred mother and father, with horrible threats that, if ever she became a Huguenot, the same would happen to her'.[15] That these members of the Gastines family were among the very first victims of the popular massacre only underscores the significance of the sectarian tension that produced riots in the capital eight months before.

Many similar examples could be cited of the bloody scene in the capital. The Protestant sources left by the memoirist and historian Simon Goulart and the martyrologist Jean Crespin, while certainly not without bias, provide a number of useful clues about popular participation in the massacre. Mathurin Lussault, for just one example, was killed instantly

---

[14] See Barbara Diefendorf, 'Prologue to a massacre', p. 1091; and idem, *Beneath the Cross*, p. 96.

[15] Quoted in Diefendorf, *Beneath the Cross*, pp. 100–2, where both incidents are discussed. She argues convincingly that the accounts of the Protestant memoirist Simon Goulart and the martyrologist Jean Crespin are generally reliable in listing the names of victims, even if details of their deaths cannot be confirmed from other sources.

when he answered his door on St Bartholomew's night. When his son came downstairs to investigate the commotion, he was also stabbed and died later in the street. Lussault's wife Françoise, fearing the worst, tried to escape from an upstairs window by leaping into her next-door neighbour's courtyard. Breaking both legs in her fall, she was soon discovered despite her neighbour's attempts to hide her. 'They then took her and dragged her by the hair a long way through the streets, and spying the gold bracelets on her arms, without having the patience to unfasten them, cut off her wrists.' She was then impaled on a spit and dragged through the streets for a time, before she was eventually dumped into the Seine. Her hands were still observed in the street several days later 'and were gnawed upon by dogs'.[16] Another example is the deaths of the Huguenot artisan Philippe Le Doux and his wife. Le Doux's house was broken into and he was surprised and killed while still in his bed. His wife, who was about to go into labour with their twenty-first child, was also murdered despite her pleas to the rioters to be allowed to give birth first. When she was rebuffed, she made a desperate and unsuccessful attempt to escape. She was stabbed in the abdomen and then hurled into the street below, as her nearly-born infant, with its head already protruding from its mother's corpse, eventually died in the gutter. Their killers then ransacked and looted the house.[17]

What do such accounts tell us? What do they reveal about the popular violence steeped in religious difference? The repeated incidents of theft and pillage might suggest economic motives were a factor, while the unusually harsh treatment of women might suggest sexual motives played a role. What stands out more clearly than these economic and social factors, both endemic to the pre-industrial world, are the differences between the two cultures of Protestantism and Catholicism. Viewed by Catholics as threats to the social and political order, Huguenots not only had to be exterminated – that is, killed – they also had to be humiliated, dishonoured, and shamed as the inhuman beasts they were perceived to be. The victims had to be dehumanized – slaughtered like animals – since they had violated all the sacred laws of humanity in Catholic culture. Moreover, death was followed by purification of the places the Huguenots had profaned. Many Protestant houses were burned, invoking the traditional purification by fire of all heretics. Many victims were also thrown into the Seine, invoking the purification by water of Catholic baptism. In fact, upon closer inspection the grisly deaths of hundreds of Protestants in Paris on St Bartholomew's night and after reveal distinct

---

[16] Quoted in ibid., p. 100.   [17] Analyzed in ibid., pp. 100–1.

patterns of what Professor Natalie Davis has called the 'rites of violence'.[18] Many of the participants in the massacre saw themselves as carrying out clerical roles of priests and purifiers and magisterial roles of judges and executioners. The young Agnes Le Mercier being 'baptised' in her parents' blood and threatened with death herself if she should ever become tainted with heresy, or the corpse of the wife of Mathurin Lussault being skewered on a spit like animal flesh (dehumanization) and then dumped in the river (purification) are just two examples among many that could be cited.

Perhaps best of all is the example of the corpse of the dead Admiral Coligny. When local Catholics discovered Coligny's body after the duke of Guise had killed him, they quickly mutilated it, cutting off the admiral's head, hands, and genitals. The corpse was then dragged through the streets, set afire as a heretic, and then thrown into the Seine. A contemporary, Claude Haton, noted that the Catholics who had seized Coligny's body conducted a mock trial of the admiral 'just as if they were judges and officers of the court'.[19] Thus, the massacre of St Bartholomew that filled the Seine with blood in August 1572 was the result of something more than the unconscious fears, the uncontrolled rage, or the random violence so endemic to the period. This violence was not random at all, but patterned after the rites of the Catholic culture that had given birth to it. Despite efforts by the king and many other notables to stop the spread of the violence, it continued off and on in the capital for nearly three days, resulting in as many as two thousand deaths. Over a thousand corpses washed up on the banks of the reddened Seine downstream from Paris over the next few days.

What had caused this unusually bloody outburst of violence, far more lethal than any previous incident in the religious wars? And why did it go unchecked for so long? Two related points need to be stressed if any sense is to be made of these 'rites of violence'. First, the sources make it very clear that many of the participants fully believed that they were carrying out the will of the king. The duke of Guise was even overheard saying as much during the murder of Coligny: 'It is the king's command.' While it seems clear in retrospect that Guise was referring just to the assassination of the admiral and the Huguenot leadership, and not to any kind of general massacre, it is obvious that word of royal endorsement of the killings spread far faster than any of the authorities could imagine. It was

[18] See the classic article by Natalie Zemon Davis, 'The Rites of Violence: Religious Riot in Sixteenth-century France', *Past and Present*, no. 59 (May 1973), 51–91; reprinted in the same author's *Society and Culture in Early Modern France* (Stanford, 1975), pp. 152–87.
[19] Quoted in Diefendorf, *Beneath the Cross*, p. 103.

yet another mistaken perception – that the king had condoned the killing of all the Protestants in the capital – that doubtless led many Catholics who were otherwise law-abiding to seize the moment and take part in the spree of killing. Moreover, as Barbara Diefendorf has pointed out, 'these words transformed private passion into public duty'.[20] The belief that Charles IX had issued a 'command' to kill the Huguenots not only gave all Parisian Catholics the opportunity to wield the magisterial power of the crown, but it made it their duty to do so. Those words overheard from the duke of Guise transformed the ritualized killings of St Bartholomew's night into public service. When Charles IX entered the Parlement of Paris two days later on 26 August and announced that 'everything that had occurred was done by his expressed commandment', participants in the massacre had every reason to feel that their actions were justified.[21] Was the king simply accepting blame for the violence (as his apologists claimed), or was he admitting that he had ordered it as well as the limited attack on the Huguenot leadership (as Protestant sources have insisted)? It is far from clear exactly what he meant, though the historical record does suggest that Charles did make efforts to try to prevent the general massacre once it broke out. The point here is that those Catholic participants in the massacre clearly believed that the king had condoned the killing of all Protestants in the capital.

A second and related point is that participants in the massacre also felt that extermination of the Huguenots was God's will. The escalating rhetoric of Parisian pamphleteers and preachers after the Edict of St-Germain was a principal factor in this perception. What were Catholics in the capital able to conclude from such constant and repetitious admonitions? René Benoist penned a short tract on the issue of the Gastines cross in which he argued that the removal of that symbol of Christ's passion and sacrifice would surely trigger God's vengeance. Moreover, Benoist reminded his readers that God often used the common people to exact his revenge on those who flouted divine will, by putting 'force in the heart and stones in the hands of the rude and imbecilic people as executors of his just sentence'.[22] This sentiment was reinforced by Catholics such as Simon Vigor, perhaps the best-known preacher in Paris. His sermons were full of references to the evils that would befall the capital if heretics were allowed to continue to live side by side with those of the true faith. Heresy was a putrid infection of the social body that would contaminate

---

[20] Ibid., p. 99.
[21] This was recorded by a *parlementaire* in the court, Etienne Pasquier, *Lettres historiques pour less années 1556–1594*, ed. Dorothy Thickett (Geneva, 1966), p. 207.
[22] Quoted in Diefendorf, *Beneath the Cross*, p. 151.

the whole if not treated immediately. Therefore, he argued that it was God's will that all heretics should be exterminated 'by a bitter death'. These 'wild beasts from Geneva' had entered God's vineyard and it was time that divine justice be done. Vigor urged all his listeners to 'keep a close watch over their city' and not to put down their weapons because of the Protestant threat. He concluded that 'in the end they will kill you, either by poison, or some other means'.[23] So convinced were the Parisians that God was growing ever more angry with them for continuing to allow the pollution of heresy in their city, that every severe storm, every freak occurrence of hail or sleet, every flood of the Seine, and particularly events such as a spectacular solar eclipse on St Michael's day 1571, were all perceived as signs of God's anger. Above all, the sudden blooming of a long dormant hawthorn tree in the cemetery of the Holy Innocents just a few days after the massacre in Paris was proof to even the most doubting sceptics that killing the Huguenots was God's will.[24] It must be remembered that it was in this cemetery where the Gastines cross still stood. Alluding to the white crosses that were pinned to the clothing or stuck in the hats of Parisian Catholics once the killings began on St Bartholomew's night (in order to distinguish them from the Huguenots), one contemporary remarked: 'By God's grace . . . where one cross has been torn down, many thousand have now sprung up.'[25] Thus, the popular 'rites of violence', whether they consisted of rioting against the removal of the Gastines cross in December 1571 or killing Huguenots in August 1572, were grounded on the solid foundation of divine will.

All the surviving evidence suggests that the popular massacre that broke out in Paris on St Bartholomew's night was neither planned nor condoned by the king's council. The king himself issued orders as soon as the popular violence broke out for everyone in the city to return to their homes. And apart from the radical fringe of the city militia who did encourage and even led the populace in many of the attacks, the bulk of the king's and the city's forces seem to have been trying to maintain order rather than participating in the murders. Even Henry, duke of Guise, who personally took charge of the murder of Coligny, made efforts to prevent the unnecessary deaths of other Protestants in the capital. Like a number of other Parisian Catholics who sheltered and hid Huguenots in their own homes, Guise harboured a young Protestant girl named Renée Burlamaqui and her two younger siblings for a week to prevent their

---

[23] Quoted in ibid, pp. 152–8.
[24] These and a host of other similar signs are discussed in Crouzet, *Les guerriers de Dieu*, II, 82–106.
[25] Diefendorf, *Beneath the Cross*, p. 106.

deaths (though he did have plans to baptise them into the Catholic faith). He also intervened to save the daughter of the former chancellor, Michel de l'Hôpital, as well as dozens of other Protestants.[26] Thus, all the Protestant sources claiming that the king, the Queen Mother, Anjou, or Guise had ordered the general massacres – which many historians have simply taken at face value – need to be balanced by the evidence of the strength of popular religious feeling in the capital at the time of the attempted assassination of Admiral Coligny. While the general massacre might have been prevented, there is no evidence to suggest that it was intended by any of the political elites at court.

The fourth and final stage of the St Bartholomew massacres encompassed the spread of the violence from Paris into the provinces over the next six weeks (Map 5). Violence erupted in a dozen different cities all over the kingdom, in most as soon as news arrived of the grisly scene in the capital, but in some over a month later: Orléans, La Charité, Meaux, Bourges, Saumur, Angers, Lyon, Troyes, Rouen, Bordeaux, Toulouse, and Gaillac. As many as 3,000 additional Protestant victims in these provincial cities were slain.[27] Rather than presenting a detailed examination of these massacres, it might prove more useful to ask a few pertinent questions. Why did the violence spread to some cities and not to others? Who was responsible for these provincial massacres, given that Charles IX sent out orders to his provincial governors on 24 August to do their best to prevent violence and to maintain the peace edict of 1570? And finally, what connections can be found between the massacre in the capital and the provincial massacres?

All twelve cities where provincial massacres occurred had one striking feature in common: they were all cities with Catholic majorities that had once had *significant* Protestant minorities. That is to say, these were towns in which sizeable Huguenot communities existed and had raised the same spectre of contamination of the body social as in the capital. All of them had also experienced serious religious division in the previous decade during the first three civil wars. Moreover, seven of them shared a further experience: Rouen, Orléans, Lyon, Meaux, Bourges, Angers, and La Charité had actually been taken over by Protestant minorities during the first civil war (and the Huguenots came perilously close to doing so in Toulouse). And while all had been returned to Catholic control since, there remained a feeling of hostility, tension, and sectarian strife similar to that in the capital. Even though there had not been a Gastines cross in these towns,

---

[26] Ibid., p. 104; and Jean-Marie Constant, *Les Guise* (Paris, 1984), p. 71.
[27] This is the estimate of Philip Benedict, 'The Saint Bartholomew's Massacres in the Provinces', *The Historical Journal*, vol. 21 (1978), 205–25.

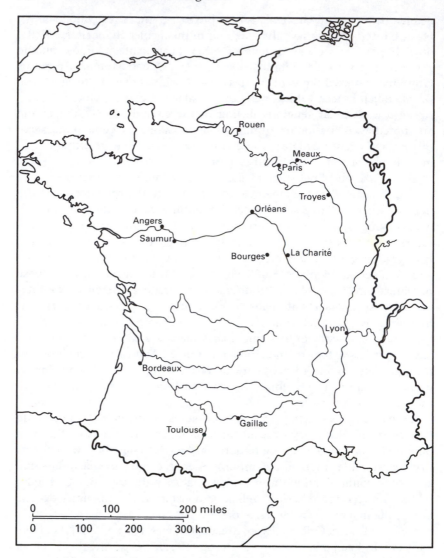

Map 5 The St Bartholomew's Massacres, August–October 1572

their own local pasts provide clues enough as to why they experienced
bloodshed and violence in the wake of St Bartholomew's night in Paris.
Clearly, in cities controlled by the Huguenots – such as La Rochelle,
Montauban, and Nîmes – there was little danger of a massacre against the
Protestants. The same was true of Catholic strongholds where Protestant
communities were too small to have created much religious division, or

where Catholic authorities ruled so securely that such tension had already been diffused. The Burgundian capital of Dijon is a good example of the latter, where pressure by the lieutenant-general of the province, the sieur de Tavannes, in concert with the city council and the confraternity of the Holy Ghost, had effectively reduced the Protestant community by 1572 through arrest and abjuration to such a level that religious tension had subsided.[28] Those towns that experienced violence in the late summer of 1572 were those where the two cultures of Catholicism and Protestantism still threatened one another openly and publicly.

What started the massacres in the provinces? Were they simply a reaction by provincial Catholics who were responding to events in Paris? The chronology of the provincial massacres suggests otherwise, as the violence in Rouen did not break out until mid-September, while the massacres in Bordeaux, Toulouse, and Gaillac did not occur until the first week in October, long after news of the events in the capital had reached them.[29] It is far likelier that local events were responsible, though doubtless news of the killings in the capital encouraged and emboldened many local Catholics. In Angers and Saumur, for example, the count of Montsoreau, the governor of Saumur, was instrumental in propagating the massacres. Upon receiving a missive from an agent of the duke of Anjou claiming that it was Anjou's as well as the king's will that he should go to Saumur and Angers 'to kill any Huguenots you find here', Montsoreau was only too happy to carry out what he took to be the king's wishes.[30] Similar roles were played by the duke of Nevers in La Charité and by Pierre Belin, an agent of the Guises, in Troyes.[31]

In most of the twelve provincial towns, however, the principal agents of violence were the local populace. In those cities, as in the capital of Paris, the masses played a significant role in the killing of Protestants. And like their counterparts in the capital, they also believed they were acting on behalf of the king and with the full support of God's divine will.[32] This is the most basic link between the provincial massacres and

[28] Mack P. Holt, 'Wine, Community and Reformation in Sixteenth-Century Burgundy', *Past and Present*, no. 138 (February 1993), 58–93.

[29] For the chronology, see Benedict, 'Saint Bartholomew's Massacres'; and [Garrisson-] Estèbe, *Tocsin pour un massacre*, pp. 142–55.

[30] Quoted in Holt, *The Duke of Anjou*, p. 20. It is unclear whether this letter was instigated by the duke of Anjou or his agent, Puygaillard. Again, there is no evidence to suggest that it was the king who desired the massacres to spread.

[31] Benedict, 'Saint Bartholomew's Massacres', p. 233, n.51. In the latter case, the duke of Guise's behaviour in the Paris massacre would suggest that his agent, Belin, was acting on his own authority rather than that of the duke.

[32] That all the participants fully believed they were acting on behalf of the king is a central point of Benedict, 'Saint Bartholomew's Massacres'.

the violence in the capital. The provincial cities experienced the same ritualistic murders, the same mutilation of corpses, and the same treatment of pregnant women as in the capital; they each experienced their own version of the Parisian 'rites of violence'. In Orléans, for example, where the massacre of Protestants took place on 26 and 27 August 1572, popular participation was very evident. The participants, largely members of the lower classes according to one historian, roamed throughout the city in bands celebrating the killing of the Huguenots accompanied by singing, lutes, and guitars. They interrupted the slaughter only in order to refortify themselves with drink in a few local taverns, where they bragged about their deeds. In Toulouse both the provincial parlement and the city magistrates were doing their best to maintain order as well as prevent any violence against the sizeable Protestant community there. Their initial success was only due to the fact that they had managed to imprison many of the leading Protestants for their own protection. Violence erupted on 3 October, however, when the Catholic populace stormed the jail and murdered the prisoners, including three Protestant judges from the Parlement of Toulouse, among them Jean de Coras. The violence had been sparked by the arrival earlier that day of two merchants claiming that they carried the verbal orders of Charles IX to begin the massacres in the provinces. And a similar scene was played out in Rouen, where the local officials had also imprisoned those Protestants they could round up for their own protection. Many Huguenots went voluntarily, thinking they were safer in the hands of local magistrates than in their own homes, while others fled abroad or into the countryside. On 17 September, however, Catholics seized control of the town, locked the gates to prevent any Protestants from escaping, and began a rampage of killing that lasted four days. When the violence ended, 300 to 400 Huguenots lay dead. Apart from Bordeaux, in all the towns where provincial massacres took place between 25 August and 6 October there is evidence of popular participation on a scale similar to that in the capital. Interestingly, even in Bordeaux, where the killings were carried out almost entirely by six companies of soldiers under the command of Montferrand, a Catholic zealot who claimed to have orders from the king to commence the killing of Protestants, popular religious tensions played a significant role. The Catholics in the city had their hatred for the Huguenots built up to such a fever pitch by the Jesuit preacher, Edmond Auger, in the weeks following the Paris massacre, that local authorities chose not to intervene when Montferrand's soldiers initiated the killing on 3 October. Thus, even there the religious tensions among the popular classes were one of the principal causes of the massacre of Protestants. This was a common bond that linked all the St Bartholomew's massacres.[33]

All told approximately 2,000 Huguenots were killed in the massacre in Paris, and an additional 3,000 or so were slain in the provinces. What impact did these events have on the Wars of Religion generally and on the Protestant movement in particular? For the Protestants the massacres proved to be catastrophic. Five thousand of their fellow Calvinists lay dead, including their leader, Admiral Coligny, and the rest of the Huguenot leadership. Of the leading Protestant nobles, only the newly-wed Henry of Navarre was spared, doubtless on account of his recent marriage to the king's sister as well as the fact that he was forced to abjure his Calvinist faith and rejoin the Catholic church as the price for his life. The victims of the massacres, however, formed only the tip of the iceberg of Huguenot casualties. In the weeks and months following the massacres thousands of Huguenots who survived the violence made their way to Catholic churches, asked to be rebaptised into the Gallican faith, and abjured their Protestant faith. Thus, the real impact of the St Bartholomew's massacres was felt less in the actual killings than in the defections that took place over the next few months. In Rouen, for example, several hundred members of the Protestant community were slain in the massacre there in the first week of October 1572. Over the next few months perhaps fifty times that number abjured their faith and returned to the Catholic church. From its number of about 16,500 souls before the St Bartholomew's massacres, the reformed community in Rouen shrank to fewer than 3,000 in the massacres' aftermath. And Philip Benedict has also shown that this defection occurred in towns throughout France, even in those where there were no provincial massacres.[34] Thus, the massacres not only put a permanent end to the growth of the reformed faith in France; they brought about an immediate and catastrophic decline in the numbers, strength, and zeal of the Protestant movement.

The intellectual and psychological impact of the massacres on the Huguenots was just as great, however. The optimism of the 1560s, when growth and expansion of the reformed movement was at its apex, paled significantly in the wake of St Bartholomew's night. Not only had the king turned against the Huguenots, but to many it seemed as if God had abandoned them as well. When the Calvinist minister Hugues

---

[33] For the massacres in Orléans, Toulouse, Rouen, and Bordeaux, see Benedict, 'Saint Bartholomew's Massacres', *passim*; [Garrisson-]Estèbe, *Tocsin pour un massacre*, pp. 144–54; and Benedict, *Rouen during the Wars of Religion*, pp. 126–8.

[34] Benedict, *Rouen during the Wars of Religion*, pp. 128–38.

Sureau reluctantly abjured after the massacres, he made it clear that he considered the massacres to be a sign of God's displeasure with the Protestant movement. 'I began to consider it [the massacre] to be an expression of God's indignation', he noted, 'as though he had declared by this means that he detested and condemned the profession and exercise of our Religion'.[35] Despair and impotence were the principal feelings of many Huguenots, who must have recognized how powerless they were to defend themselves against the overwhelming majority of Catholics in the kingdom. While many, like those Huguenots in Rouen, ultimately abjured their Calvinist faith and returned to the fold of the majority, many others chose to abandon France altogether for foreign reformed communities in Geneva, London, and elsewhere, where they could continue to keep the faith. This likely only increased the feeling of isolation by those French Protestants who remained, as now they were even being abandoned by their own members. For those Huguenot survivors of the massacres who resisted both abjuration and emigration, life was clearly never the same.

The St Bartholomew's massacres thus stood as a watershed in the Wars of Religion. Not only did it mark the breaking and decline (though *not* the complete elimination) of the Protestant movement in France, it marked the beginning of a new form of French Protestantism: one that was openly at war with the crown. This was much more than a war against the policies of the crown, as in the first three civil wars; it was a campaign against the very existence of the Gallican monarchy itself. The solitary and unrepresentative calls for resistance to the monarchy heard before 1572 became much more shrill in the aftermath of the massacres. Indeed, Huguenot political rhetoric after 1572 brought resistance theory into the public arena with proposals for popular sovereignty. In the short term, Huguenot opposition to the crown resulted in the renewal of the civil wars, as a number of Protestant towns – most notably La Rochelle, Montauban, and Sancerre – refused to recognize the authority of the king who had ordered their leaders murdered on St Bartholomew's night. Moreover, these same Protestant strongholds began negotiating with foreign powers such as England and the Dutch rebel provinces for protection from their own king.

As a result of its unique origins in the massacres, the fourth civil war was unlike the previous three. While the Protestants had raised arms in many parts of the Midi, it was their citadel of La Rochelle that became the

---

[35] Quoted in Robert M. Kingdon, *Geneva and the Consolidation of the French Protestant Movement, 1564–1572* (Geneva, 1967), p. 117n; and in Benedict, *Rouen during the Wars of Religion*, p. 147.

principal focus of the war, as the Rochelois had refused to admit their royal governor, the Catholic Armand de Gontaut, marshall Biron in September 1572. Although the city's leaders had no desire to secede from the realm, they openly refused to pay either allegiance or any royal taxes to the crown because of the massacres. Charles IX was determined to force them to submit, and on 6 November he declared war on the city and ordered Biron to begin a siege as soon as a royal army could be raised. Aided by Henry, duke of Anjou, Biron and the royalist forces did not effectively begin the siege until February 1573. It was a fiasco from the beginning, however, as internal intrigue and division divided Biron's forces while La Rochelle's advantageous position on the coast made it relatively easy for food and supplies to be shipped in to the besieged fortress. With rumours circulating of an English armada ready to land in La Rochelle to aid the Huguenots in their struggle, Charles suddenly called off the siege and concluded another peace treaty in May. The timing was facilitated less by an English attack (the rumours of an armada were entirely false) than by Catherine de Medici's desire to secure the election of her third son, the duke of Anjou, to the vacant throne of the kingdom of Poland. Even though the siege had not succeeded, the casualties were great. There were substantial losses on both sides, and the cost to the royal treasury of this ineffectual operation was more than half a million *livres* per month.[36]

This farce of a war resulted in an even greater travesty of a peace: the Peace of La Rochelle signed on 2 July 1573. While the Huguenot leadership sought the renewal of the terms of the Peace of St-Germain of 1570, Charles and the Queen Mother were clearly determined to eliminate many of the privileges and guarantees the Protestants had been granted three years before. And although the final peace resembled the earlier treaty in its structure and wording, the reality was very different. In effect, the new terms allowed the Huguenots freedom of conscience in theory, but in practice Protestant worship was only allowed in the private homes of the reformed in three towns: La Rochelle, Montauban, and Nîmes. It was not allowed in public even there, and elsewhere in the kingdom Protestant worship was forbidden entirely. Nowhere was the changed position of relative strength since the massacres more marked than in the Peace of La Rochelle. As one historian has remarked, it was 'a disastrous

---

[36] For the siege of La Rochelle see Holt, *The Duke of Anjou*, pp. 28–33; and James Westfall Thompson, *The Wars of Religion in France, 1559–1576* (New York, 2nd edn, 1958), pp. 454–68. For the costs to the crown, see Bibliothèque Nationale, Paris, Fonds français 4554, fols. 92–100.

edict, rashly concluded and crudely drafted'. Moreover, it would become 'the cause for still worse trouble'.[37]

For Charles IX the illusion of peace was only temporary. The Huguenots had been decimated by the massacres, but they were not eliminated altogether. And in parts of the Midi, their strength was still very significant, as the open defiance of the ban on Protestant worship proved. Moreover, they still refused to submit to royal authority, something the king was unable to enforce throughout his kingdom. Finally, in the spring of 1574 they even attempted to liberate Henry of Navarre and Charles IX's youngest brother, the duke of Alençon, from court in a bungled escape attempt.[38] Before a fifth civil war was initiated, however, Charles suddenly died in May 1574, not yet 24 years old. The young king who had agreed to the murder of Coligny on St Bartholomew's night was mourned by most French Catholics. He left a kingdom to his younger brother Anjou (already installed in Cracow as king of Poland) that was significantly changed by the St Bartholomew's massacres, yet a kingdom still divided by the two cultures of Protestantism and Catholicism. And even though the massacres had significantly weakened the Huguenots, Henry, duke of Anjou – now Henry III – could not know that the bloodiest and most violent of the civil wars still lay ahead in the future. For the Catholic fears and anxieties that exploded on St Bartholomew's night still remained undiminished. France clearly required a stronger and more resourceful monarch than Charles IX had been, and most Catholics in 1574 looked to the new king as a saviour who would finally restore the entire kingdom to 'one king, one faith, one law'.

[37] Sutherland, *Huguenot Struggle for Recognition*, p. 360.
[38] For the failed escape plot of 1574 see Holt, *The Duke of Anjou*, pp. 34–44.

4   The rhetoric of resistance: the unmaking of the body politic, 1574–1584

Although the St Bartholomew's massacres dealt a devasting blow to the Protestant movement in France, the violence far from exterminated the Huguenots. They were still protected under the law after the Peace of La Rochelle, though they were much more alienated from the crown than before the massacres, and the peace edict included no general toleration clause. This further polarization of Protestants and Catholics was nowhere more evident than in the post-massacre political manoeuvrings of the few remaining Huguenot leaders. With Jeanne d'Albret, Louis of Nassau, and Gaspard de Coligny all dead, and Henry of Navarre forced to convert to Catholicism in August 1572, only the young son of Condé – Henry de Bourbon, prince of Condé – remained among the national leaders, and he had also been forced to convert at the time of the massacres. This put all the more responsibility on the local Huguenot leaders in the south of France, especially Languedoc, where their remaining numbers were strongest. That they should decide to try to link the remaining fortified towns still in Huguenot hands together in a defensive alliance was unsurprising after the massacres. The decision to form a Huguenot republican constitution, however, was more radical.

Though we do not know its author, who subscribed to it, or even if it was ever implemented, such a constitution emerged in late 1572, and it was decidedly anti-monarchical. Consisting of forty articles, it opened by declaring that the Huguenots had grown tired of 'waiting until it pleased God (who has the hearts of kings in his hand) to replace the one who is their king and restore the state of the nation in good order, or to inspire a neighbouring prince, who is distinguished by his virtue, to be the liberator of these poor, afflicted people'. They were thus forced to elect in each community – that is, in each Protestant church – 'a head or elder [*majeur*] to be their commander, as much for the war (for their defense and and protection) as for civilian jurisdiction, so that everything was done for [the maintenance of] proper order'.[1] Each elder then selected 24 councillors

---

[1] Bibliothèque Nationale, Paris [hereafter B. N.], Fonds nouvelles acquisitions françaises 7191, article 4. The bulk of this constitution is printed (in French) in Gordon Griffiths, ed., *Representative Government in Western Europe in the Sixteenth Century* (Oxford, 1968), pp. 276–9.

'either from the nobility or among the people' to assist him in governing each local community. These 25 then selected 75 others 'as many taken from the towns as from the countryside' to hear appeals and criminal cases. And while the Council of 24 could make war and administer justice, 'matters of the greatest importance' such as making treaties and levying taxation, required the imprimatur of the Council of 100: that is, agreement of all the representatives.[2] The elders and councils of all of the Protestant communities then elected the young prince of Condé as 'a general head' to command an army in the field, and whom all civilians would obey since 'his charge was for the common benefit of their protection'. Thus, like 'the twelve flourishing cities of ancient Greece', the Protestant communities formed themselves into a republic, not only better to safeguard their future existence, but also to ensure the continuation of Calvinist discipline, 'so that by this means, one sees clearly the reign of God and the sceptre of his word established and implemented, and the reign of Satan, with his cohort of vices established by the world of the flesh, destroyed, extirpated, and abolished among the faithful, the true children of light'.[3]

Meetings of this general Protestant assembly were held in Montauban and Millau in 1573 and 1574, and by the latter date the Huguenots had even forged an alliance with the royal governor of Languedoc (where the bulk of the Protestant churches remained): Henri de Montmorency, sieur de Damville. Son of the Constable, Anne de Montmorency, Damville was a powerful noble in Languedoc. With a strong strain of Protestantism in his family (Coligny and his brothers were Damville's first cousins) as well as the largest concentration of Protestant communities in his governorship, he had always been ambivalent on the religious question, even though he was a practising Catholic. To take a public stand in support of an anti-monarchical constitution was still surprising, however, from someone whose position and office were gained via royal appointment. In a radical strike against the monarchy, the royal courts, the royal army, and the Gallican clergy, this Huguenot constitution was a vivid sign of the new political ideology of the Protestants following the massacres of 1572. Although not published until 1574, when it was included in a pamphlet almost certainly written by Nicolas Barnaud, *The French Alarm Bell*, this constitution was a ringing wake-up call to all French Catholics.[4] Many had always suspected the Huguenots intended to overthrow the traditional political and social order; now they were openly advocating it.

[2] Ibid., articles 5–7.   [3] Ibid., articles 14–16 and 25.
[4] For Barnaud as the author of *Le Reveille-matin des français* (Edinburgh [Basel], 1574) see Donald R. Kelley, *The Beginning of Ideology: Consciousness and Society in the French Reformation* (Cambridge, 1981), pp. 301–6.

Moreover, they had established their state within the state, whose military presence stood as a threat to the sacral monarchy of the new king, Henry III. Though the Huguenots stopped short of renouncing their loyalty to the king altogether, their anti-monarchical rhetoric was unmistakable.

Other Protestant voices were even more caustic in their message of resistance to the crown in the aftermath of the massacres of St Bartholomew. Among the earliest of them was François Hotman's *Francogallia* published in 1573. Although the work was begun in 1568 and was largely completed before the massacres of 1572, *Francogallia* was certainly read in a different light in the wake of the Huguenot 'state within the state'. Arguing that the ancient Franks and Gauls had elected their first joint king – Childeric, son of Merovech – Hotman strongly suggested that the French monarchy was elective rather than hereditary, and that a 'public assembly' elected and deposed all French kings until this tradition was overturned by the innovations of Louis XI in the late fifteenth century. The implications of the author's subtle constitutional fiction were very vivid in the wake of the massacres: Protestants were not necessarily required to obey a king who threatened them, as he could be deposed. Hotman went on to evoke the clarion call of republicanism, first made by Cicero in *On the Laws* in the first century BC and echoed by Machiavelli in his *Discourses on Livy* in the early sixteenth century: 'Let the welfare of the people be the supreme law (*Salus populi suprema lex esto*).'[5] This was not in itself a very radical statement, even for the sixteenth century, as every monarch and prince claimed to protect the *salus populi*. In the aftermath of St Bartholomew, however, Cicero's words took on a much more republican connotation. Theodore Beza, Calvin's lieutenant and successor in Geneva, went even further. In his *On the Right of Magistrates over their Subjects* published in 1574 he argued that subjects were not required to obey a king who had offended God and Christianity, and that it was the duty of 'inferior magistrates' to overthrow such tyrants.[6] Both Hotman's 'public assembly' and Beza's 'inferior magistrates' were presumed to be the Estates-General, a corporate representative body of the French state divided into the three traditional estates of the realm: those who prayed (clergy), those who fought (nobility), and everyone else (third estate). And it was not coincidental that both authors called on the assembly of the Estates-General, historically convoked to deal with

---

[5] François Hotman, *Francogallia*, ed. and trans. Ralph E. Giesey and J. H. M. Salmon (Cambridge, 1973), pp. 296–300 (see also the editors' superb introduction, pp. 3–134); Cicero, *De legibus* (Loeb edn), p. 464; and Niccolò Machiavelli, *The Discourses*, ed. Bernard Crick (Harmondsworth, 1986 edn) p. 513.

[6] Theodore Beza, *Du droit des magistrats sur leur subjets*, ed. Robert M. Kingdon (Geneva, 1970).

constitutional or fiscal crises, to meet in order to resist the unworthy and tyrannical Valois monarchy.

The most militant of the Protestant voices after St Bartholomew's Day, however, belonged to the authors of the anonymously published *Political Discourses on the Various Forms of Power Established by God in the World*, which appeared in 1574, and the *Defense of Liberty against Tyrants*, which was begun in the mid-1570s and published in 1579. The author of the *Political Discourses* claimed that 'the sovereign community [the people] is superior to him [the king] ... The community gave [public] power to the prince ... If he abuses it they can invoke the law which holds that the thing given [public power] can be revoked due to culpability of the one to whom it was rendered.' The author further argued that it was not just the duty of the Estates-General to resist a tyrant, it was the responsibility of the princes, peers, officers of the crown, provincial governors, and members of the parlements to indict a tyrannical king and then to depose him from office if convicted. The author of the *Defense of Liberty against Tyrants* (almost certainly Philippe du Plessis-Mornay) followed the *Political Discourses* in expanding the base of those who could legally resist the tyranny of a legitimate monarch. Arguing that it was lawful to resist a tyrant who opposed God's law, the church, or the state, the author expanded the coalition of nobles and judges whose duty was to oppose him to include foreign princes, thus giving the debate an international dimension.[7] Thus, Protestant discourse after St Bartholomew's Day became a call to arms against the Valois tyranny perpetrated in the massacres of 1572. Set in the context of the Huguenot republic in the south, this rhetoric of resistance tore at the fabric of the Gallican monarchy.

Although he was far from the only defender of the Valois monarchy in this period, the legist and political theorist Jean Bodin responded with a traditional defence of sacral monarchy combined with a novel constitutional framework of great subtlety. In his *The Six Books of the Commonwealth*, first published in 1576, Bodin argued that all political authority came from God and that kings were thus answerable to God

---

[7] For the *Discours politiques des diverses puissances establies de Dieu au monde* see Sarah Hanley, 'The French Constitution Revised: Representative Assemblies and Resistance Right in the Sixteenth Century', in Mack P. Holt, ed., *Society and Institutions in Early Modern France* (Athens, GA, 1991), pp. 36–50. Also see Etienne Junius Brutus (pseudonym), *Vindiciae contra Tyrannos*, ed. and trans. H. Weber *et al.* (Geneva, 1979). For a general discussion of all this resistance literature, see Quentin Skinner, *The Foundations of Modern Political Thought*, II: *The Reformation* (Cambridge, 1978), chaps. 8–9; and Robert M. Kingdon, 'Calvinism and Resistance Theory, 1550–1580', in J. H. Burns and Mark Goldie, eds., *The Cambridge History of Political Thought, 1450–1700* (Cambridge, 1991), esp. pp. 206–14.

alone. Moreover, Bodin asserted that sovereignty was indivisible and could not practically be shared or divided among individuals or institutions in a state. It had to reside completely and absolutely with one individual or group, and in the case of France, Bodin was in no doubt that sovereignty rested indivisibly with the king, who was both the executive and legislative arm of the crown. Unrestricted and unlimited by any 'inferior magistrates' or 'popular assembly', the power of the king was undivided; he could not be deposed by his subjects. While Bodin made it clear that the power of kings was not completely unlimited – kings were subject to the laws of nature, the laws of God, and the fundamental laws of the realm – he offered a sharp rebuke to those Protestants advocating resistance: their prescriptions could only result in anarchy and political disorder. And it was this 'licentious anarchy, which is worse than the harshest tyranny in the world' as Bodin noted in his preface, that was the ultimate target of his treatise.

But when I perceived on every side that subjects were arming themselves against their princes; that books were being brought out openly, like firebrands to set Commonwealths ablaze, in which we are taught that the princes sent by providence to the human race must be thrust out of their kingdoms under a pretense of tyranny, and that kings must be chosen not by their lineage, but by the will of the people; and finally that these doctrines were weakening the foundations not of this realm only but of all states; then I denied that it was the function of a good man or of a good citizen to offer violence to his prince for any reason, however great a tyrant he might be; and contended that it was necessary to leave this punishment to God . . .[8]

In defending the Gallican monarchy from its Protestant critics, Bodin thus made a strong argument for absolute monarchy.

This rhetorical struggle to define the French constitution was made in the context of monarchical crisis. When Charles IX died in May 1574 his brother and heir, Henry III (1574–1589), was in Poland. He took his time returning to France despite the pleas of his mother, preferring a leisurely tour of Italy before making his royal entrance at Lyon in September. He returned to find his younger brother, François, duke of Alençon, and Henry, king of Navarre still closely guarded at court after their recent attempts to escape, and rumours were rife that further plots were afoot to liberate the princes. With the escalating rhetoric of resistance resonating throughout the Protestant portions of the realm, what was sorely needed was a strong, resourceful monarch. Unfortunately, if Jacques-Auguste de Thou's judgment is at all accurate, the new king was just the

[8] Jean Bodin, *The Six Bookes of a Commonweale*, ed. Kenneth Douglas McRae (a facsimile edition of the 1606 English translation) (Cambridge, MA, 1962), pp. A71–A72.

reverse: 'It is no longer possible to find in this prince those qualities which had elevated him above the rest, that is to say, his military prowess and warrior courage which was so much admired. Now he never gets on a horse or shows himself to his people as his predecessors have always done.' De Thou went on to say that what France's new king was most noted for now was 'ostentation and laxity ... together with an unfortunate penchant for frivolous living'.[9] This may have been an overly negative view of the new king, but it does show that French men and women had high expectations for the military hero of Jarnac and Moncontour.

De Thou might also have added inexperience, which showed itself immediately. Not only did Henry III manage further to alienate his younger brother Alençon and the king of Navarre over the next year, but he could not prevent either from escaping from court. When the maverick duke of Alençon fled from court during the night of 15 September 1575, both the king and Queen Mother feared that he might seek the refuge of the Protestant princes in the south. Although Alençon himself had no Protestant sympathies, his political ambitions far exceeded his limited abilities and he had long sought a spotlight and recognition. Though Protestants such as Condé and Navarre were wary of Alençon's support, the presence of a royal prince could bring some legitimacy to the cause of the opposition. And when just three days after his escape from court Alençon issued a public manifesto at Dreux, much of his rhetoric echoed the themes of Protestant pamphleteers. Portraying himself as an 'inferior magistrate' Alençon noted that when kingdoms fell into ruin and civil war, God often 'raises up when it pleases him heroic and worthy persons to oppose the tyranny of those who only seek to render all things in disorder'. He deplored the heavy taxes, imposts, and subsidies levied by his brother's royal officers, 'nearly all foreigners, who have monopolized the king and the principal offices and governments of his kingdom'. This last reference was to a group of Italian nobles at court as well as the Guises from Lorraine. Finally, Alençon hoped 'to restore this kingdom to its former splendour, glory, and liberty by a general and free assembly of the three estates of this kingdom, convoked in a secure and free place', and he vowed 'to take under our protection and safe-keeping everyone, those of one as well as the other religion'.[10] Despite his pleas that his quarrel was not with the king but the king's advisors, Alençon's declaration firmly tied him to the Huguenot resistance theory of Hotman, Beza, and the others. And when the duke soon attempted to

[9] Jacques-August de Thou, *Histoire universelle*, 11 vols. (Basel, 1742 edn), V, p. 101.
[10] B. N., Fonds français 3342, fols. 5–6. For a summary see Mack P. Holt, *The Duke of Anjou and the Politique Struggle during the Wars of Religion* (Cambridge, 1986), pp. 52–4.

attach his small band of followers to the gathering Protestant forces in the south led by the prince of Condé (and after his escape from court in February 1576, the king of Navarre), resistance had turned into open rebellion.

What made Alençon's participation in the rebellion so dangerous was that he was Henry III's heir presumptive. Should something happen to Henry, his younger brother could rightfully claim his place on the throne. Moreover, Condé had managed to secure a military alliance with the Calvinist elector Frederick III of the Palatinate, with the result that by the spring of 1576 20,000 German mercenaries under the command of Frederick III's son, John Casimir, had crossed the Rhine and approached the French frontier ready to join the Protestant forces commanded by Condé, Navarre, and Damville. And despite the best efforts of Henry III and Catherine de Medici to prevent the duke of Alençon from joining this threatening force, the maverick prince ignored them and revelled in the spotlight of attention he was getting from the Huguenots.

It soon became clear why the king and Queen Mother had worked so feverishly to talk Alençon out of aligning himself with the Protestant princes. Within weeks of Henry of Navarre's flight from court in February 1576, the various Protestant princes agreed to let Alençon represent them in an attempt to win greater concessions from the crown. Deputies from Alençon, Navarre, Condé, and Damville presented a long remonstrance to Henry III demanding 'the free, general, public, and complete exercise of the Reformed religion ... without any modification or restriction to time, place, or person'. The demands also included the creation of *chambres mi-parties* in the various parlements, sections of the court divided equally between Protestants and Catholics, as well as a number of fortified towns to maintain their military defences. The princes also demanded that the French crown pay the wages and arrears of the German mercenaries commanded by the duke of Casimir. Moreover, each of the princes wanted some personal benefit included in any peace settlement.[11] This was the most sweeping set of demands made by the Protestants since the start of the religious wars, and Henry III and Catherine de Medici found themselves in a very weak position from which to bargain. The king was in no financial position to raise an army to thwart the combined Protestant forces of Alençon, Navarre, Condé, Damville, and Casimir, close to 30,000 men. Even worse, the large force of German mercenaries captained by Casimir had already reached central France and by April was encamped with the other Protestant forces near Moulins, threatening the fortified towns along

[11] Bibliothèque de l'Institut de France (hereafter B. I. F.), Fonds Godefroy 95, fols. 10–28, 19 February 1576, autographed by Alençon.

the Loire. If this large army were to cross the Loire, there was no way the king could prevent a march toward the capital of Paris. The only recourse left to Henry and Catherine was capitulation.

The fifth war of religion was thus brought to a close by the Edict of Beaulieu on 6 May 1576. Apart from a brief skirmish the previous October between a royal company commanded by the duke of Guise and an advance party of German mercenaries led by Guillaume de Thoré, younger brother of Damville, hardly a shot had been fired. The very real presence in central France of this large Protestant army, coupled with the king's utter inability to defeat the Huguenots, resulted in an edict of pacification that would have been unimaginable four years earlier at the time of the massacres of St Bartholomew. And his younger brother's participation in the Protestant campaign only increased Henry III's problems, for with Alençon as the legitimate heir to the throne a Protestant victory might even spell the end of Henry's reign as king. Thus, the 'peace of Monsieur' – so-called because to contemporaries it appeared to be forced on the king by his brother, the duke of Alençon – was a dramatic turnaround for Protestant fortunes only four years after the massacres. But it must be remembered that it was dictated in arms; neither Henry III nor Catherine de Medici had experienced any *volte-face* in their policies toward the Huguenots.[12]

The peace edict of sixty-three articles did pay lip service to Catholic sensibilities. The edict required the Huguenots to restore Catholic worship in all Protestant towns where it had been abolished (article 3), forbade the public worship of Protestantism in the capital (article 8), and made it mandatory that all Protestants celebrate Catholic feast days (article 15). Moreover, the edict made it clear that 'in all acts and public actions where the said [reformed] religion is mentioned, these words will be used: the so-called reformed religion (*religion prétendue réformée*)' (article 16). By and large, however, the 'peace of Monsieur' was a victory for those of 'the so-called reformed religion'.

The terms were essentially those dictated in arms by the Protestant princes. For the first time in the religious wars, French Protestants were accorded the right of 'a free, public, and general exercise of religion' everywhere in France outside Paris. Thus, for the first time the Huguenots were allowed not only to worship openly and publicly anywhere in France save the capital, they could also build Protestant churches anywhere outside the capital (article 4). The *chambres mi-parties* were to be created in all the sovereign courts in order to prevent

---

[12] Holt, *Duke of Anjou*, pp. 63–7; and N. M. Sutherland, *The Huguenot Struggle for Recognition* (New Haven, 1980), pp. 223–31.

discrimination in cases involving litigants of different religions (articles 18–21 and 45). And as most of the Protestant resistance literature had demanded, and as the duke of Alençon had echoed at Dreux in September 1575, the edict called on the king to convoke the Estates-General within six months (article 58).[13] The Protestant princes were duly rewarded for their part in a set of so-called 'secret articles' that were not part of the published peace edict. No one benefitted more than François, duke of Alençon, who was granted the duchies and revenues of Anjou, Touraine, and Berry, as well as an additional annual pension of 300,000 *livres tournois*. In taking his brother's former title of duke of Anjou, the young prince had finally received the recognition he had long sought.[14] In essence, only four years after the massacres, the Protestants seemingly had won nearly everything they had been seeking since the start of the Wars of Religion. Yet two principal obstacles still remained before them: the king had no intention of enforcing these liberal concessions, and most French Catholics stoutly opposed the edict altogether. Catherine de Medici openly boasted that she and the king 'had made the peace in order to get back Monsieur [the duke of Alençon] and not to re-establish the Huguenots, as everybody now realizes'.[15] Meanwhile, the Parlement of Paris refused to register the peace edict and the Paris populace, led by the Catholic clergy, demonstrated vehemently against it with placards and hostile demonstrations during the month of May. Some of the fortified towns ceded to the Huguenots in the edict refused to admit any Protestant troops. Peace was, as ever, still just an illusion.

Moreover, the meeting of the Estates-General, which opened at Blois on 24 November 1576, did little to satiate Protestant demands. Despite the constant Huguenot demands for the convocation of the Estates-General, the elections of the deputies from the three estates resulted in a virtually all-Catholic assembly. Out of a total of nearly 400 deputies, there were naturally no Protestant deputies representing the clergy, only one noble deputy (who left shortly after the meeting opened), and only a handful of Protestant deputies in the Third Estate. In many areas the time and place of the elections were only announced at Catholic mass, and in some jurisdictions Protestants were simply prevented from participating

---

[13] The treaty is printed in André Stegmann, ed., *Edits des guerres de religion* (Paris, 1979), pp. 97–120; while a very useful summary is in Sutherland, *Huguenot Struggle for Recognition*, pp. 228–31 and 361–2.

[14] B. I. F., Fonds Godefroy 94, fols. 2–4 for the 'secret articles', and Fonds Godefroy 316, fol. 79 for the grants to Alençon. For a summary see Holt, *Duke of Anjou*, pp. 66–8.

[15] Lalourcé and Duval, eds., *Recueil des pièces originales et authentiques concernant la tenue des Estats Généraux*, 9 vols. (Paris, 1789), III, p. 18.

in the elections.[16] The result was not only a nearly all-Catholic assembly, but a collection of deputies that was collectively hostile to the edict of pacification and desirous of a renewal of the war against the Huguenots. Henry III was still strapped for cash, however, and also wanted the deputies to support the levy of new revenues, monies that would be vital if there was to be a renewal of the war. Thus, the Catholic deputies of the Estates-General of Blois found themselves in a dilemma: they generally favoured overturning the recent peace edict and renewing the war against the Huguenots, but they were being asked to pay for it out of their own pockets.

Of the three estates the clergy were the most united in their determination to overturn the peace edict and renew the civil wars, unsurprising given the militant nature of the Catholic clergy throughout the religious wars. They unanimously agreed that the king ought to maintain the uniformity of religion throughout the kingdom and even agreed to grant subsidies to the crown for this purpose. In the second estate the nobility also agreed to support the uniformity of religion, though a small handful – about half a dozen – did speak out that the king 'ought to maintain his subjects in peace'. In the third estate there was much less consensus as a faction led by Jean Bodin, the author of *The Six Books of the Commonwealth* published earlier in the year, argued loudly that peace was preferable to war, and that in any case, it would be most imprudent to grant the king's wish for a sharp increase in taxes. This might appear to be a strange position for the defender of absolute monarchy to take, though Bodin did not intend his opposition to the king's request for higher taxes to be seen as a constitutional check on the monarchy. He was simply defending a political decision he believed to be in the best interests of the crown; not to ask more in taxes from an already weakened populace.[17] While a majority of the third estate did eventually vote to support the uniformity of religion, they hoped it could be achieved 'without war'; there was also very little support for a tax increase. The result was that when the meeting concluded in late February with each of the three estates presenting its own *cahier de doléances* (list of grievances), the king was left with his own dilemma. The three estates had endorsed overturning the peace edict, but apart from the clergy they had firmly refused to levy any additional monies to carry out this mandate.

---

[16] Georges Picot, *Histoire des Etats-Généraux ... de 1355 à 1614*, 4 vols. (Paris, 1872), II, 305; and B. N., Fonds nouvelles acquisitions françaises 7738, fols. 288–91, 'Protestation faicte par ceux de la religion sur la tenue des Estats generaux de France'.

[17] Julian H. Franklin, *Jean Bodin and the Rise of Absolutist Theory* (Cambridge, 1973), pp. 88–92; and Martin Wolfe, 'Jean Bodin on Taxes: The Sovereignty–Taxes Paradox', *Political Science Quarterly*, vol. 83 (June 1968), 268–84.

Moreover, Henry III's position was further undermined at the meeting by attempts by Catholic militants among the first two estates to organize a 'catholic association' to deal with the Huguenots if the king was either unwilling or unable to do so. Supported by the Guises (now led by Henry duke of Guise, as the Cardinal of Lorraine had died in 1574), this association or league threatened the king's own authority. He made a feeble attempt to counteract this threat by claiming to be the head of this association in December 1576. He even sent out letters to all the royal governors in the provinces requiring them to swear their loyalty to him as head of the association. His actions only underscored his weakness, however, as he was left with a strong mandate for war by the first two estates but a stout refusal to pay for it by the third estate.[18]

Finally, there was a vocal minority at Blois that steadfastly refused to endorse the majority platform of overturning the recent edict of pacification. Bodin's opposition in the third estate has already been mentioned, but there were also reservations among the nobility. On 28 February 1577 Louis de Bourbon, duke of Montpensier, and one of the most ardent persecutors of the Huguenots in the early religious wars, astonished a number of deputies with his concerns about renewing the war.

I believe, gentlemen that there is not one of you who doubts the zeal and devotion I have displayed for the advancement of God's honour and for the support for the Roman Catholic church ... Nevertheless, when I consider the evils which the recent wars have brought us, and how much this division is leading to the ruin and desolation of this poor kingdom ... and the calamities such as those which I saw on my journey here, of poor people immersed in poverty without hope of ever being able to raise themselves from that state except by means of peace ... I am constrained to advise their Majesties to make peace ... being the only remedy and best cure that I know of for the evil that has spread all over France ... I do not mean to give the impression that I favour any other than the Roman Catholic religion, but I would advise the toleration and sufferance of those of the new opinion for a short time ... until by means of a council, another meeting of the estates, or any other means, their Majesties having thus reunited and reconciled their subjects, God can bless us with only one religion, the Roman Catholic faith held and followed by all previous kings, and in which I protest to live and die.[19]

The very same day of Montpensier's speech another group of noble deputies submitted a remonstrance to the king protesting the decision taken by the second estate to renew the war against the Huguenots.

[18] On the Estates-General see Mack P. Holt, 'Attitudes of the French Nobility at the Estates-General of 1576', *Sixteenth Century Journal*, vol. 18 (1987), 489–504; idem, *The Duke of Anjou*, pp. 76–87; and Sutherland, *Huguenot Struggle for Recognition*, pp. 246–69.
[19] Lalourcé and Duval, eds., *Recueil des pièces originales*, II, pp. 210–13.

Recorded in the diary of Pierre de Blanchefort, noble deputy from Nivernais, this minority remonstrance from the second estate echoed the speech of Montpensier:

It is highly desirable for the people of France to live in one Roman Catholic and apostolic religion, under which they remain in your obedience. And it is true that when people have only one religion, a king is better obeyed and served. But as the people are subject to kings, so are kings subject to God ... And one of the greatest afflictions occurs when the people are torn apart, as when the children of one house at the wish of their father are banded together one against the other ... The war is so entirely contrary to the establishment of proper order and the increase of your grandeur ... Your Majesty will be aware, however, that we by no means approve of the so-called reformed religion ... but we beseech you very humbly, Sire, to believe that anyone who favours civil war is ungodly.[20]

Twenty noble deputies signed this remonstrance – fully one-fourth of the second estate – and the duke of Montpensier presented it to the king that same day.

The minority voices of Montpensier and Blanchefort in the second estate and Jean Bodin in the third estate were indicative of a growing apprehension of what the Wars of Religion were doing to the kingdom of France. The advocacy of peace and temporary toleration of Protestantism in order for tranquility and order to be restored throughout the kingdom was a platform that would later grow into a *via media*: a possible compromise between the extremist rhetoric of militant Protestants and Catholics. Dubbed *politiques* by the most militant Catholics because they appeared to be placing political considerations above the Catholic faith, figures such as Montpensier, Blanchefort, and Bodin were excoriated for being willing to accept the temporary co-existence of Protestantism as the price to be paid for ending the civil wars. Several modern historians have attempted to unite these sporadic, minority voices into a movement, or even a party, that favoured some modern notion of religious toleration. At the same time, it is claimed that these so-called *politiques* were the birth of the modern view that political considerations should always take precedence over religious considerations: in other words, the decline of confessional politics. Nothing could be more misleading, however, as there was neither a *politique* movement nor organized party in the 1570s. Moreover, as we have already seen, figures such as Montpensier and Blanchefort explicitly favoured the uniformity of religion with all French men and women eventually reunited within the Gallican church. To suggest that these *politiques* were sympathetic to any permanent

---

[20]   The diary of Blanchefort is in Bibliothèque municipale de Blois, Mss. 89 (quote on fols. 193v–96r).

religious co-existence, much less any modern notion of religious toleration, is simply inaccurate. Montpensier, Blanchefort, and Bodin were
simply expressing at Blois many of the same concerns that Catherine de
Medici and others had voiced since the beginning of the religious wars:
that civil war would eventually result in the destruction of the kingdom. In
any case, their voices were drowned out in early 1577 by the majority of
the deputies who favoured a return to war.

Henry III had managed to win back the loyalty of his brother, now duke
of Anjou, as a result of the peace settlement with the Huguenots.
Moreover, in March 1577 Damville, the governor of Languedoc, also
abandoned the Huguenots. As a Catholic nobleman and royal governor,
he found too many disagreements with the Huguenots to remain as their
protector in the Midi. Nevertheless, Henry III knew that without any new
tax revenues, which the deputies at Blois had opposed, he would be
unable to defeat a Protestant army that was aided and abetted by
Protestant forces from abroad. Yet militant nobles on the royal council,
such as the dukes of Guise and Nevers, continued to demand the renewal
of the war against the Huguenots, which put the king in a very awkward
position. 'Gentlemen, each of you has seen how hard I have tried to
honour God and how much I have wanted only one religion in my kingdom', Henry noted to his councillors in March. 'Needless to say, I have
even solicited the deputies of the three estates and have asked them to
vote for religious uniformity, in the belief that they would help me carry
out this holy resolution. But seeing what little money they have given me,
I have little hope of executing my intentions, which I want each of you to
understand.'[21] In order to maintain his authority among the Catholic
militants on the council, and in order to carry out the mandate of the
deputies at Blois, Henry resolved to renew the war against the Huguenots,
who were already in the process of rearming. But without adequate
resources to defeat the Protestant army – and this, after all, is why the
crown was forced to submit to the Huguenot demands a year earlier – the
sixth war of religion was destined to be both short and inconclusive.

A small royal force was cobbled together and placed under the nominal
command of the new duke of Anjou, an obvious royal sign to the
Huguenots that Anjou's loyalty to the crown was re-established. Anjou
was young and inexperienced, however, and the army was actually under
the *de facto* command of the duke of Nevers, who had a long history of
persecuting Protestants. The army was so badly equipped and outfitted
that it was unclear whether it could survive more than a month or two in

---

[21] Marin le Roy, seigneur de Gomberville, ed., *Les Mémoires de monsieur le duc de Nevers*,
2 vols. (Paris, 1665), I, 176–7.

the field. Nevers's targets were the eight fortified towns that had been ceded to the Protestants in the peace edict of May 1576, with the Loire fortification of La Charité being first on the list. When La Charité fell to the besieging royal army on 2 May 1577, followed by Issoire to the south in Auvergne a month later, it appeared that the king was again on the offensive. But Nevers and his troops struggled through the Limousin, out of ammunition and foodstuffs. The duke was forced to billet his troops on the civilian population – or force donations of cash with the threat of billeting – and ultimately recommended that the king recall his army. With Henry of Navarre and the prince of Condé still at large with the bulk of the Huguenot forces, and aid forthcoming from the English Queen Elizabeth in August, the king had no alternative to another peace settlement with the Protestants.

The Peace of Bergerac, where the settlement was negotiated in the southwest, was issued by the king on 17 September 1577. It was clearly a compromise between the generous terms offered the Huguenots in the edict of May 1576 in the so-called Peace of Monsieur and the harsh repressive policy advocated by the Estates-General at Blois, clearly a result of the circumstances of the crown in the summer of 1577. If the last edict had been the Peace of Monsieur, the edict signed at Bergerac was clearly the king's. It outlawed all leagues and associations throughout the kingdom, and it pared down the general freedom of Protestant worship outside Paris of the last edict to only one town in each administrative district of the realm. In most other respects, the text of the edict repeated the last edict of pacification virtually word for word.[22]

In the autumn of 1577 Henry III and Catherine de Medici continued to experience the same problems they encountered after the Peace of Monsieur in May 1576: many Catholics refused to recognize the new settlement, many royal officials in the provinces refused to enforce it, and most French Protestants still saw no reason to trust the monarchy given the legacy of St Bartholomew's Day. Thus, in late 1577 Henry's authority was questioned and repudiated by many throughout the kingdom. If he was unable to sustain a war long enough to defeat the Huguenots, he was equally incapable of maintaining peace for any extended period. The Protestants' rhetoric of resistance to the crown made them rebels as well as heretics to many French Catholics, while the king's and Queen Mother's involvement in St Bartholomew's Day prevented most Protestants from willingly disarming. It was a paradox that haunted Henry III's entire reign and made a genuine peace almost

---

[22] See Sutherland, *Huguenot Struggle for Recognition*, pp. 270–3 and 362–3 for a summary of the peace. The actual treaty is in Stegmann, ed., *Edits des guerres de religion*, pp. 131–53.

impossible to achieve. Many better leaders than Henry would have been equally powerless to resolve this dilemma.

The peace came painfully close to dissolving into civil war once again on several occasions during the years 1578–80; in each instance, however, religious and confessional differences quickly became submerged in general peasant revolts (see Map 6). A variety of factors – including the loss of authority of the crown, seigneurial repression in many rural areas, a rising population, and the general economic impact of fifteen years of civil war on the countryside – explain how confessional differences could get buried beneath a myriad of socio-economic complaints among the popular classes. In Provence, for example, a group of peasants called Razats grew tired of being forced from their homes by billeting troops and of being pressed for revenues from both sides. In 1578 they raised arms in order to defend themselves from soldiers of any political or religious denomination. Their principal target was the militant Catholic count of Carcès and his many noble clients. The Razats not only were made up of peasants of both faiths, but they sought allies of both faiths among the rivals of Carcès in Provence. In April 1579 a band of peasants from the region near Toulon secretly assembled and massacred 600 noble clients of Carcès in the village of Cuers. At about this same time another group of peasants in the village of Callas sacked the château of their local seigneur, which set off a frenzy of looting and burning of noble properties in the region, with their inhabitants fleeing for safety.[23]

Even more widespread peasant revolts took place just to the north in the Vivarais and Dauphiné. In the region of Vivarais just west of the Rhône (the modern-day Ardèche), the first risings took place in the town of Largentière where Catholic parishioners had been provoked by soldiers from both sides in the fifth and sixth religious wars. The year 1575, when Protestant troops had seized and garrisoned 26 towns and the Catholics 78, was described by a local chronicler as the worst year the province had ever known: 'The peasants removed tiles and beams from their houses and brought them to sell in Aubenas in order to keep alive through war and famine. The countryside was despoiled by the treachery of the soldiers of both religions. They cooperated with each other in betraying wealthy civilians, and in committing atrocities, thefts, and all kinds of evils.'[24] It was a small-town lawyer named Jean La Rouvière,

---

[23] J. H. M. Salmon, *Society in Crisis: France in the Sixteenth Century* (New York and London, 1975), pp. 208–9.
[24] Quoted in J. H. M. Salmon, 'Peasant Revolt in Vivarais, 1575–1580', in *Renaissance and Revolt: Essays in the Intellectual and Social History of Early Modern France* (Cambridge, 1987), p. 217.

Map 6 Areas of Peasant Revolts, 1579

however, not a peasant, who eventually drew up a petition to present to the king in February 1579, on behalf of 'the poor people of the third estate of Your Majesty's barren desolated countryside of Vivarais – poor, miserable, martyrized, and abandoned men'. And like the local chronicler of 1575, this petition targeted 'the insolence, authority, and power of the *gentil-shommes* [nobles], captains, and soldiers' as the cause of their misery. La Rouvière then went on to outline a long list of atrocities that he implored the king to remedy. They had been

buried alive in heaps of manure, thrown into wells and ditches and left to die, howling like dogs; they had been nailed in boxes without air, walled up in towers without food, and garrotted upon trees in the depths of the mountains and forests; they had been stretched in front of fires, their feet fricasseed in grease; their women had been raped and those who were pregnant had been aborted; their children had been kidnapped and ransomed, or even roasted alive before the parents ... There had been burnings, ransoms, sackings, levies, *tailles* [taxes], and tolls together with seizures of goods, grain, and livestock. In one year impositions placed upon them first by the Catholic and then by the Protestant garrisons had exceeded the amount of the *taille* in [the last] thirty years.

The petition concluded with an excoriation of the local nobility:

In as much as the seigneurs of the said region, together with their officers of one religion or the other, have permitted and do continue to permit, with connivance and dissimulation, infinite crimes and excesses, and do maintain, shelter, defend, and sustain the murderers, robbers, rebels, and disturbers of the public peace, may it please Your Majesty to command and enjoin most expressly that they must abstain from withdrawing the above named into their houses and from giving them comfort, help, and aid.

While the complaints against further taxes, tolls, and impositions might suggest that this was just an anti-fiscal riot – common enough in the sixteenth and seventeenth centuries – and though the charges against the seigneurs might even suggest a social revolution, it was clear that the principal targets were the garrisons of troops these revenues and seigneurs supported. The peasants' ultimate goal was 'to purge the country of this vermin' who consistently broached the peace.[25] The king read and ultimately replied to the petition, even showing some sympathy with the Vivarais peasants' complaints. It was only some months after Catherine de Medici restored a semblance of royal authority in the south with a truce signed with Henry of Navarre at Nérac that same month, however, that any semblance of order was restored. The alliance of Calvinists from the towns and rural Catholics in Vivarais was never defeated or subdued, but the revolt did eventually cease once the marauding bands of troops were dispersed and contained.

Across the Rhône in the province of Dauphiné, a similar large-scale peasant revolt broke out in the town of Romans. In February 1579 during the Carnival celebrations leading up to the beginning of Lent, a local

---

[25] Quoted in ibid., pp. 221–2.

textile-worker and former soldier named Jean Serve, also known as Paumier, was elected 'king' of the drapers' 'kingdom', one of the traditional festival groups that traditionally took part in pre-Lenten festivities. He managed to raise troops and unite the artisans and peasants of both faiths under his banner as La Rouvière had done in Vivarais. On the feast day of St Blaise (3 February) – the patron saint of drapers, carders, and woolcombers – this peasant band mounted an armed demonstration that soon led to physical confrontation. According to the town notable, Antoine Guérin, Serve-Paumier commanded 'with so much indiscretion and bestiality that he made the gentlefolk dread him'. The notables' fears were well founded when the armed peasants stormed Romans's town hall, 'replaced the council, and instead of the gentlefolk who had filled it, he had others of his own following take over, who were as unworthy of this responsibility as a shoemaker would be as presiding officer of a High Court'.[26] This social tension between commoners – made up of rural peasants and urban artisans – and the elites was also echoed by the diarist Eustache Piémond: 'In Romans, the common folk, having elected Paumier as their chief, took the keys [to the city's gates] from the captains of the said town, and especially captain Antoine Coste and other notable personages who were the keepers of the town.'[27] Like their counterparts in Vivarais, the Romans peasants parlayed this rhetoric of social tension to underscore other demands: a suspension of the *taille* and the many indirect taxes placed on goods produced, bought, and sold in Romans, as well as an end to the systematic pillage and plunder of their homes and property by the various noble warlords in the province. The most visible successes of this insurrection came with the sacking and burning of the châteaux of Châteaudouble and Roissas, where two such warlords had set up their bases of operations. The peasants remained an effective force for the next twelve months, however, as they continued as a guerrilla force in the countryside.

The insurrection came to a bloody climax during Carnival 1580. The elites of Romans organized their own military force and took part as their own 'kingdom' in the pre-Lenten festivities. Having elected Guérin as their 'king', they conspired to use the traditional mock battles between the various 'kingdoms' of Carnival to defeat the peasant 'kingdom' of Serve-Paumier. The mock battles turned to genuine violence on Mardi Gras itself, 16 February 1580, the highlight of Carnival. Heavily armed, Guérin's supporters drove the peasant militia out of town, with the

---

[26] Quoted in Emmanuel Le Roy Ladurie, *Carnival in Romans*, Eng. trans. Mary Feeney (New York, 1979), p. 103.
[27] Quoted in ibid., p. 104.

peasant leader being killed in the process. Other peasant bands in the countryside were unable to aid Serve-Paumier and his Romans supporters. The latter fled in retreat up the valley of the Isère, where they were trapped and massacred by royal forces on 26 March 1580 in the town of Moirans. On that date more than a thousand 'already most harrassed and frightened' men, according to the diarist Piémond, were slaughtered by a small contingent of royal troops. Once Guérin had incarcerated and then executed the last of Serve-Paumier's supporters in Romans itself, the peasant insurrection was over.[28]

What can we make of these peasant revolts in the southeast in the years 1578–80? Clearly, they are evidence that there were many socio-economic as well as political factors that could motivate French men and women to violence in addition to religious differences. The rhetoric of class war is certainly evidence of acute social tensions that were inherent in most sixteenth-century communities. These tensions were exacerbated by the hardships of nearly two decades of civil war and erupted into the violence that was witnessed in Provence, Vivarais, and Dauphiné. But should these incidents be understood as symptoms of a class war of haves against have-nots, where religious differences receded into the background as one's social station counted for more than one's faith? Not at all. What all three of these insurrections demonstrate is how fearful the elites – both bourgeois and noble – were of any threat to the social and political order. They used the same language and rhetoric to describe the peasant insurgents as they had been using to describe Protestants for two decades: as disturbers of the public peace and threats to proper order under a Gallican monarchy. Of particular interest is the public propaganda that Guérin propagated to justify his harsh repression and retribution against the supporters of the peasant 'king' in Romans in the aftermath of Mardi Gras 1580. The 'rebels', as he referred to them, planned

to begin on Mardi Gras to kill the nobility, the judiciary, and even Messieurs of the Court of Parlement, the clergy, all the notable bourgeois and merchants of the town of Romans, and afterwards even kill their own women, and marry the wives of the said notables whom they had killed and whose property they had seized and divided up, and after all this bring the Huguenots into the said town.[29]

Here in a nutshell is evidence of the mentality of Catholic elites about both peasant rebels and Protestants, which Guérin linked together: they were murderers who would even stoop to kill their own wives out of economic and sexual revenge. In short, they planned to turn the social

---

[28] Ibid., pp. 229–63 (quote on p. 258), and Salmon, *Society in Crisis*, pp. 210–11.
[29] Quoted in Le Roy Ladurie, *Carnival in Romans*, p. 254.

and political order upside-down. Thus, the legacy of the peasant uprisings of 1578–80 was twofold: the fear of the Catholic elites who opposed
them, as well as a heightened consciousness and anger among the common people. Although it was but a foretaste of more widespread (and
more genuine) social upheaval to come in the 1590s, these events underscored the difficulties any *politique* or compromise solution to the civil
wars would surely have to confront.

While peasant uprisings occupied both Protestant and royalist forces in
the southeast, the shortest and least significant of the French religious
wars occurred in the southwest in the spring and summer of 1580. Using
the excuse that not all of Marguerite de Valois's dowry had been turned
over to him as promised upon their marriage in August 1572, Henry of
Navarre set out to take possession of several Catholic strongholds along
the Lot and Garonne valleys. The only confrontation occurred at Cahors,
which Navarre successfully besieged in May. As neither side was able to
sustain any kind of offensive long enough to defeat the other in any
significant way, yet another compromise settlement was in order. It was
the king's younger brother, François, duke of Anjou, who supervised the
negotiations with Navarre in the fall, and the Peace of Fleix was signed on
26 November 1580 ending the seventh civil war. The peace edict simply
restated the terms of the previous peace (signed at Bergerac in 1577) and
the truce signed at Nérac between Navarre and the Queen Mother in
1579.[30] Unsurprisingly, the legal rights granted to the Huguenots proved
as impossible to enforce in 1580 as they had in 1576 and 1577.

It was no coincidence that the duke of Anjou was in the southwest
anxious for peace in the autumn of 1580, as his own interests in foreign
policy required a peace settlement at home. His activities, which had
become more rather than less worrisome after he abandoned the
Huguenots after the Peace of Monsieur, had threatened further dangers
in the late 1570s; and not the least of these worries was the prospect of
foreign invasion. Although he had abandoned the Huguenots after the
Peace of Monsieur when he was rewarded with his new titles, and even
participated in the renewal of the wars against them in 1577, Anjou had
nevertheless become a focus of international intrigue in two different
Protestant circles. At the Protestant court of Queen Elizabeth in
England, Anjou re-emerged as a possible marriage suitor to the queen
in 1578. At the same time, the Dutch Calvinist provinces of Holland and
Zeeland under the guidance of William of Orange had made overtures to

---

[30] See the peace treaty in Stegmann, ed., *Edits des guerres de religion*, pp. 192–203. It is
summarized and analysed in Sutherland, *Huguenot Struggle for Recognition*, pp. 276–7 and
363–4.

Anjou about replacing Philip II of Spain as their sovereign prince. The common link between these two initiatives was the impact of Spanish hegemony in the Netherlands and Spain's resulting ability to dominate both the North Sea and the North Atlantic. Thus, for heads of state such as Henry III of France, Elizabeth of England, and Philip II of Spain, the confessional struggle in Europe was complicated by the practical politics that predated the Reformation. As much as Henry III may have shared similar sensibilities with Philip II concerning Protestantism, the political rivalry of Spain and France that had begun in 1494 in Italy in the form of the Habsburg–Valois Wars was not dissipated by the Peace of Cateau-Cambrésis in 1559. Henry and Catherine de Medici had no more desire to see Spain dominate the Netherlands than did Elizabeth, and both monarchs had much to gain by supporting the rebellion in the northern provinces of the Netherlands against Spanish rule. Their policies throughout the 1570s, however, were tempered by their mutual fear of Spanish reprisal should they appear openly and publicly to side with the Dutch rebels. This explains the delicacy of Anjou's position. Henry and Catherine de Medici, as well as many French Catholics, were loath on one hand to see Protestants such as Elizabeth and William of Orange lend support to the Huguenots in France; after all, it was the foreign support of John Casimir that had forced the Peace of Monsieur upon them in 1576. On the other hand, they were prepared to help them defeat the Spanish army in the Netherlands to weaken Habsburg preponderance on their northern frontier. The trick was to do this privately rather than publicly, in order not to provoke a Spanish invasion in retaliation, making vacillation a prudent but necessary foundation of their foreign policy.

The duke of Anjou's relationship with the Dutch rebels took a revolutionary turn in September 1580, when he signed an agreement at Plessis-lès-Tours with deputies from the seven northern provinces still in revolt against Philip II, making him the successor to Philip II as their sovereign prince. Although the Dutch rebels did not officially repudiate Philip's sovereignty until July 1581 in their 'Declaration of independence', they had made every effort to line up a suitable prince as replacement before-hand. Anjou was their reluctant choice, since Elizabeth had turned down a similar offer several times before. Anjou agreed to provide significant troops and military support, as well as a promise from his brother Henry to do likewise, in return for the titles of prince, duke, count, and lord in the respective Dutch provinces as well as a pension of 2,400,000 florins per year to carry out the war against Spain. This was an enormous sum, which the Dutch were never able to pay. Moreover, it was clear that the limitations and checks on Anjou's power as titular sovereign prince were much greater than Philip II had experienced. He had no authority in the matter of religion, for example, as each province decided that issue for itself. In addition, unlike previous sovereigns, Anjou had no authority over the Dutch army or the sole authority to convoke and disband the States-General, the representative body representing all the Dutch provinces still in revolt.[31] Nevertheless, Anjou's treaty with the Dutch further threatened Spanish reprisal against the kingdom of France, as the heir to the French throne was now openly cavorting with Protestant rebels against their legitimate prince.

Anjou's relationship with Queen Elizabeth was, despite a façade of propaganda, underpinned by similar motivations. The English queen was by more than twenty years Anjou's senior – and well beyond child-bearing age – a crucial factor given the paucity of heirs to both crowns. Moreover, they were of different religions: she the conservative Protestant and he the traditional Gallican Catholic despite his links with the Huguenots in 1575–76. And finally, Elizabeth found Anjou to be physically repulsive when they first met in 1579, as he had been disfigured by smallpox as a child. Why, then, would she be interested in this Valois prince as a marriage suitor? And that she was definitely interested was the conclusion that everyone who witnessed her second interview with Anjou in England in the autumn of 1581 drew. It was certainly what the Spanish ambassador, Bernardino de Mendoza, thought as he observed the scene at Whitehall on Ascension Day:

On the 22nd at eleven in the morning, while Anjou and the queen were strolling through the gallery accompanied by the earl of Leicester and [Francis] Walsingham, the French ambassador entered and said that he wanted to write to his master, who had ordered him to find out from the queen's own mouth what she planned to do concerning the marriage with his brother. She responded: 'You can write this to the king, that the duke of Anjou will be my husband.' At the same moment she kissed Anjou on the mouth and gave him a ring which she took from her finger as a token of her pledge.[32]

It was all a ruse, however, as Elizabeth only wanted to give Henry III the impression she was going to marry his younger brother Anjou. It had become painfully clear to her in 1579, upon Anjou's first visit to England, that her privy council and the majority of the population were unwilling to accept a Catholic consort for their queen. Elizabeth did intend to help fund Anjou's enterprise in the Netherlands against Philip II, and she only wanted to ensure it was not going to be money wasted by making sure that Henry III would support his brother too. Henry had pledged to support

[31] Holt, *Duke of Anjou*, pp. 134–40.
[32] M. F. Navarrete *et al.*, eds., *Colección de documentos inéditos para la historia de España*, 112 vols. (Madrid, 1842–95), XCII, 193–4, Mendoza to Philip II, 24 November 1581.

Anjou's Dutch venture only if Elizabeth would do likewise, and he insisted on her pledge of marriage to make good on her support. So, Elizabeth's gambit on Ascension Day in the garden at Whitehall was propaganda aimed squarely at Anjou, Henry III, and Catherine de Medici.[33]

The ploy worked admirably as Anjou departed England for the Netherlands without a wife but £60,000 richer. He was duly installed as 'prince and lord' of the Dutch provinces still in revolt against Spain – the seven northern provinces – in Antwerp on 19 February 1582 amidst great fanfare and celebration. His rule proved to be very short-lived as the Dutch provinces never managed to make good on their promise of his annual stipend. Relying on Elizabeth's money plus what little he could get from his brother, Anjou proved incapable of defeating the Spanish army. Ultimately, his own incompetence as a military commander, and even treachery when he tried to seize Antwerp by force in January 1583, cost him what little good will he had in the Dutch provinces, and he was forced to return home to France after only a year. He was clearly not the saviour that William of Orange and the Dutch provinces had been hoping for. Nevertheless, the significance of his activities of the preceding three years for the religious wars in France was considerable. He had openly pledged his hand in marriage to the Protestant queen of England. Moreover, he had openly and publicly allied himself with the Calvinist-led Dutch rebels in the Netherlands against their legitimate Catholic prince, Philip II. For militant Catholics in France, this did not bode well, as the opportunist, chameleon-like Anjou seemed to be heading back toward the Protestant cause that he had dallied with back in 1575–76. As Henry III was distressingly childless and perceived to be incapable of producing an heir of his own, the duke of Anjou was in all likelihood the next king of France, not to mention maybe king consort of England and 'prince and lord' of the Dutch provinces in revolt against Spain. For many French Catholics, Anjou was not just cavorting with heretics; he was thought to be a genuine threat to the sacral monarchy in France that he would one day surely inherit.

When the duke of Anjou suddenly died in June 1584, however, he proved even more dangerous in death than in life. With splendid irony, the passing of the last Valois heir meant that the next in line to the throne (at least according to most jurists) was the Protestant Henry of Navarre. The death of the duke of Anjou at his estate in Château-Thierry on 10 June 1584 proved to be the second major watershed of the Wars of

---

[33] Holt, *Duke of Anjou*, pp. 146–65.

Religion. If the St Bartholomew's massacres marked a significant turning-point in 1572 as a critical blow to Protestant growth and strength throughout the kingdom, the death of Anjou proved to be a different kind of turning-point. If Anjou's prospect as the next king of France was perceived as a threat to the Gallican monarchy, the thought of the Protestant king of Navarre on the throne was an outright abomination. The rhetoric of resistance of all the Protestant literature of the 1570s now sounded even more shrill in 1584. To many Catholics Navarre as king meant not only the end of the Gallican monarchy, but perhaps the demise of Catholic culture altogether. Contemporaries were immediately aware of the implications and consequences of Anjou's passing. Two days after he died, the king's secretary of state wrote that 'Their majesties and all of France are saddened, and with good reason, since the king has no children.' The priest who gave the duke of Anjou the sacrament of last rites and was with him when he died was even more explicit: 'The tenth of June will forever bear witness to our misfortune ... the year 1584 is indeed a year of revolution.' And finally, the Florentine ambassador in France reflected 'that the death of the duke of Anjou was the ruin of France'.[34] All these prognostications sadly proved to be true, as Anjou's death spawned the longest and bloodiest of all the civil wars.

[34] All quoted in ibid., pp. 211–12.

While most French Catholics mourned the death of the duke of Anjou in June 1584, the Parisian diarist Pierre de l'Estoile noted cynically that the Guises 'took great heart'. 'It came at a very opportune time for them, facilitating and advancing the designs of their League, which from that moment began to grow stronger as France grew weaker.'[1] L'Estoile was referring to the organization known as the Holy Union, usually called the Catholic League, that emerged when Henry of Navarre became presumptive heir to the throne at Anjou's death. Composed of a variety of different Catholic cohorts and loosely directed by the Guise family, the League was held together by one common goal: to prevent the monarchy of the 'Most Christian King' from falling into the hands of a heretic. Whatever the social and political tensions that divided French Catholics following Anjou's death, they all shared a common vision of a sacral monarchy. This vision went beyond any general theory of 'divine right', a notion shared by all sixteenth-century princes throughout Europe, and singled out France as a unique Christian commonwealth, whose 'Most Christian King' received God's special favour in return for a promise to fight heresy throughout his kingdom. Made explicit in his coronation oath, it was a promise that Henry III found even more troubling now that the legitimate heir to the throne was the Protestant Henry of Navarre. Although not traditionally recognized as such by legists, most French Catholics readily accepted the Catholicity of the crown as one of the fundamental laws of the unwritten constitution. As the Parisian barrister and member of the League, Jean de Caumont, wrote in 1587, 'Jesus Christ will conquer; Jesus Christ will reign; Jesus Christ will be king in France and will have His lieutenant render His justice, always "Most Christian".'[2] For all of its political machinations aimed against Henry III and Henry of Navarre and

---

[1] Pierre de l'Estoile, *Journal pour le règne de Henri III* (*1574–1589*), ed. Louis-Raymond Lefèvre (Paris, 1943), p. 357.

[2] Quoted in Frederic J. Baumgartner, *Radical Reactionaries: The Political Thought of the French Catholic League* (Geneva, 1975), p. 75.

their many clients, and despite the social tensions that attracted many of its supporters, it is clear that a fundamentally religious strain was part of the foundation of the League: its various members were 'godly warriors'.[3]

The Catholic League appears to be a revival of the Catholic associations that sprang up in opposition to the Peace of Monsieur in 1576. And while those associations tended to dissolve once the Estates-General at Blois repudiated that peace settlement, the situation in 1584 was more lasting: whatever the king's policies concerning the Huguenots, Henry of Navarre was still heir to the throne. This was such an alarming possibility that even Philip II of Spain thought it worthwhile to support the League's efforts. The result was a formal treaty signed by the Guises with Spain at Joinville in December 1584. Besides recognizing that a heretic could not be king of France, and that both parties would work together to abolish Protestantism in France and the Netherlands, the terms of the treaty not only strengthened the hands of the Guises, they also brought the wealthiest and most powerful state in Europe into the French civil wars. In return for a monthly subsidy of 50,000 escudos paid by Philip to the League to wage war against the Huguenots, the Guises promised to help Spain recover the French-occupied city of Cambrai – the one gain of Anjou's in his military venture in the Netherlands – as well as Henry of Navarre's territories in Béarn along the Spanish border. Moreover, the Guises promised to promote and publish the decrees of the Council of Trent, which the crown and the French church had long resisted as a threat to Gallican liberties. The Treaty of Joinville was an agreement that would ensure Spanish influence on League policies for the next decade.[4]

The League at its revival in 1584 existed on two levels. At the top was the aristocratic league of noble clients of the Guises, largely concentrated in the north and east of the kingdom. In addition to the Guise family holdings in Lorraine just outside France along the northeastern frontier, the duke of Guise's own base was in Champagne where he was royal governor. His brother Charles, duke of Mayenne, was likewise governor in Burgundy and had a large client base there. A distant cousin, the duke of Mercoeur, was governor of Brittany and was equally powerful in that province; while two first cousins, the duke of Aumale and the duke of Elbeuf, had very strong client bases in Picardy and Normandy respectively. Along with a number of other nobles who allied themselves with the Guises, the aristocratic cohort of the League provided their cause with

---

[3] I have taken this term from the title of Denis Crouzet, *Les guerriers de Dieu: La violence au temps des troubles de religion vers 1525–vers 1610*, 2 vols. (Seyssel, 1990).

[4] For the treaty see DeLamar Jensen, *Diplomacy and Dogmatism: Bernardino de Mendoza and the French Catholic League* (Cambridge, MA, 1964), pp. 51–5.

a significant military arm. Aided and sustained with Spanish money, the League was thus in a position to dictate policy both to the king as well as to the Huguenots.

The more visible as well as the larger cohort of the League was composed of urban notables and magistrates who would eventually organize League cells in city halls throughout the kingdom. This urban base of the League began in the capital of Paris, which was always the foundation of popular support for the movement, where Leaguer cells emerged independent of Guise control. By early 1585 groups of lay Catholics began to organize in private homes and various chapels across the capital. Founded by a group of lawyers, royal officers, and curates, the Paris cell was known as the Sixteen because it established a revolutionary committee of public safety in each of the sixteen *quartiers* of the city. The Sixteen managed to channel the overwhelming Catholic sentiments of the populace into a political machine that was not only independent of the Guises, but soon came to be independent of the Paris municipal authorities and even the crown itself. In its early years prior to the spring of 1588, the Sixteen consisted largely of fairly well-to-do members of the established middle classes. Of the 41 members whose occupations are known, 5 were from the clergy, 6 were magistrates from the sovereign courts, 5 were wealthy merchants of status, 5 were middle-echelon officers of justice or finance, 10 were lawyers or procurers from the Parlement of Paris, 11 were minor functionaries of the Parlement, and only 2 were artisans or shopkeepers – in short, a cohort representing the social attitudes of the establishment.[5] They were not, at least at this early stage, the 'men of low condition' or 'petty tradesmen' that their opponents claimed they were. What gave this revolutionary movement credibility, however, was the widespread popular support the Sixteen enjoyed throughout the Parisian petty-bourgeoisie and lower classes. This popular support was built on the Sixteen's opposition to Protestantism and its announced intention of keeping the monarchy Catholic.

Indeed, religion was the principal astringent that bound the masses of the capital, the establishment middle-class leaders of the Sixteen, and the aristocratic clients of the Guises together into a Holy Union. They shared the common goal of reuniting France under the traditional rubric of 'one king, one faith, one law', that is, the restoration of all French Protestants

---

[5] J. H. M. Salmon, 'The Paris Sixteen, 1584–1594: The Social Analysis of a Revolutionary Movement', in idem, *Renaissance and Revolt: Essays in the Intellectual and Social History of Early Modern France* (Cambridge, 1987), pp. 243–4. For a complete analysis of the 225 individuals who made up the Sixteen, see the very useful book of Robert Descimon, *Qui étaient les Seize? Mythes et réalités de la Ligue parisienne (1585–1594)* (Paris, 1983).

to the Gallican Catholic church of their forebears. This was evident in the manifesto issued by the League at Reims in March 1585. Not only did the Leaguers reject Henry of Navarre as heir, they recognized instead his ageing uncle, the Catholic Charles, cardinal of Bourbon. And although much of the manifesto concerned political issues such as the call for a general reduction in taxation, it was above all a harsh criticism of Henry III and Catherine de Medici for having tolerated and legally recognized Protestantism in the various edicts of pacification. And that the League planned to use their aristocratic arms and Spanish money to assure their goals was made very clear in the oath all members were required to swear: 'We have all solemnly sworn and promised to use force and take up arms to the end that the holy church of God may be restored to its dignity and [reunited in] the true and holy Catholic religion.'[6]

Just as he had attempted to do in late 1576 when Catholic associations began forming as a rival to his authority, Henry III made an initial effort to superimpose his own authority on the League. The resulting Treaty of Nemours in July 1585 has been traditionally depicted as a capitulation and submission to the League. Given the king's financial position, however, just as precarious as it had been in 1576–77, it is difficult to know what Henry could have done differently. The treaty revoked all the former edicts of pacification, and the practice of the 'so-called reformed religion' was forbidden everywhere in the kingdom. Pastors were to be banished and all Protestants were forced to abjure within six months or be exiled. The legal and military provisions for Huguenot protection were also revoked, as the *chambres mi-parties* were abolished, all Protestants were made ineligible for any royal office, and all garrisoned towns had to be evacuated. Finally, Henry, duke of Guise was rewarded with the governorships of Verdun, Toul, Saint-Dizier, and Châlons-sur-Marne. Thus, the Huguenots lost in one blow everything they had gained since the Edict of January 1562. It was now illegal even to be a Protestant, no matter how loyal to the crown.[7] Two months later in September 1585 Catholic passions were further aroused, as Pope Sixtus V excommunicated Henry of Navarre and the prince of Condé and barred them from inheriting the French crown.

Henry III's capitulation to the League ought not to be taken at face value, however. Although perhaps the favourite of Catherine de Medici's four sons, and easily the most talented and intellectual of the group,

---

[6] Quoted in J. H. M. Salmon, *Society in Crisis: France in the Sixteenth Century* (London and New York, 1975), p. 238.

[7] For the Treaty of Nemours, see N. M. Sutherland, *The Huguenot Struggle for Recognition* (New Haven, 1980), pp. 279–80.

Henry was much more independent of the Queen Mother than either Francis II or Charles IX. And though not a dominating or charismatic personality, the king had a widespread following of nobles, military and legal officials that belies the traditional view of him as a foppish weakling only interested in his minions. Moreover, Henry had a devout streak of dedication to Catholicism that showed itself in his own personal piety as king. He founded new religious orders, such as the aristocratic Order of the Holy Spirit in 1578 (partly to try to win back Huguenot nobles to the traditional faith), and the confraternities of White Penitents (dedicated to the Annunciation) and Blue Penitents or Hieronymites (dedicated to St Jerome), both in 1583. Moreover, he also favoured older orders, such as the Franciscan-influenced Minimes, for whom he built a new house in the Bois de Vincennes just east of Paris, and above all the Capucins, a reformed Franciscan order, with whom the king spent much of his time. During his reign Henry participated in more religious processions than any king in living memory, and perhaps more than any previous king in French history. The king even preached with his fellow *confrères*. Yet this very Catholic piety led Henry to do things many Parisians found unking-like, such as extended fasting, or most shocking of all, participating in religious processions and ceremonies without his distinguishing symbols of sacral power. As Pierre de l'Estoile recorded on several occasions, the king appeared in public just like any other ordinary Catholic. 'On the day of the feast of the Annunciation, which was on Friday the 25th of March of the present year of 1583, there was a solemn procession of the confraternity of the [White] Penitents ... In this procession the king marched without guards or any other distinction from the other confrères, either of dress, rank or order.' To many French men and women, Henry was simply an enigma. As l'Estoile so famously remarked, Henry 'lived more as a Capucin than as a king'. (See the illustration on the cover of this book.)[8]

Although the League manifesto and the Treaty of Nemours proved popular with many Catholics throughout France, they also marked the renewal of the civil wars in late 1585 and early 1586, as various forces led by League noblemen throughout the provinces attempted to execute the Treaty of Nemours by force. As the League managed to purge most of northern and eastern France of Protestantism, many Huguenots either

---

[8] L'Estoile, *Journal*, pp. 326, 446. For the recent revival of Henry's reputation, see Jacqueline Boucher, *La cour de Henri III* (Rennes, 1986) and Robert Sauzet, ed., *Henri III et son temps* (Paris, 1992). On his piety, see Frances A. Yates, 'Religious Processions in Paris, 1583–1584', in her *Astraea: The Imperial Theme in the Sixteenth Century* (London, 1975), pp. 173–207, as well as her *The French Academies of the Sixteenth Century* (London, 1947), pp. 152–76.

abjured or fled like refugees, as the only alternatives for many of them were arrest, confiscation of property, or death. The leadership for this campaign came not from the chastened Henry III, but from Henry, duke of Guise. Armed with the subsidy from Philip II of Spain, the League appeared to be trying to win the Wars of Religion on its own after more than two decades of warfare. The other Henry, king of Navarre, did his best to maintain control of the Huguenot fortifications still occupied by his forces and those of the prince of Condé in the south. Moreover, they made every effort to seek foreign support from both Queen Elizabeth and the German Protestant princes just as they had done in the past. The eighth in the series of civil wars, the 'war of the three Henries', which was initiated by the death of Anjou in 1584 and would last more than a decade, would prove to be the longest, costliest, and most violent of all the Wars of Religion.

In the summer of 1587 negotiations between Condé, Queen Elizabeth, and John Casimir of the Palatinate resulted in another army of German mercenaries crossing the border into eastern France to aid the Huguenots, just as they had done a decade earlier. The duke of Guise immediately put together a Leaguer army to repel the Germans, while a royal force under the command of one of the king's favourites, the duke of Joyeuse, was dispatched to Périgord in the southwest to prevent Henry of Navarre's Protestant troops from joining them. Navarre's army surprisingly routed the royalist troops at Coutras in October, killing Joyeuse in the process. This success was balanced by a heavy defeat inflicted by Guise on the German mercenaries a month later just outside Chartres. The Protestant cause suffered further blows in early 1588 with the deaths of two of Navarre's most important noble allies – Henry, prince of Condé, and Guillaume-Robert de la Marck, duke of Bouillon – leaving Henry of Navarre as the sole Protestant leader. With a resurgent aristocratic League led by the duke of Guise and the increasingly popular Sixteen in Paris putting further pressure on the king to disavow Navarre as his heir, the likelihood of a Catholic victory seemed imminent.

French Catholics were by no means united, however, as League preachers in the capital as well as numerous published pamphlets excoriated those French Catholics who continued to support Henry III or who recognized Navarre as the legitimate heir to the throne. Etienne Pasquier, an officer in the Parlement of Paris and target of some of these barbs, noted that those who criticized the League or showed more support for the king than for Guise were called 'sometimes politiques, sometimes Machiavellians, that is to say, completely without religion'. The term 'politique' thus came to be used by Leaguers as a term of derision for anyone who opposed their agenda. As Pasquier further explained, these so-called 'politiques' were hardly without religion; indeed, most, like Pasquier, wanted to reunite France under the Catholic faith. The charge was a difficult one to counter, however, as the Sixteen's popularity continued to grow in the capital. 'Catholics are today divided into two groups: the ones called Leaguers, who are tightly embraced by the preachers, and the ones called politiques, whom they detest.' The Leaguers maintained that 'it is necessary to exterminate the heretics by blood and by fire', while the 'politiques' claimed that 'all that would accomplish is the ruin of the state and by consequence, our religion as well, which is a part of it'.[9] Many Leaguers were also angered that many pockets of Protestantism still persisted, especially in the south, and that Henry III was not doing enough to reduce them. This animosity between royalist Catholics and supporters of the League was further exacerbated in April 1588 when Henry III ordered the duke of Guise to stay away from Paris, where the king's popularity ebbed as Guise's rose. When the Sixteen derided the king and requested that their hero come to the capital anyway, a showdown of some kind appeared inevitable.

The events in Paris on 12 May 1588, called by contemporaries the Day of the Barricades, marked the nadir of royal authority in Henry III's reign. Without the participation or knowledge of Guise, the Sixteen had been planning a revolution in Paris for some time. While it appears that Mayenne may have at least known about these plans, Guise himself was disturbed at the independent and revolutionary turn the Sixteen was taking. Nevertheless, he was reluctant to pass up the opportunity to be praised as a conquering hero and to embarrass the king further at the same time. When the Spanish ambassador Mendoza urged Guise to occupy both the king and Navarre so that Philip II's armada might sail into the English Channel unmolested, Guise wasted no time in making his move. The popular uprising in the capital on 12 May was precipitated less by Guise's arrival, however, than by the sight of 4,000 Swiss guards who had been hired by the king to occupy several strategic locations throughout the city. Henry III, in an effort to defend his royal power, had hoped to use these troops as a show of force and as a sign of his authority in the face of resistance from Guise and the Sixteen. His plan backfired badly, as the Parisian Pierre de l'Estoile noted in his diary that day. 'The king's design completely failed to accomplish what was intended, as the people, seeing all his troops dispersed throughout the city, began to grow excited and to fear something worse, and to murmur that no one had ever seen or heard of a foreign garrison being deployed in

---

[9] Etienne Pasquier, *Lettres historiques pour les années 1556–1594*, ed. Dorothy Thickett (Geneva, 1966), p. 282.

Paris.' The uprising that followed was supported by the populace in the capital, as Parisians from every social level rushed to support the League in what they feared might be another royal massacre. 'At this, everyone took up arms to safeguard the streets and neighbourhoods and made barricades by stretching chains across the streetcorners. The artisan put down his tools, the merchant left his deals, the university its books, the solicitors their briefs, the barristers their bonnets, and the presidents and the judges [in the Parlement] themselves took up halberds.'[10] This was the moment the Sixteen had been waiting for, as they and Guise made the most of the opportunity. With 4,000 Swiss guards awaiting an order to arrest Guise and the leaders of the Sixteen, or at least to break up the barricades and disperse the angry mobs, Henry III procrastinated and lost the initiative. Locked up in the Louvre, he could not bring himself to exert his authority in the face of a capital that was now clearly behind the cause of the League. With shouts of 'Long live the duke of Guise!' ringing outside the royal palace to make his humiliation complete, the king decided to abandon Paris. He and a few nobles and officers of his household sneaked out to the royal stables in the Tuileries, quickly mounted horses, and hastily beat a retreat along the road heading west toward St Cloud and eventually southward to Chartres. As l'Estoile noted in his diary, the Day of the Barricades marked the beginning of a new 'time of troubles'.

The revolution in Paris was made complete as Guise and the Sixteen supervised the takeover of nearly every major institution in the city. The mayor and aldermen on the city council were summarily dismissed and replaced by members loyal to the League in the Hôtel de Ville. Thirteen of the sixteen colonels of the city militia were also replaced by officers loyal to the League. The Arsenal and the Bastille were seized, and the former mayor and a number of others thought to be sympathetic to the king were locked up. The officers of the Parlement of Paris and other sovereign courts (like Etienne Pasquier) had been the most vocal critics of the Sixteen for several years, and plans were put in motion to occupy the Palais de Justice where the Parlement met, as well as the two sovereign courts of the Châtelet, the Chambre des Comptes and the Cour des Aides. A number of the judicial and fiscal officers were put in the Bastille, while the rest of the king's supporters followed Henry III's example and fled Paris. All the gates of the city were eventually secured, as the Sixteen made it clear that no one was to leave or enter without express command of the new revolutionary government. The Sixteen also

---

[10] L'Estoile, *Journal*, p. 552.

appointed a committee of public safety in each of the sixteen *quartiers* of the city, giving the Parisian League a way to supervise the populace. A bloodless *coup d'état* had occurred in the capital and a radical government had replaced the royal court. It was still not clear, however, exactly how much control either the duke of Guise or the Sixteen had in the king's absence.

Henry III was no longer master of his capital or the institutions of government within it. His humiliation was underscored by the Edict of Union in July 1588, in which Henry was forced to recognize virtually all the demands of Guise and the Sixteen. He reaffirmed the Treaty of Nemours and his coronation oath to fight heresy, 'without ever making any peace or treaty with the heretics nor any edict in their favour'. He recognized the cardinal of Bourbon as his rightful heir and urged all French Catholics not to recognize the heretic Navarre as his successor. Moreover, he was forced to recognize the legitimacy of the revolutionary government in Paris, as well as the authority of the duke of Guise in all military matters, which was completed by naming Guise lieutenant-general of the realm (the commander-in-chief of the royal army). Finally, the king was required to convoke a meeting of the Estates-General for the autumn, to plan an all-out war against the Huguenots.[11]

When the Estates-General eventually assembled in Blois in October 1588, it was evident that the League had thoroughly dominated the election of the deputies. The cardinal of Bourbon – the League's would-be heir to the throne – and the cardinal of Guise, brother of the duke, were elected as presidents of the clergy. The Guises themselves dominated the noble deputies. And the Sixteen dominated the third estate, with the new Leaguer mayor of Paris, a man named La Chapelle-Marteau, being elected as its president. If the king had any thoughts that the Estates-General might be able to curb the activities of the Guises or the League, he quickly abandoned them. The first and third estates tended to dominate the early sessions. The clergy's main ambition was to renew the war on heresy and to defeat the Huguenots as quickly as possible, while the deputies of the third estate wanted some revolutionary reforms implemented: an overhaul of the judicial system, reduction in taxes, abolition of venality of office, some real constraints placed on the king's fiscal powers, regular meetings of the Estates-General, and a total reform of morals and manners in the church, the state, and throughout society. Just as in the previous meeting at Blois in 1576, however, all discussions hinged on new taxes that were needed to renew the war

[11] Sutherland, *Huguenot Struggle for Recognition*, pp. 365–6.

against the Protestants. And just as in that last meeting of the Estates, the deputies of the third estate balked at raising new taxes (from which most of the clergy and nobility claimed exemption).

With his authority diminished at Blois amidst the quarrelling of the Leaguer deputies, Henry III gambled on a decisive strike to win back the initiative and authority he had surrendered to the League in Paris the previous May. On the morning of 23 December the duke and cardinal of Guise were summoned to the king's chamber in the château at Blois. There the duke was ambushed and murdered by the king's guards. In the next room, where he overheard the struggle and his brother's cries for help, the cardinal of Guise was also arrested. The next morning, 24 December, he suffered the same fate as his brother in his cell. Henry III also arrested and detained the duke of Guise's mother and son, a number of other nobles and prelates sympathetic to the League, as well as the leading members of the third estate, including La Chapelle-Marteau and other members of the Paris Sixteen. Later that day the bodies of the two Guise brothers were hacked into pieces and burned to ashes. Not wishing to leave any relics or symbols for martyrdom, the king then ordered that the ashes be dispersed to the wind, after which he calmly went to Christmas mass.[12]

Henry III's desperate gamble to regain his authority from the League backfired miserably. Although he managed to settle the score with Guise for his humiliation on the Day of the Barricades, his efforts to diminish the influence of the League, and especially the Sixteen, only added fuel to the flame. As Pierre de l'Estoile recorded, there were cries in the streets of Paris of 'Murder! Fire! Blood!' and 'Vengeance!' as soon as the news of the killings reached the capital, and for more than a week angry mobs of demonstrators, urged on by numerous preachers, begged God to seek vengeance on the tyrant Henry III. Guise's youngest brother, Charles, duke of Mayenne, took command of the aristocratic League, most of whom were still at Blois. In Paris the Sixteen replaced La Chapelle-Marteau and the other members who were imprisoned at Blois, and they appointed the duke of Aumale as governor of the city. The doctors of the Sorbonne, not waiting for a formal bull of excommunication from the Pope, declared the king deposed and urged all true Frenchmen to rise up in arms against him. The revolution of the League that had been consummated on the Day of the Barricades was now much more radical, as royal authority was openly flouted. Amidst all the chaos in the capital, Catherine de Medici died quietly at Blois on 5 January 1589. The Queen

---

[12] Details of the murders are in L'Estoile, *Journal*, pp. 581–2.

Mother had worked zealously to maintain the peace and to safeguard the crown worn by her husband and three successive sons. According to l'Estoile, she was already ill at the time of the murders of the Guises and the desperate action of her last surviving son snuffed out whatever will she had to go on living. This seventy-one year old woman, despite the many errors of judgment she had made in the previous forty years, recognized all too clearly the impact of her son's grisly deed. When told of the news of the two murders, she scolded Henry: 'What do you think you have done? You have killed two men who have left a lot of friends.'[13]

The truly revolutionary turn taken by the League in response to the murders at Blois is most visible in the pamphlets and propaganda cranked out by Parisian presses. Up until the murders of the Guises Leaguer political polemic had largely followed one of two arguments: (1) that the Law of Catholicity took priority over the Salic Law (to justify the cardinal of Bourbon as heir presumptive), or (2) that it was legitimate to oppose the authority of a king who defied God and his coronation oath. As early as 1586 Leaguer polemicists such as Louis Dorléans, an *avocat* in the Parlement of Paris, had written a great deal on the origins of the Salic Law under the pagan king of the Salian Franks, which clearly could not supersede the Law of Catholicity of the crown which came from God. Dorléans also made much of the king's *sacre*, his anointment with the oil from the Holy Ampulla, and his oath to protect and defend the Catholic religion from heretics. Finally, in a reference to the Protestant resistance theory that emerged after the St Bartholomew's massacres, Dorléans borrowed a page from the monarchomach authors: 'In their *Franco-Gallia*, which is one of the most detestable books ever to see the day and which was composed to place France on fire, they [the Huguenots] cry that it is lawful to choose a king to their desire; tell the heretics then that the king of Navarre is not to our desire.'[14]

After December 1588, however, Leaguer resistance theory went far beyond any arguments made by the Protestant monarchomachs. One of the most widely read of these works was *The Just Deposition of Henry III*, written in Latin in the spring of 1589 by the curate and theologian of the Sorbonne, Jean Boucher. Boucher was one of the founding members of the Sixteen in Paris, and besides his official duties as curate of St Benoît and faculty member of the Sorbonne, he was best known as one of the most forceful and demonstrative preachers in any Paris pulpit. *The Just Deposition* raised three essential questions: Is it just and lawful for the church to depose Henry III? Is it just and lawful for the people to depose

[13] L'Estoile, *Journal*, p. 604.   [14] Quoted in Baumgartner, *Radical Reactionaries*, p. 72.

Henry III? And is it just and lawful for the people to take up arms and even kill this tyrant before a formal act of deposition is received from the Pope? As any reader might conclude from the work's title, Boucher resolutely answered all three questions in the affirmative. Like Hotman's *Francogallia* and *The Defense of Liberty against Tyrants*, Boucher's arguments made numerous references to the Bible and classical and medieval authors. There was much discussion of what constituted a tyrant, the role of the Estates-General, the contract between the king and the people who elected him, and the right of the people to resist such a tyrant. Unlike the Huguenot resistance literature of the 1570s, however, which limited the right to resist evil kings to other princes, lesser magistrates, or other divinely ordained officials, Boucher justified tyrannicide, even regicide, on behalf of individuals. Because he equated the people with the *respublica*, or Godly-ordained commonwealth, Boucher also eliminated the monarch from the contract between God and the people. Thus, in his view the people were above the monarch. And by natural extension, any individual member of the *respublica* was not only justified, but required to take up arms to remove a tyrant who had ignored and violated God's laws. Boucher left no stone unturned in his effort to tabulate all the crimes against God committed by Henry III, starting with the violation of his coronation oath by permitting heresy within the kingdom and recognizing a heretic as his heir, and culminating in his murder of the Guises. He noted that ultimately the Pope would also be forced to depose Henry with a formal bull of excommunication, but the Sorbonne having already declared the king to be deposed made it perfectly legitimate for the people to act on their own prior to the inevitable papal bull. Moreover, he argued that the League could not wait any longer for the Pope to act formally, and any private person could act on behalf of the *respublica* and kill this tyrant of France.[15]

Henry III could no longer pretend to be loyal to the terms of the Edict of Union. Murdering the duke of Guise had brought the wrath of the League upon him in the form of an army raised by Mayenne in the early spring of 1589. Assassinating a cardinal of the church also brought the wrath of the entire Gallican church and Rome upon him, with the inevitable papal retribution to follow. He thus came to conclude that his only option for survival was to make peace with Henry of Navarre. Apart from religion, the king certainly had far more in common with the Protestant leader than with the Catholic nobles of the League who threatened them both. So it came as no surprise when the two kings

---

[15] Ibid., pp. 123–44.

signed a truce and formal pact on 3 April 1589 to make war against their common enemy. It was couched in very Catholic language to protect Henry III from charges of caving in to the Huguenots, and it was also accompanied by the king's announcement that he hoped Navarre would soon convert to Catholicism. Nevertheless, the terms of the agreement were wholly favourable to the Protestant cause. Given that the Treaty of Nemours (July 1585) and the Edict of Union (July 1588) had totally rescinded all the Huguenot gains in the previous edicts of pacification, the pact between the two Henries restored a great deal. The truce was to last for one year, during which time the Protestants were allowed to keep whatever towns were currently in their control. Furthermore, Navarre was granted one additional town in each bailiwick in the kingdom, plus the fortified town of Saumur. Above all, a general ceasefire was announced between the crown and the Huguenots, who were not to be persecuted during the truce, so that royal and Huguenot forces might join together to defeat the League.[16] The two kings joined forces immediately and initiated a military campaign whose target was the repossession of the capital. Defended by Mayenne and Aumale, Paris was nevertheless threatened in the summer of 1589 as the royalist army was reinforced with several thousand new Swiss and German mercenaries. Just when it appeared that the shoe was on the other foot and the king might reverse the Day of the Barricades, on 1 August a Jacobin monk named Jacques Clément assassinated Henry III in the royal camp at St Cloud just west of the capital. Caught up in the excitement and religious enthusiasm of the Leaguer rhetoric in the capital, this young zealot ended the life of the last of the Valois. Jean Boucher's tract, still on the presses and not yet published, now became an *ex post facto* justification of this deed.

The revolutionary impact of Clément's deed was instantly recognizable to contemporaries everywhere. Demonstrations of rejoicing and exultations of divine will were common in Paris and in most towns held by the League. Protestant reaction was more mixed; though overjoyed that their leader should succeed the late king, they recognized that the crown was all that stood between them and the fury of the League. Their future was by no means certain. Navarre himself was equally torn by his loyalties: to his Protestant allies who had stood by him so long, and now as King of France to the Catholic nation and the Gallican church. The new king would clearly have to recognize, defend, and protect the Catholic religion, as he immediately promised to do, but how could he square his personal religion and his confessional loyalties with his coronation oath,

[16] Sutherland, *Huguenot Struggle for Recognition*, pp. 293–6 and 366–7.

which required him to persecute all heresy? There was no easy answer. And finally, what about the loyalties of the many Catholic subjects of the new king? For those under the sway of the League, the answer was easy: Navarre was a heretic deposed by the Pope and could never be recognized as king of France. He and all Huguenots would continue to be persecuted. For most of those Catholics outside the jurisdiction of the League, however, and even for many moderate Catholics within the League, the answer was less clear-cut. According to the Salic Law, Navarre ought to be recognized as Henry IV; yet according to the Catholicity of the crown, a Protestant was ineligible. Both were perceived by many Catholics as equally binding fundamental laws of the realm, so how could one possibly choose between them? Again, there were no easy answers, unless Navarre abjured his Protestant faith and converted to Catholicism. While always a possibility and much discussed even by Navarre himself, such a conversion seemed unlikely, at least in the short run. Many Catholic nobles, such as the dukes of Epernon and Nevers, abandoned Navarre and the royal army after Henry III's assassination, to retire to neutrality or even to support the moderate wing of the League. The political theorist Jean Bodin, the advocate of strong monarchy, was another who turned to the moderate faction of the League. Several others, such as the baron of Biron and the duke of Montpensier, recognized Navarre as the legitimate royal successor and stayed with him to continue the fight against the League. But whether to recognize Navarre as Henry IV, or to continue to oppose him as a heretic usurper, was the choice that faced most French Catholics in the wake of the assassination of the last Valois. How did they make these choices? Etienne Pasquier, an officer in the Parlement of Paris, who after much deliberation opted to recognize Navarre as king, perhaps offers a clue for those the Leaguers called 'politiques': 'Thus I deliberated to live and die under the one who will govern us in future, without entering into any examination of his conscience. Since he is the one God has given us, we must accept him. God knows better than we ourselves what is necessary.'[17]

The revolutionary nature of the events that unfolded between May 1588 and August 1589 was clearly reflected in the towns under the control of the League. On the Day of the Barricades in May 1588, although they enjoyed widespread support in many places, the League controlled only a handful of towns outside Paris: Sens, Troyes, and Auxerre among them. A few more joined the movement after May 1588, but it was the murder of the Guises at Blois in December that

[17] Pasquier, *Lettres historiques*, p. 448.

Map 7 Principal cities of the Catholic League

transformed the urban cells of the League into a dynamic force. In early
1589 Leaguer cells seized control in many of the major cities of France
(Map 7). Cities that had refused to embrace the League before quickly
turned against Navarre to support the Leaguer cause: Agen, Amiens,
Bourges, Dijon, Le Mans, Nantes, Poitiers, Rouen, and Toulouse to

name only the most important. Only Lyon of the major cities held out, and it would fall to the League very soon. Many of the urban moderates were purged by the more radical and militant factions of the League, while others began to abandon it as it became clearer after December 1588 that the Guise aristocratic clienteles had no control over the numerous urban cells throughout the kingdom. Most of these urban cells of the League were controlled by local notables who were either merchants, lawyers, or officers from the middle and lower echelons of the venal system. Their goals and ambitions were more shaped by local issues than national policy. In any case, many of them viewed the aristocratic leadership of Mayenne and Aumale as a threat to their own interests, as social tension threatened to obscure the League's common ambition of keeping the monarchy Catholic. In Paris the Sixteen had replaced the municipal and royal governments altogether in early 1589 with a General Council of the Union, forty members appointed by the Sixteen, most of whom (apart from seven officers from the Leaguer army) were not nobles but members of the middle classes. A system of provincial councils was established throughout the kingdom to coordinate further the interests of the urban notables, all of which was independent of the aristocratic leadership of Mayenne. And there were even some towns, such as Marseille and Arles, where Leaguer dictatorships were established which were totally outside the control of the Guises, the Sixteen, and the provincial councils. This revolutionary situation of 1588–89 had produced a structure of government in the League towns that ignored the Old Regime notions of privilege and distinction, as radical members of the middle classes set up a participatory system that by-passed the traditional elites.[18] And what was particularly disturbing to most Catholic members of the establishment, including many Leaguers, was that this radical urban federation initiated a reign of terror in 1589 that threatened to shake the entire social order even more severely than the Protestants. A brief look at four League towns – Paris, Rouen, Toulouse, and Dijon – will delineate how violence and the threat of it became the staple of a Leaguer reign of terror. In all of them, the crucial dynamic was the internal tensions within the Leaguer leadership between the militants, who favoured the pro-Spanish policies of the Sixteen as well as their inclination to use violence, and the moderates, largely conservative officeholders who wanted to re-establish a strong Catholic monarchy. Both factions realized, however, that gaining the support of their respective urban populations was crucial to staying in power.

[18] Salmon, *Society in Crisis*, p. 252; and Elie Barnavi, 'Centralisation ou féderalisme? Les relations entre Paris et les villes à l'époque de la Ligue (1585–1594)', *Revue historique*, vol. 526 (1978), 335–44.

In Paris this violence was highly visible, as the Sixteen purged the Parlement and the other sovereign courts in early 1589. A small group of parlementaires was clearly committed to the Sixteen's radical agenda, but most of these conservative figures of the establishment were not. Some fled Paris and were later established as a royalist Parlement of Paris at Tours in March by Henry III. Of those who stayed behind in the capital, only a small core was truly sympathetic to the goals of the Sixteen. Most were simply unable to support Henry III, or after August 1589, Henry of Navarre as king; they either kept quiet in Paris or did what they could to try to steer the Sixteen away from some of its more radical ideas. Nevertheless, they were always suspect in the eyes of the militants. This was evident on 16 January 1589 when Bussy-Leclerc, a leading member of the Sixteen, entered the Grand Chambre and arrested the First President of the Parlement, Achille de Harlay, and twenty-two other judges. All the other members of the court, even those most sympathetic to the League, were dumbfounded, and they followed their colleagues in procession to the Bastille. Although most of the twenty-two were eventually released, the moderate Harlay was relieved by the Sixteen of the first presidency and replaced by the more activist Barnabé Brisson. 'Never in any age or memory or history', noted one anonymous Leaguer, 'has the said court of Parlement, since it was first created in the city of Paris, received such a bad blow as it got on the said Monday, the sixteenth of January 1589'. More radical members of the Sixteen were also appointed to fill a number of other judicial offices. Edouard Molé was named the new solicitor-general, while Jean Le Maistre and Louis Dorléans, the latter the author of earlier League propaganda, became *avocats du Roi*. Le Maistre is also interesting because his father, a president of the court, had fled Paris and later joined the royalist court at Tours. The other sovereign courts in the Châtelet, the city militia, the Bastille, and the city government of Paris were also purged as the Sixteen seized firm control of the capital.[19] The extremists in the Sixteen also waged a war on the populace of Paris throughout 1589. Anyone suspected of 'politique' or royalist sympathies was likely to be a target of beating and confiscation of property. Even members of the rump Parlement were not immune from such treatment. In November Oudin Cruce, a radical who was a solicitor in the Châtelet, began a new wave of terrorism and nearly fifty suspected 'politiques' were publicly hanged in the market places throughout the capital.

[19] Elie Barnavi, *Le parti de Dieu: Etude sociale et politique des chefs de la Ligue parisienne, 1585–1594* (Brussels and Leuven, 1980), pp. 129–36 (quote on p. 130).

One reason for the increased violence in Paris was that the aristocratic League was faring poorly against the royalist troops of Henry IV. The new king recognized that the heart of the League's resistance was in Paris and that he could never hope to capture the loyalty of most French Catholics as long as he was opposed by the capital. In September 1589 his forces defeated the Leaguer army led by Mayenne at Arques, near the Normandy coast, while the following spring Henry inflicted an even greater defeat on Mayenne and the League at Ivry in March 1590. This confrontation was much closer to Paris, and Henry used the victory as a springboard for laying siege to the capital itself. Moreover, the League suffered another blow in May when the ageing cardinal of Bourbon died. Held in captivity by his nephew Henry IV, the cardinal had been the League's surrogate king, whom they recognized as Charles X in place of the Protestant Navarre. Now they were left without a suitable candidate for the throne, which only increased the tensions within the League. With the news of the cardinal's death and military defeat on the battlefield outside the capital to spur them on, the Sixteen stepped up their campaign of terror within.

The siege of Paris in the late spring and summer of 1590, however, was an unexpected shock for all Parisians including the radicals of the Sixteen. Bolstered by his recent victories as well as the addition of 5,000 fresh troops from England, Henry IV managed to secure all the surrounding towns around the city by late April with the intention of cutting off all supplies and foodstuffs from the capital. For the next four months the inhabitants of Paris faced their most extended period of hardship and suffering of the civil wars. Most of the food in the city was consumed by the beginning of July and starvation set in among the very young, the ill, and the elderly. Although there are no accurate accounts of how many actually died from starvation, Pierre de l'Estoile, who lived through the siege, estimated that it was in the hundreds, as many turned to catching dogs and rats to stay alive. Rumours of cannibalism even surfaced. Even the wealthiest and most influential in the capital felt the sting of the siege, with the result that the militant preachers and the radicals of the Sixteen became even more alienated from Mayenne and the more moderate wing of the League.[20]

With Mayenne unable to relieve the siege, the Sixteen turned to the king of Spain for a lifeline. Bernardino de Mendoza, the Spanish ambassador in the capital, had long since pushed for such a strategy, and by mid-summer

---

[20] For two good contemporary accounts of the siege of Paris, see the anonymously written 'Bref traité des misères de la ville de Paris [1590]', in M. L. Cimber and F. Danjou, eds., *Archives curieuses de l'histoire de France depuis Louis XI jusqu'à Louis XVIII*, 1st series (Paris, 1834–50), vol. 13, pp. 271–85; and Pierre de l'Estoile, *The Paris of Henry of Navarre*, ed. and trans. Nancy Lyman Roelker (Cambridge, MA, 1958).

he finally managed to persuade his master that this was in Spain's best interest. Ever since the defeat of the Armada in 1588, the only possible way Philip II could relieve the siege of Paris was by diverting his army in the Netherlands under the command of Alexander Farnese, duke of Parma. Parma argued strenuously against such a strategy, rightly predicting that the Dutch rebels would be able to mount a successful offensive in the absence of Spanish forces. But Philip reasoned that if Paris fell to a heretic king, the rest of France could quickly follow, which would totally destroy Spanish foreign policy. Thus, in late August Parma's army crossed the frontier into France and headed south toward Paris. In a masterpiece of military strategy, Parma lured the French king's troops out of Paris feigning battle, and then slipped behind them into a starving capital. Henry was forced to withdraw his army into Normandy as the four-month siege was lifted. The Sixteen and other radical Leaguers were now indebted to the Spanish king and even further alienated from Mayenne and the moderates. With a Spanish garrison left behind to protect the inhabitants, contemporaries recorded that shouts of 'Long live Philip II!' were echoing in the French capital.[21]

The aftermath of the siege of Paris was that the radicals continued their purge of suspected 'politiques' and moderates throughout the rest of 1590 and 1591. Although the purges resulted in still more beatings and executions, the last bastions of moderation and support for Mayenne were still in the Parlement and the Hôtel de Ville. When the Sixteen proved unable to dominate the latter completely – the aldermen were elected annually each summer and were thus not entirely under the radicals' control – they turned their attention to the Parlement, with the high magistry becoming their principal target. In November 1591 the Sixteen met secretly to plan a further purge of the Parlement of Paris. The first president, Barnabé Brisson, whom the Sixteen thought not to be militant enough, and two other magistrates were summarily executed in the apogee of the Sixteen's reign of terror in the capital. While many had been put to death at the hands of the radicals ever since the Day of the Barricades, the entire membership of the Parlement and the Hôtel de Ville were terrified at the execution of Brisson, whom the Sixteen had appointed to the first presidency less than three years before. Mayenne could wait no longer and entered Paris on 18 November despite the presence of Spanish troops. Four of the radicals were hanged and six others arrested, while Bussy-Leclerc, Crucé, and a number of others were expelled from the city. The radicals' reign of terror had come to a violent end.

[21] Jensen, *Diplomacy and Dogmatism*, pp. 208–9.

An examination of the forty-six most radical members of the Sixteen who had planned the attack on the Parlement reveals that a decisive social shift had taken place in the Paris League since the Day of the Barricades. In November 1591 the radicals were composed of 7 clergymen, 2 magistrates, 3 wealthy merchants, 3 mid-level judicial and financial officers, 18 barristers and solicitors, 8 minor functionaries, 4 shopkeepers, and one of undetermined status. While upper-class members made up 34 per cent of the Sixteen before the barricades, they contributed only 17 per cent in November 1591. In contrast, the barristers and solicitors, who had made up 21 per cent of the revolutionary elite before 1588, contributed 39 per cent of the group that planned the attack on the Parlement in 1591. The social make-up of the revolutionary group known as the Sixteen had led to an anti-aristocratic and more popular movement in Paris, which in turn alienated them from the duke of Mayenne and League moderates. This led the Sixteen in turn to a closer reliance on Spain. While some radicals may have actually favoured overturning the monarchy and establishing a Catholic republic, as Mayenne feared, many more were willing to look to Philip II to provide a Catholic candidate to place on the French throne. Although Mayenne had successfully checked the radicals' excesses, the balance of power in the Paris League was still tilted heavily toward the Sixteen. Perhaps better than any other city, the experience of Paris illustrates the problems the League faced in trying to keep all its constituent parts united behind the common goal of keeping the monarchy Catholic.[22]

The experience of the League in the Norman capital of Rouen was altogether different. No such social antagonisms divided the League as in Paris, and Rouen's experience in the early civil wars was markedly different from that of the capital, as Rouen had actually been seized by the Protestants in a coup in the first civil war. There was no extremist group like the most radical of the Sixteen in Rouen either, as the Rouennais eventually opted to side with the crown after the Day of the Barricades in May 1588 and even welcomed Henry III to the city the following month with cries of 'Long live the king!' This situation changed after the murder of the Guises at Blois in December, however, and all the efforts of the royal lieutenant-general in Rouen, the seigneur of Carrouges, to maintain the peace proved fruitless. With Jesuit preachers fanning the passions of Rouennais Catholics, and shipping along the Seine interrupted by the League-controlled cities of Paris upstream and Le Havre downstream, many of the city's merchants and notables began to wonder if declaring for the League might be in their best interest.

---

[22] This and the previous paragraph are based on Salmon, 'The Paris Sixteen', pp. 252–9.

Matters quickly came to a head in the Norman capital, however, and proved beyond the control of the city fathers. Rouen experienced its own Day of the Barricades on 5 February 1589 when a Leaguer coup seized the city by force. The previous day a member of the Parlement of Rouen, Richard Regnault, seigneur Du Pont, organized barricades to be set up in the streets to forestall the arrival of royal troops that Carrouges had requested from the king. The next day, a Sunday, a large religious procession was scheduled to wind its way through the city to the Franciscan monastery in the centre of town. The Leaguers had infiltrated the procession with members of the city's militia, and at some point along the route they broke ranks and turned the procession into a rebellion. The militia quickly seized the Hôtel de Ville, just a block from the monastery, and took possession of the keys to the city gates and the municipal arsenal. After securing the rest of the city, Du Pont and his followers went to an abbey where Carrouges and thirty of his men had fled. After some intense negotiation Carrouges was eventually persuaded to turn over control of the two royal strongholds outside the city walls overlooking the Seine: the Château and the Vieux Palais. Two days later on 7 February the League met at the Hôtel de Ville to pack the Parlement, militia, and city council with League sympathizers. The take-over of the city was thus complete.

Contrary to the situation in Paris, where mainly solicitors, merchants, and minor functionaries were brought into the revolutionary government of the Sixteen, the new leaders of Rouen were drawn from the highest social ranks. Virtually all of them were already part of Rouen's power elite before the coup: three were parlementaires, two others were members of the court's Chamber of Requests, and three others had already served as aldermen in the past. Two were also secrétaires du Roi, one was a maître des requêtes, and seven possessed seigneuries as well as accompanying noble titles. This was not a group of frustrated middle-class officers without access to the highest echelons of government; and there was no anti-aristocratic feeling in the Rouen League either. What separated them from their royalist counterparts was not social tension, but two other distinctive characteristics: their religious zeal and hard-line commitment to the Catholic faith, as well as their length of service and age. An examination of the Parlement of Rouen reveals this division most clearly.

When Henry III ordered royalist parlementaires in early 1589 to form their own parlements outside those cities where the League had taken over the sovereign courts, royalists in the Parlement of Rouen followed the example of their Paris counterparts and established a royalist Parlement in Caen. The Rouen court split roughly in half, as 27 parlementaires chose to stay in Rouen and side with the League, while

27 members opted to support the king in Caen. As a cohort the Leaguer parlementaires had been in office much longer than the royalist judges; the median length of service for the League members was eighteen years, while that of the royalist members was only four years. Thus, a generational divide seems to have split the Rouen court down the middle. Most of the League magistrates had come of age at the dawn of the religious wars and remembered vividly the Protestant take-over of the city in the first civil war when confessional tensions were at their highest. The younger judges would have been too young to remember much of those years, and the differing experiences may explain why some chose the League in 1589 while others opted to support the king.

What needs to be stressed about the rise of the League in Rouen, however, is that its members were drawn from the highest levels in society and they already held positions of authority with much experience. They were also loyal to Mayenne throughout the next few years, and while the duke could not control the League in Rouen it proved a much more reliable ally for him than the Sixteen in Paris. Although there was some violence in Rouen, there was nothing like the reign of terror in Paris under the Sixteen. Many suspected royalists and 'politiques', and virtually all the English living in Rouen, were frequently imprisoned or exiled. And groups of vigilantes among the populace at large or from the militia did occasionally ransack the homes of any who were thought to be insufficiently committed to the cause of the League. But on the whole, violent and disorderly conduct generally died down after the first couple of years under League control. This was largely because in Rouen the leadership of the League eventually passed from the Parlement and Hôtel de Ville to the military governor, who from early 1590 was a Burgundian noble, Jean de Saulx-Tavannes, son of the famous military captain and lieutenant-general during the early civil wars, Gaspard de Saulx-Tavannes. It was the noble Leaguers who benefitted most, in fact, from the League in Normandy, and the good relations with Mayenne proved beneficial when Henry IV laid siege to Rouen in November 1591 as he had done to the capital eighteen months earlier. This time the royalist army was swelled with an English contingent led by the earl of Essex, making survival for the Rouennais even more difficult. Although the outcome was the same – a second sortie by Parma with his Spanish army from the Netherlands broke the siege five months later in April 1592 – there was never the rancour or anti-aristocratic tension in Rouen that there had been in the capital. Nor was there the accompanying reign of terror. What there was in Rouen between early 1589 and the end of the siege in 1592 was the introduction of new confraternities and religious orders, clerics participating in politics for the first time in the commune's history, and godly magistrates attempting to remake the earthly city into a more holy community through a rigorous dose of Catholic spirituality.[23]

The city of Toulouse in Languedoc offers yet a third example of the League. Like Rouen, Protestantism attracted large numbers there in the 1550s and early 1560s, as nearly every institution in the city including the Parlement became affected. Unlike the Norman capital, however, an attempted Protestant coup in 1561 failed to take over the city government of Toulouse. It was repressed, as was Protestantism generally thereafter; indeed Toulouse acquired a deserved reputation as a bastion of Catholic solidarity throughout the civil wars, as the massacres of Protestants there in 1572 would indicate. It thus came as no surprise when the murders of the Guises at Blois in December 1588 set in motion Catholic passions that resulted in a takeover by the League in Toulouse.

Nevertheless, the early signs were that the League takeover in Toulouse would be entirely peaceful without violence or barricades. The rumors from Blois were not formally corroborated until 6 January 1589, and the following day the grand vicar and provost of the city's main cathedral, Jean Daffis, proposed to the city council that a special governing committee be established to maintain the Catholic unity of the city. Called the *Bureau d'état*, this committee was composed of eighteen members: six each from the Parlement of Toulouse, the clergy, and the bourgeois of the city. The following day, 8 January, the council approved the provost's proposal unanimously. Toulouse had thus created its own committee of public safety, in effect its own cell of the League, peacefully and without any pressure or assistance from either Mayenne or the Sixteen. Moreover, the new *Bureau d'état* did not replace existing city institutions, restock them with its own members, or threaten them in any way. It existed alongside and as an appendage of the municipal magistrates called *capitouls* in Toulouse (the same as *échevin*, or alderman, elsewhere) and the judges in the Parlement. The halcyon beginning of the League in Toulouse concealed several significant fissures, however.

The first of these emerged only a fortnight later in the person of one of the six clerical members of the *Bureau d'état*: Urbain de Saint-Gelais, bishop of Comminges. In the third week of January Saint-Gelais accused the bourgeois members of the Bureau of being 'politiques, changeable creatures of the first president [of the Parlement of Toulouse] who, by open or secret means, directs everything to his own purpose'.[24] The

---

[23] The preceding five paragraphs are all based on Philip Benedict, *Rouen during the Wars of Religion* (Cambridge, 1981), pp. 167–232.

[24] Quoted in Mark Greengrass, 'The *Sainte-Union* in the Provinces: The Case of Toulouse', *Sixteenth Century Journal*, vol. 14 (1983), 467–96 (quote on p. 483). All of my discussion of the League in Toulouse is indebted to this article.

bishop further demanded that the first president of the Parlement, Jean-Etienne Duranti, convoke a free and open meeting of the entire city as well as incarcerate all suspected Huguenots and 'politiques'. When Saint-Gelais presented these demands to a full meeting of the Parlement on 25 January, a mob of angry and armed citizens packed the lobby of the Palais de Justice in support. Fearing that a riot might break out if he opposed the bishop's proposals, Duranti reluctantly gave in to keep the peace. As he was entering his coach after the meeting, however, the first president was jostled by the crowd and approached by a priest armed with a sword. Although one of his own bodyguards intervened and he managed to escape, Duranti's coach was stabbed several times as he fled the scene. A contemporary noted that the crowd wanted to turn him 'into sausage meat'. Thoroughly aroused, the mob erected the requisite barricades in the streets as a general riot seemed inevitable.

Ironically, Saint-Gelais himself diffused the violence the next day by organizing a religious procession through the city. When the procession reached the cathedral, however, the scene turned ugly once again. The crowd demanded the execution of all 'politiques' in the city, particularly those on the Parlement 'who care more for the cause of the Valois than that of Jesus Christ'.[25] His supporters also clamoured for the bishop to declare himself governor of the city, which Saint-Gelais tried to refuse. Ultimately, he consented, but only if the appointment was registered in Parlement, and if it was recognized that it was just a provisional appointment until Mayenne appointed a 'proper prince'. As the Parlement had already given in to his earlier demands, they registered Saint-Gelais's appointment the following day and he immediately took over control of the city guards. Duranti and the advocate-general of the Parlement were unwilling to accept defeat so lightly, however, and one of them wrote to a royalist judge in the Parlement of Bordeaux as well as to the royal lieutenant in Guyenne seeking help to overthrow the influence of Saint-Gelais. Copies of these letters were discovered by the Bureau a few days later, and Duranti and his colleague were both arrested. When the Parlement refused to try their colleagues, on 10 February a mob of more than 4,000 broke into the Jacobin church where the two were held and summarily executed them both, as well as one of Duranti's servants, without a trial.

Although the same tensions as in Paris might appear to be at work in Toulouse, with the League forging a revolutionary government aimed against the high magistrates of the Parlement, this was not exactly the

---

[25] Quoted in ibid., p. 485.

case. The Parlement of Toulouse did not evacuate en masse after the murder of the first president and advocate to form a royalist court outside the city, as between February and August 1589 only two judges departed the Parlement. The proximity of the Huguenot-occupied strongholds outside Toulouse kept the city and the Catholics of the Parlement united to such an extent that the kind of royalist support that barely survived in Paris, and flourished in Rouen, simply evaporated in Toulouse altogether. As a result, the bulk of the judges in the Parlement banded together and stayed in Toulouse to support the independent League.

What finally threatened the regime of Saint-Gelais were the inner tensions that only emerged after the assassination of Henry III. This was most evident in the rivalry between Saint-Gelais and the military leader Mayenne assigned to Languedoc, Guillaume de Joyeuse, who had just lost Carcassonne to a royal army. When Joyeuse entered the city on 30 September 1589 with what remained of his troops, he sought a temporary ceasefire agreement with the Protestants so his army could recover. Joyeuse also demanded that Saint-Gelais disband the Confraternity of the Holy Sacrament he had founded since coming to power, as he felt it was a threat to civil order. The bishop's reaction was predictable, as he retired to the small island of Thunis in the middle of the Garonne with a number of armed men. On 1 October he preached a sermon urging the citizens of Toulouse 'to arm themselves for Jesus Christ', and about 500 or 600 of his supporters stormed the residence where Joyeuse was staying. The expected violence was averted, however, when Joyeuse managed to secure the city with the help of his son. More importantly, he won over the confidence of a significant segment of the Parlement, the *capitouls*, and the *Bureau d'état*, who agreed to negotiate with him and Mayenne. The result was an agreement reached on 27 November which marked the end of the Toulouse League's independence and brought it back into the Leaguer mainstream. The *Bureau d'état* was disbanded, Saint-Gelais left the city, and Joyeuse remained the head of the League in Toulouse thereafter. Although some of the parlementaires later fled to Carcassonne in the early 1590s, where a rival royalist Parlement was established, for the most part Joyeuse maintained the civic support of the city. The independence of the regime under Saint-Gelais was its strength as well as its weakness, since the bishop was unable to tie in his interests with any of the surrounding towns or other League strongholds, especially Bordeaux. While there was never the alienation and social tension against Mayenne that there was in Paris, there was also never the closer bond with the rest of the League towns that both Paris and Rouen enjoyed. As most of the fighting of the Leaguer armies took place in northern France, the League in Toulouse remained isolated and on the periphery of the Holy Union. Its experience shows just how fragile and disunited the union really was.

A final example of the League is the Burgundian capital of Dijon. The Guises had controlled the royal governorship in Burgundy since the 1540s, and Mayenne himself had been governor of the province since 1573, so the military head of the League had a large and loyal clientele that reached down to nearly every Hôtel de Ville in the province as well as all the sovereign courts in Dijon. Even in Burgundy, however, Mayenne's ability to control politics and dictate policy was limited. At the time of the assassination of the Guises at Blois in December 1588, his agent Jacques La Verne was the mayor of Dijon and fully dominant in the Hôtel de Ville in the Burgundian capital. Another of Mayenne's closest clients, Pierre Jeannin, was a president in the Parlement of Dijon, and other clients, such as Etienne Bernard, were councillors in the Parlement as well. Finally, Mayenne hoped to secure complete control of the province by appointing another close client as lieutenant-general in February 1589: Guillaume de Hautemer, sieur de Fervaques. Fervaques was a distinguished military nobleman who had served the duke of Anjou in the Netherlands, who became a client of the Guises after Anjou's death. His appointment replaced the unreliable Léonard Chabot, count of Charny as the lieutenant-general of the province, that is, head of the military in Burgundy during Mayenne's absence. Yet even with these loyal agents in the principal positions of power in Dijon, Mayenne could not completely control events.

When news from Blois reached Dijon on 28 December 1588, for example, the mayor and aldermen in the Hôtel de Ville made their first priority maintaining order in the city. But rather than offering any encouraging words to Mayenne, La Verne made an impassioned plea to the aldermen to swear 'to God on the saints and sacred gospels that they will maintain and continue the faithful service that they pledged to the king'. Each of the aldermen circulated in his own parish, exhorting his constituents to 'the obedience of the king'. Moreover, a small cohort of about a dozen royalist judges and barristers from the Parlement tried to secure the city for the king. Nearly all of them had taken up their offices in the court in the previous two years, and now they hoped to seize the armed fortification known as the Château and the city of Dijon with the aid of armed troops. This secret cohort dissipated quickly when Mayenne arrived in Dijon on 5 January 1589, as a handful of royalist parlementaires fled the city. They would eventually make their way to Flavigny to set up a royalist Parlement in opposition to the one in Dijon. Nevertheless, Mayenne could never be certain of controlling events in his own governorship, much less the rest of the League.[26]

---

[26] Henri Drouot, *Mayenne et la Bourgogne: Etude sur la Ligue (1587–1596)*, 2 vols. (Dijon and Paris, 1937), I, pp. 197–233 (quotes on pp. 219–20).

Mayenne did go on to secure the Château and the city of Dijon, and they would remain among his most loyal bastions of support during the period of the League. His foundation of support, however, was the Hôtel de Ville as in so many other League towns, not the Parlement. There was no violence or barricades of any kind associated with the formation of the League in Dijon, as Mayenne persuaded the city fathers and a loyal nucleus of the sovereign courts that it was in their best interest to trust him. He called for an assembly of all the city council, the sovereign courts, and captains of the parishes on Monday, 16 January 1589, at six o'clock in the morning. After mass was heard at the Sainte-Chapelle in the ducal palace, the assembly crowded into the council chamber at the Hôtel de Ville where Mayenne cited 'numerous passages of Holy Scripture, focusing on the duty and obedience that the said inhabitants owed first to God, then to the king'. The entire group then promised the duke not to admit any troops whatsoever into the town without his express permission, and they recognized the mayor, La Verne, as his chosen deputy within the city during his absence. Although Fervaques commanded the Château, La Verne controlled the city militia inside the city walls. The entire assembly then took an oath 'to guard and conserve the said town of Dijon in the service of God, the apostolic and Roman Catholic faith, and the French crown under the government of the said lord, duke of Mayenne'.[27] Mayenne then set up a Council of State of the Holy Union to supervise the League in Dijon, much like the *Bureau d'état* in Toulouse. It had equal numbers of members from the Hôtel de Ville and the Parlement, but the power of the mayor was still very dominant within the city.[28]

Mayenne's authority was not absolute, however, since the office of mayor in Dijon was elected annually from among all the male heads of households in the city. When the opportunist La Verne proved to be more interested in protecting his own authority than serving the cause of Mayenne and the League, he proved difficult to check. In April 1589 he actually imprisoned Fervaques in a struggle over control of the Château. When the mayoral elections were held the following June, Mayenne used the duke of Nemours's influence to get an experienced solicitor in the Parlement elected mayor, Pierre Michel. The popular La Verne was reelected in 1590 nevertheless with more than 99 per cent of the vote, and again in 1591, despite the fact that Mayenne himself had nominated and supported the candidacy of the parlementaire Etienne Bernard. During this year in office La Verne's dictatorial nature became more visible, as he had executed one of the judicial officers who tried to stand

---

[27] Archives municipales de Dijon, B 226, fols. 146v–47r.
[28] Drouot, *Mayenne et la Bourgogne*, I, pp. 243–4; II, pp. 41–64.

up to him. Thus, in the June 1592 election Etienne Bernard was duly elected, although with only 28 per cent of the vote he barely beat out La Verne. La Verne's ties in the Hôtel de Ville were still evident, however, when the four-times mayor was elected for a fifth term in June 1593. Thus, Mayenne could not completely control the office of mayor he himself had made so powerful in January 1589. Mayenne did finally oust La Verne from office in the June 1594 elections, after which the defeated mayor sold out to the royalists in August. Ultimately, Mayenne was forced to execute La Verne when the latter, forever looking out for his own interests, attempted to turn the Château over to the army of Navarre.[29]

The experience of Paris, Rouen, Toulouse, and Dijon makes it clear that in each town loyal to the League, local factors and local tensions played as large a role in internal politics as any overall guiding policy from either Mayenne, the League's general council, or the Sixteen. There was a general tension between the aristocratic leadership of the League and the various urban oligarchies that made up the rank and file of League membership. This was partly due to the general social tension in such a hierarchical society that showed up most clearly in Paris. But all the examples show that the League in any town could be riven with internal rivalries that left Mayenne helpless to intervene. What held all the various factions and cohorts of the League together was not any shared sense of a common experience or a united loyalty to Mayenne, but a fervent desire to extirpate Protestantism and to safeguard the Gallican monarchy from a heretic. It was their Catholic sensibilities that held the League together; in this sense it was a Holy Union.

Mayenne could delay no further the necessity of selecting a League candidate to place on the throne if Navarre, or Henry IV to royalist Catholics and Huguenots, could be defeated. He had agreed to the many calls for a meeting of an Estates-General of the League, and in the autumn of 1592 he authorized the election of deputies to take place in all the Leaguer towns, with the clergy and nobility selecting their own deputies. The meeting of the Estates opened in Paris in January 1593 with only 128 deputies (well down on the roughly 400 deputies who attended the meetings in Blois in 1576 and 1588), as royal armies prevented many from the outlying provinces from reaching the capital. Moreover, many others were deterred from attending because of the illegality of the meeting. Only a legitimate king could convoke the Estates-General, and Henry IV did not recognize the assembly as legal. The principal goal of the

[29] Ibid., I, pp. 423–8, II pp. 327–57.

assembly was to set aside the Salic Law in order to elect a Catholic king. There were many candidates: Mayenne himself, the young duke of Guise (son of the murdered duke at Blois), the Habsburg Archduke Ernst, and the prince of Savoy. The Spanish ambassador, loudly supported by the Sixteen who dominated the delegation of the third estate from Paris, demanded that whoever was elected ought to marry Philip II's daughter: the Infanta, Isabella Clara Eugenia, granddaughter of Henry II and Catherine de Medici through their daughter Elizabeth, who married Philip II in 1559. The internal bickering at the Estates-General was characteristic of the entire history of the League, as nothing near a consensus was reached for the first five months. On 28 May the Spanish delegate proposed that the Infanta marry Archduke Ernst and that they be elected king and queen. This proved a shock, as even some of the Sixteen balked at electing two foreigners to the French throne. Finally on 20 June Philip II initiated another proposal: his daughter the Infanta would marry a French prince (and he intimated that the young duke of Guise was his choice), who would jointly be elected king and queen.

The Gallican sentiments of the deputies finally got the best of them, however. Many of them had been willing to bend to ultramontane (literally 'beyond the mountains') pressures ever since the Day of the Barricades – across the Alps to Rome as well as across the Pyrenees to Madrid – but this proposal was too much for all but the Sixteen. When Mayenne tried to get the assembly to agree to a marriage between his own son and the Infanta, some of the delegates walked out. On 28 June Guillaume du Vair, a judge of the Parlement of Paris as well as a leading moderate delegate representing the capital in the third estate, made a ringing defence of the Salic Law in the Parlement. He persuaded the court, with the support of Le Maistre the first president, to issue a decree that no transfer of the crown to a foreign prince or princess would be tolerated since it violated the fundamental laws of the kingdom. Although Mayenne and the Sixteen denounced the decree, its Gallican defence of the fundamental laws of the kingdom won over many deputies. For all practical purposes, the Spanish influence, so powerful in Paris under the guidance of the Spanish ambassador and a Spanish garrison of troops, proved unable to dominate the League as Philip II had hoped.[30]

After the jolt from Du Vair on 28 June, a second thunderbolt struck at the heart of the League and the meeting of the Estates less than a month later: Henry IV abjured his Calvinist faith and recognized the Catholic religion as the true church of God at St Denis on 25 July 1593. In an

[30] Peter M. Ascoli, 'The Sixteen and the Paris League, 1585–1591', PhD dissertation, University of California at Berkeley, 1971, pp. 642–52.

orchestrated move that showed his political genius, Henry IV eliminated at a stroke the *raison d'être* of the Estates-General and dissolved the one unifying thread that had held the League together since 1588. His abjuration having eliminated the conflict between the Salic Law and the law of Catholicity, many Catholics began to abandon Mayenne and the League. Although it would take another two years to defeat most of the Leaguer holdouts, and longer still to restore peace in the kingdom between Protestants and Catholics, Henry's conversion marked the final watershed in the Wars of Religion. The ceremony in the basilica at St Denis, repository of the bodies of French kings past, ended with Henry taking mass, receiving both the bread and the wine as a sign of his sacral kingship and universal kinship with his royal ancestors. Though many refused to accept the conversion as genuine, at least without papal absolution, Gallicanism carried the day as absolution by French bishops proved sufficient for most. The flood of popular support the League enjoyed immediately after the assassination of the Guises in December 1588 was now reversed by Henry III's successor. Leaguer moderates and 'politique' Catholics everywhere soon shifted their loyalty and allegiance to their newly Catholic king. In short, Henry IV's conversion effectively pulled the rug out from under the Holy League.[31]

What is the final judgment on the Catholic League? It would be a mistake to treat it, as so many historians have, as nothing more than a body motivated purely by partisan politics or social tensions. While political and social pressures were doubtless present, and even significant in the case of the Sixteen in Paris, to focus on these factors exclusively overlooks a very different face of the League. For all its political and internecine wrangling, the League was still very much a Holy Union. Its religious role was significant, as the League was the conduit between the Tridentine spirituality of the Catholic Reformation and the seventeenth-century *dévots*. Often overlooked is the emphasis the League placed on the internal and spiritual renewal of the earthly city. Moving beyond the communal religion of the late Middle Ages, the League focused on internalizing faith as a cleansing and purifying agent. New religious orders and confraternities were founded in League towns, and the gulf separating clergy and laity was often bridged as clerics joined aldermen in the Hôtel de Ville where both became the epitome of godly magistrates. To overlook the religious side of the League is to overlook the one bond that did keep the Holy Union holy as well as united.

---

[31] Michael Wolfe, *The Conversion of Henri IV: Politics, Power, and Religious Belief in Early Modern France* (Cambridge, MA, 1993), pp. 134–58.

One work that is very representative of the League's spiritual goal of recreating the city of God on earth is the *Very Humble Remonstrance to the King of France and Poland ... on the Disorders and Miseries of this Kingdom, Causes of the Same, and Means of Remedying Them to the Glory of God and the Universal Tranquility of this State* written by Nicolas Rolland in 1588 on the eve of the Estates-General at Blois. Rolland was a newly elected alderman in the Paris Hôtel de Ville and a member of the Sixteen. After an opening section outlining abuses in the fiscal and judicial systems, Rolland launched into an attack on the evils of society. Sorcery, blasphemy, and debauchery seemed to be everywhere, he argued, even at the royal court. Feast days were not observed and worldly business was conducted as usual on Sundays, when people were seen gambling and going to taverns and theatres instead of worshipping the Lord. All of these things were corrupting the youth and the *menu peuple*, he went on, but the worst thing of all is that 'all this filth is maintained by you, since you give letters of permission to continue this abuse'. Rolland also complains of the breakdown of the social order, with servants refusing to obey masters, wives their husbands, and children their parents. Even murder goes unpunished when committed by one of the king's courtiers. Being a member of the Sixteen, Rolland singled out the magistrates in the Parlement and all the nobility of the robe for special abuse. They lived an overly luxurious lifestyle unbecoming their social station.

Rolland paralleled the abuses in society and the state with a list of abuses in the Gallican church. Most Catholics did not go to mass, take the sacraments, or even know their own priest. Fast days were routinely not observed, and confession was all but ignored. Above all ecclesiastical offices were handed out as political spoils, to men, women, soldiers, and heretics indifferently. Virtue and spirituality seemed to be entirely absent from the church altogether. How to remedy all these ills? Rolland's answer to Henry III was a short and simple one: do not allow a heretic to succeed to the throne, and implement a total moral and spiritual reform which can only occur if the kingdom is united under the one true faith.[32]

This perception of a divine mission or a crusade to create a new society, or new world order, was a constant thread running throughout most League literature and propaganda. Even those tracts normally cited by historians to illustrate political or social tensions provide clear testimony to the spirituality of the League. In *The Dialogue between the Courtier and the Labourer* written by François Morin de Cromé in 1593 there is clearly

[32] This work is discussed in Ascoli, 'The Sixteen and the Paris League', pp. 209–26 (quote on p. 216).

evidence of the kind of social tension expressed by the Sixteen in Paris generally. Yet there is also clear evidence of the perception that the League was founded and chosen 'by the particular hand of God', and that God led the League from its inception, just 'as he led the people of Israel out of the deserts of Egypt'. God provided the League with leaders, 'just as God, in order to found and lead the league of the children of Israel, raised up a Moses to give order to all that was to be done, and then gave him several lieutenants like his brother Aaron'. Although comparing Guise and Mayenne to Moses and Aaron did serve to elevate the authority of the League's leaders, it also underscored the spiritual nature of that leadership. Cromé made it very plain that nothing the League did was achieved by human effort, especially something as secular in appearance as the Day of the Barricades. 'God alone [is] the author of such enterprises.'[33]

Finally, it is evident that the League, like Henry III before them, was closely involved in the founding of new religious confraternities whose goals for spiritual purification were the same as those mentioned by Rolland and Cromé. In Paris the Franciscans created new confraternities of penitents, in particular the Grey Penitents established at the Capuchin monastery on the rue Saint-Honoré. Older devotional forms were also renewed in the capital during the rule of the League, with the display of the Corpus Christi chief among them. Religious processions winding through the streets of Paris displaying the body of Christ became more numerous in the decade 1584–94 than at any time since the reign of Francis I. As Pierre de l'Estoile noted in his diary on Mardi Gras (14 February) 1589, just after the murder of the Guises at Blois: 'Throughout the day there were in Paris fine and devout processions instead of the dissolution and trash of mascarades and Shrove Tuesday revelries with which people besotted themselves during previous years.'[34] These religious processions were truly popular in that soldiers and priests marched together as 'godly warriors' along with women and children. The same was true throughout other League towns: creation of new confraternities and an upsurge of penitential piety.[35] Despite all its political machinations and its emphasis on social mobility, the League blazed the trail of the Catholic Counter-Reformation in France and introduced the basic tenets of Tridentine spirituality in a systematic way. Just as Madame Acarie, who founded a Carmelite order in Paris in

---

[33] Quoted in Crouzet, *Les guerriers de Dieu*, II, pp. 427–50 (quotes on pp. 435–7).
[34] Quoted in Denis Richet, 'Sociocultural Aspects of Religious Conflicts in Paris during the Second Half of the Sixteenth Century', in Robert Forster and Orest Ranum, eds., *Ritual, Religion, and the Sacred: Selections from the Annales* (Baltimore, 1982), pp. 182–212 (quote on p. 205).
[35] For a very good example, see Benedict, *Rouen during the Wars of Religion*, pp. 190–208.

1604, was the widow of a member of the Sixteen, it is no exaggeration to say that the dévots of the early seventeenth century were the descendants of the 'godly warriors' of the Holy League.

The other legacy of the Holy Union was much more immediate: a radical political ideology that focused on tyrannicide and popular sovereignty, going far beyond any of the resistance theories of the Huguenots. Fanned by the zealots of the militant clergy and radical press, the flames of this revolutionary rhetoric reached their peak in Paris following the murder of the Guises at Blois in 1588. It is no wonder that a royalist broadsheet would excoriate this rhetoric in no uncertain terms:

What is the invention of this League doing today but visibly preparing to overturn the state and to assail the living forces of the monarchy? What can the League be but a public attempt and a public assault on royalty? And what is the people but a recognition of its force, its many heads and arms, and its desire to dissolve in an instant the power of the monarchy created over so many centuries?[36]

The abjuration of Henry IV certainly dissipated the Leaguer political theory based on tyrannicide and popular sovereignty and restored the traditional support of sacral monarchy. The most noticeable difference on the political landscape after 1593, however, was not just the absence of resistance theory; this rhetoric was quickly replaced by the discourse of order and royal absolutism.

[36] Quoted in Barnavi, *Le parti de Dieu*, p. 149.

Henry IV and the Edict of Nantes: the
remaking of Gallicanism, 1593–1610

The decision taken by Henry IV to abjure his Calvinist religion and accept instruction in the Roman Catholic faith was not taken lightly. He clearly never said that 'Paris is worth a mass,' as so many historians have long insisted. That statement was just propaganda from the League, who wanted French Catholics to believe that Navarre's conversion was neither genuine nor sincere, and was simply a cynical ploy to gain the crown. Although it is impossible to know everything that Henry was thinking in July 1593, all the evidence suggests that his conversion was rendered in good faith. If dogma and doctrine were never his strong points, it is nevertheless clear that Navarre was a man who had risked his life for his religion on the battlefield and off for nearly two decades. To suggest that he was either unprincipled or cared little for religion is contrary to the evidence. Equally unlikely is the notion put forward by some scholars that Henry was a modern-thinking king who put reason of state, order, and politics ahead of religion as a priority. While there is no doubt that Henry's decision to abjure was made for political reasons – to end the civil wars and to restore the authority of the monarchy – we ought not to conclude from this that Henry's conversion was either insincere or cynically made. What may not have been evident to contemporaries at the moment of his abjuration was that Henry IV did indeed have a plan to restore order and bring an end to the fighting: by reuniting all French men and women under one religion, the Catholic faith of all French kings since Clovis. The goal of 'one king, one faith, one law' was as important to Henry IV as it was to his predecessors. Just as he was forced by circumstances to remake his religious commitments in order to adapt to the Gallican monarchy, so were his subjects required to put down their arms and remake the Gallican unity and concord so necessary for a lasting peace.

Another factor forcing Henry's hand was the rising tide of popular antagonism to the civil wars, particularly among the lower classes who bore the brunt of the economic disruption and political disorder of the previous thirty years. Already by the summer of 1593 various groups of peasants across the realm had begun to band together to try to prevent both royalist and Leaguer armies alike from further pillage of their barns and granaries and continued disruption of their harvest cycle (Map 8). Peasant bands had already attacked groups of soldiers and individual noblemen in Brittany and Normandy, and in 1593 armed villagers in Burgundy's wine region organized to protect themselves from further transgressions by warring troops. Winegrowers from the villages of Pommard, Volnay, Meursault, Auxey, Santenay, St-Aubin, Gamay, Beaune, and Nolay banded together and promised to signal each other with the tocsin whenever they saw a soldier approach their villages. And according to a judge in the Parlement of Dijon, Gabriel Breunot, they had already killed thirty Leaguer soldiers who were attempting to collect subsidies for the duke of Mayenne. These peasants' fears of military hostilities against them and their property seemed real enough to the startled Breunot. He even reported seeing a group of peasants from the villages just outside the capital of Dijon parading through the Burgundian capital with carts loaded with wood dismantled from their own homes. When asked why they were trying to sell the wood from their own homes, 'they replied that they would sooner demolish and sell them themselves than see them burned and destroyed by soldiers'.[1] The peasant insurrection soon spread both northward and southward in early 1594. To the south over a thousand peasants calling themselves *Bonnets Rouges* on account of their identifying red caps mobilized to prevent troops from moving between Tournus and Mâcon. To the north groups of winegrowers in both Beaune and Dijon began to lobby their municipal magistrates to end the war and come to terms with the king. These winegrowers had been a constant and important source of support for municipal elites for decades. They had been a bedrock of opposition to Protestantism at the outbreak of the civil wars and had been ardent supporters of the League since its founding. Now that Henry IV had abjured and joined the community of the Catholic faith, however, they saw little reason to continue to hold out in the face of the continued disruption and chaos of civil war.[2]

The most serious popular opposition to the wars occurred in the southwest, in the Dordogne valley regions of Limousin and Périgord and in the Lot and Garonne valley region of the Agenais, where a number of major battles and thousands of troops had passed in the preceding thirty years.

---

[1] J. F. Garnier, ed., *Journal de Gabriel Breunot, conseiller au Parlement de Dijon*, 3 vols. (Dijon, 1864), II, 19, 31.

[2] Henri Drouot, *Mayenne et la Bourgogne: Etude sur la Ligue (1587–1596)*, 2 vols. (Dijon and Paris, 1937), II, 286–8.

Map 8 Areas of Peasant Revolts, 1593–94.

There peasants organized in greater numbers and proved to be more formidable opponents to both the royalist and Leaguer armies than anywhere else in France. Calling themselvs *Tard-Avisés*, or 'latecomers', because of their initial hesitation to seize the moment and arm themselves for self-preservation, these peasants were derisively dubbed *Croquants* by their enemies, 'country bumpkins', which also alluded to the social cleavages involved. There is little question that these peasants had some serious grievances. The Leaguer governors of both Limousin and Périgord had set new standards of personal terror and pillage as they billeted their troops in their villages, seized their property, and demanded seigneurial dues far above what was owed them. A handbill circulated in Périgord described their plight in very evocative terms:

The *plat pays* has been completely ruined by a vast horde of bandits. The poor farmers, who time after time have suffered from the quartering of the soldiery upon them by one side or the other, have been reduced to famine. Their wives and daughters have been raped and their livestock stolen. They have had to leave their lands untilled and die of starvation, while numbers of them languish in prison for failure to meet the enormous *tailles* and subsidies both parties have levied upon them.

This litany of abuse was corroborated by Jean Tarde, a canon from Sarlat, who complained 'that the *gentilshommes* forced them through imprisonment to pay two or three times more rent than they owed, that they refused to issue receipts after payment, and in every respect treated them as slaves'.[3]

While there was little coordination among the dozens of local peasant uprisings in the southwest, they tended to share a number of common goals:

(1) an end to improper administration of clerical benefices,
(2) an end to the unjust and unlawful oppression by the nobility,
(3) the appointment of a government official to enforce peasant rights and privileges,
(4) the lowering of the *taille* to its pre-war level,
(5) a requirement that nobles who purchased non-noble land would pay taxes on it just as commoners did,
(6) the substitution of local tax assessors in place of the royal *élus*,
(7) a ban on the holding of noble titles by all except the ancient *noblesse de race*,
(8) a ban on the nobility's illegally using its influence to alter verdicts in the judicial system, and
(9) the abolition of all new taxes.[4]

It is clear that there were both anti-fiscal and anti-seigneurial elements to the peasant demands. And while their rhetoric and polemic might appear to be supporting a radical social revolution to overthrow the aristocratic

[3] Both sources quoted in J. H. M. Salmon, *Society in Crisis: France in the Sixteenth Century* (London and New York, 1975), pp. 284–5.
[4] Ibid., p. 290.

order, it was primarily the gross seigneurial abuses and unlawful excesses that occurred in the chaos and disorder of the civil wars that most concerned them. This is what united Protestant and Catholic peasants together, who wanted to end the warfare altogether in order to restore the traditional seigneurial regime free of such abuses. Thus, Professor John Salmon is exactly right when he notes that 'it was not the normal administration of the seigneurial régime, but rather its gross abuse in circumstances of civil anarchy, that provoked the risings. The plight of the peasantry was the result of three decades of civil war.'[5]

What did the various peasant risings accomplish? For one thing they amassed large numbers of peasants together in assemblies to protest and occasionally even to fight. While many of these assemblies produced no more than 100 to 200 people, the largest of them were quite impressive. The peasant force that mobilized outside the walls of the towns of St-Yrieux and St-Léonard in Limousin in May 1594 numbered 2,000 men. More than five thousand peasant troops assembled at St-Priest-Ligoure, and between seven and eight thousand peasants gathered in the forest of Abzac on 23 April 1594. These were not the most impressive peasant assemblies, however. In early 1594 12,000 peasants had assembled in Dognon, and the largest recorded assembly was held in La Boule near Bergerac in Périgord in May 1594, where estimates of between 20,000 and 40,000 peasants met to express their grievances and issue a manifesto.[6] Although it is fair to say that most of these peasant bands who engaged any professional troops of either army were usually defeated, the large and vociferous outbursts of peasant discontent did not go unnoticed. Many members of the upper classes took the anti-seigneurial rhetoric of the peasant manifestos very seriously and feared a social revolution, while others were more sympathetic to the peasant grievances. In either case, the peasant revolts served as a catalyst for peace. When the 'Croquants' sent a deputation to Henry IV seeking royal redress of their grievances in June 1594, the king responded in populist fashion (at least according to the diarist Pierre de l'Estoile) that if he had not been born to become king, he would have joined the Croquants himself.[7] More importantly, he made every effort to appease them. Though the Croquants never achieved the appointment of a royal official to safeguard their rights and privileges, the arrears they owed in taxes were significantly reduced

---

[5] Ibid., p. 282.
[6] Yves-Marie Bercé, *History of Peasant Revolts: The Social Origins of Rebellion in Early Modern France*, trans. Amanda Whitmore (Ithaca, 1990), p. 77.
[7] Pierre de l'Estoile, *Journal pour le règne de Henri IV (1589–1610)*, 2 vols., ed. L-R. Lefèvre (Paris, 1948–58), I, 420.

and the tax levy was slightly reduced for forthcoming years. Above all, the king's insistence that the local authorities in the southwest not take any reprisals against the Croquants was generally accepted. There can be little doubt that the peasant risings of 1593–94 helped to convince Henry IV that a peace settlement and an end to the civil wars were urgently required.

Appeasing the peasants of the southwest proved far easier than appeasing the Leaguers who still opposed him, however. Moreover, many of his former Huguenot allies also began to show signs of discomfort and outright opposition to Henry now that he had abjured Protestantism and had become a Catholic. Thus, the king's primary goals were to try to win over the support of the principal League and Huguenot leaders. But even that would not prove very efficacious if there were still significant numbers of fortified towns, armed by either one group or the other, that continued to resist royal authority. Henry's memories of his ill-fated efforts to besiege Paris in 1590 and Rouen in 1592 must have made him cringe at the thought of trying to instill royal authority on recalcitrant subjects by force. And further complicating the equation was the continued presence of a significant number of Spanish troops in various League garrisons, above all in the capital of Paris. So, Henry decided to deal with all remaining strongholds and military garrisons that resisted his authority in the same way he dealt with the Croquants: he offered them the carrot of appeasement rather than the stick of suppression. Any chance Henry had of persuading the large number of moderate Catholics who populated every League stronghold to support him depended entirely on his ability to convince them of his sincerity as well as his willingness to offer them an olive branch rather than a sword. In this sense, Henry's politics of transition from war to peace should not be viewed cynically as a process of the king's buying off his opponents, as historians have long maintained, but rather as a very traditional way any patron might try to guarantee and assure the fidelity of his clients.

Even though Henry was granted absolution by French bishops after his abjuration and conversion in July 1593, the Pope had not yet done so, and for many Catholics the king remained excommunicate. An even more pressing problem was that Henry could not even be crowned as king in Reims, as the city was held by League radicals who refused to recognize his authority. Henry solved that problem by cleverly stretching and molding the traditions of the French *sacre* to fit his unusual political circumstances. While it is true that Reims was the traditional site of most French coronation ceremonies, some of the royal secretaries quickly discovered that some medieval *sacres* had been performed at Chartres, which was in royal hands. And even though the archbishop of Reims, a Guise, refused to administer the oaths, the bishop of Chartres, Nicolas de Thou, was willing to step in. But perhaps the greatest obstacle to a convincing *sacre* (and any other kind would have been counter-productive) was the absence of the oil from the Holy Ampulla in League hands in Reims. Again Henry, or more likely his advisors, suggested a ready substitute, the holy oil presented by the Virgin to St Martin of Tours, kept at his monastery at Marmoutier just outside Tours. After all, when Louis IX lay on his deathbed in 1483, he had asked that the Holy Ampulla from Reims as well as the ampulla from Marmoutier be brought to him. Thus, on 27 February 1594 Henry IV was consecrated and crowned king of France at Chartres. The efficacy of the oil of St Martin apparently overcame any doubts or fears that Henry was anointed and consecrated with the wrong holy oil, as his royal authority and the validity of his coronation were never called into question on account of the innovations in the ceremony.[8]

If he were ever going to win over all of Catholic France to support him as king, Henry recognized the necessity of winning the loyalty and support of the capital. The domination of the Sixteen in Paris had waned somewhat since Mayenne had arrested and hanged the radicals who had murdered President Brisson in November 1591, and especially since the Leaguer moderates defeated their plan to put the daughter of Philip II of Spain on the French throne at the Estates-General the previous summer. Since Henry's conversion in July 1593 a number of placards had already appeared in the capital calling for the immediate recognition of the newly converted king. And Henry played upon this rising groundswell of popular support to end the war by making early contact with moderate League politicians in Paris. This would be his principal tactic in dealing with all the recalcitrant League towns, in fact, as he sought to use the popular calls for peace to broker an amenable and peaceful deal with League moderates. In Paris, this turned out to be the governor of the capital, Charles de Cossé, count of Brissac. Although there were numerous moderates in both the Parlement and the municipal government, Brissac was a surprising target for the king to seek out, since Mayenne had only appointed him in December 1593 to replace another Leaguer with suspected royalist sympathies. Brissac recognized the advantage in supporting Henry IV, however, and above all could see the consequences of continuing to hold out and resist a recently consecrated and crowned king.

Unlike the starvation-filled summer of 1590 when Henry had last attempted to take the capital, the royalist recovery of Paris in the spring of 1594 was remarkably peaceful. At four o'clock in the morning of 22 March

---

[8] Richard A. Jackson, *Vive le Roi! A History of the French Coronation from Charles V to Charles X* (Chapel Hill, 1984), pp. 45–6.

1594 Brissac and Pierre Lhuillier, the *prévôt des marchands* (or mayor) of Paris, ordered two of the city gates to be opened to allow in the royalist troops of the king. Royalist supporters had already seized control of the other strategic points of access; and if there were any thoughts of resisting by any of the Sixteen or the Spanish troops still garrisoned in the capital, they never materialized. Two hours later, about six in the morning, Henry IV marched proudly through the Porte Neuve, the very gate through which Henry III had fled during the Day of the Barricades six years before. And for the first time in six years, the French capital had a resident and reigning king. Again showing his leniency and largesse, Henry allowed the Spanish troops to exit in formal military procession and sought no vengeance against those Leaguers who had fought him and resisted his authority for so long. Only those recalcitrant members of the Sixteen who still refused to accept him as king were banished from the capital, and even their property was safeguarded for a possible reconciliation. At eight o'clock Henry went to the cathedral of Notre Dame, where he celebrated Mass and a *Te Deum*, making a public display of his Catholic conversion. As his entry into Paris occurred near the end of Lent, Henry decided to remain in the capital in order to celebrate Holy Week with his loyal subjects and further demonstrate to any remaining doubters that he was indeed the Most Christian King. One week after his entry on 29 March he even took part in a religious procession led by the city's clergy from the Louvre to Notre Dame. The holiest relics from the Sainte Chapelle were displayed en route, many of them for the first time in public, including a splinter of wood from the True Cross and a thorn from Christ's crown. At Notre Dame a special Mass was celebrated marking the peaceful submission of the city as well as the defeat of the Sixteen. And Henry continued to display his personal piety and the sincerity of his new faith during Holy Week. Not only did he worship in every parish church in the city – the very sites where League preachers had vilified him for six years – but he visited the sick in the Hôtel-Dieu, pardoned prisoners in the Châtelet, washed the feet of the poor on Maundy Thursday, and even blessed several hundred victims of scrofula with the royal touch on Easter Sunday. The king made every effort to show his Catholic subjects that the body politic had been restored to the body of Christ. As one anonymous writer noted on the day Henry entered the capital, 'All good Leaguers became good Royalists and all good Royalists became good Leaguers at the festivities attending this great day of peace.'[9]

---

[9] Much of the material in this paragraph (including the final quotation) comes from Michael Wolfe, '"Paris is Worth a Mass" Reconsidered: Henri IV and the Leaguer Capital, March 1594', paper presented at the Society for French Historical Studies, Wilmington, Delaware, March 1994. I am grateful to Dr Wolfe for allowing me to cite his paper here.

The fall of Paris to the king started an avalanche of royal support, as one town after another began to submit to the royal will. Henry continued to use the carrot rather than the stick in dealing with all Leaguers who, like Brissac in Paris, negotiated a settlement rather than continuing to hold out. Brissac himself was rewarded by being made a marshal of France, and Leaguers everywhere began to rethink the advantages of submitting to the king. There were some significant holdouts: the Guise strongholds in Burgundy were still loyal to Mayenne, a number of Leaguer towns in Brittany were still loyal to Mayenne's cousin, Philippe-Emmanuel, duke of Mercoeur, and a few independent towns such as Marseille and Toulouse in the south continued to defy the king on their own. For the most part, however, the submission of Paris was the crucial first step on the road to peace. By the end of 1594 most of the major League towns in northern France submitted to the king: Abbeville, Amiens, Auxerre, Beauvais, Bourges, Orléans, Reims, Rouen, and Troyes. The Burgundian towns of Auxonne, Beaune, and Mayenne's capital of Dijon also submitted the following year, as did the duke of Mayenne himself. In all these towns, Henry dealt leniently with those Leaguers who helped to negotiate a settlement, and more harshly with those who continued to resist. He could overlook Leaguer opposition to the crown in the past if present behaviour and deference to the royal will could be counted on in future. Like Brissac's reward of a marshal's baton, the League towns of the later 1590s were littered with recipients of royal favour. Although the renegade dukes of Mercoeur and Epernon remained at large in Brittany and Provence respectively, and a few towns in the extreme south continued to hold out for a little longer, for the most part Henry IV's politics of appeasement was a success. And when Henry finally received absolution from Pope Clement VIII in late August 1595 (resulting in the submission of the duke of Mayenne just a few months later), the prospects for a lasting peace seemed bright.[10]

This tranquillity was already being threatened, however, from two very different directions. Nearly a year prior to Henry's papal absolution, dispatches had been intercepted indicating that Philip II of Spain was seriously considering another invasion into northern France from the Netherlands with his Army of Flanders, hoping to attract any remaining League rebels – Mayenne, Mercoeur, and Epernon, for example – to his cause. With other evidence that Philip's intentions were anything but pacific, Henry was virtually forced to declare war against Spain. Although

---

[10] The most complete analysis of Henry's 'politics of appeasement' is Annette Finley-Croswhite, *Henry IV and the Towns: The Pursuit of Legitimacy in French Urban Society, 1589–1610* (Cambridge, 1999).

he personally favoured making peace at home before getting involved in a foreign war, Henry was unable to resist the strong tide of argument in favour of war pushed by some of his closest advisors, especially the Huguenot duke of Bouillon. Thus, a declaration of war against Spain was published in 1595.

At the same time, a second threat to peace in the realm came from a different direction: the disgruntled Huguenots. Ever since Henry's abjuration and coronation, many French Protestants could not help but wonder what future they had in this remade Gallican France. After all, did not the king's coronation oath require him to extirpate all heresy from his Catholic realm? Moreover, Henry's politics of appeasement with the Catholic League only increased Protestant fears. In the event, the Huguenot assemblies of 1594, 1595, 1596, and 1597 became much more politicized and their demands to the king became much more militant as they sought a legal settlement guaranteeing their future, indeed guaranteeing their 'state within the state'. This militancy was clearly reflected in the noble domination of the assemblies by 1597. Whereas only 5 nobles (out of 21 deputies) attended the Saumur assembly in 1595, 22 nobles (out of 39 deputies) attended the Châtellerault assembly in 1597. Numerous Protestant communities had already stopped contributing their *tailles* to the royal treasury, and a number of Huguenot nobles, such as Bouillon and La Trémoille, even threatened armed insurrection and a renewal of the civil wars if the king did not accept their demands. So just as Henry IV was trying to restore concord and harmony to a divided France, his Huguenot subjects (and former co-religionnaires) were threatening to reopen old wounds.[11]

Although the war with Spain did allow French Protestants and Catholics to unite together in a common effort to defeat a foreign enemy, it was clear that Henry would have to continue to fight on both domestic and foreign fronts simultaneously. Spanish troops seized Cambrai early on and forced Calais to surrender to them in 1596, but the biggest blow was the loss of the frontier town of Amiens, which fell to the Spanish in the spring of 1597. Only after a long and costly siege was Henry able to recapture the town in September, but the recovery of Amiens proved to be the turning point in the war. Mercoeur, who had openly aided and abetted the Spanish, was the last renegade League noble to submit, and even he finally surrendered to the king in January 1598. Only then could Henry turn his full attention to a settlement with the Huguenots.

---

[11] N. M. Sutherland, *The Huguenot Struggle for Recognition* (New Haven, 1980), pp. 306–12; and Salmon, *Society in Crisis*, pp. 295–6.

The accord that Henry IV eventually reached with the Huguenots in April 1598, the Edict of Nantes, was also molded by his politics of appeasement. He could not afford to alienate French Catholics, however, especially former Leaguers, by granting too many favours to the Huguenots, so his task was a nearly impossible one from the start. In the end, neither Protestants nor Catholics were totally supportive of the settlement, each hoping to use it as a stepping stone for further gains. So much historical misinformation and mythology has been propagated about this edict, that before analysing its contents, it is necessary to explain what this edict was not. The Edict of Nantes did not introduce a systematic policy of religious toleration. As will be explained below, it allowed for temporary religious co-existence, but its ultimate goal was religious concord – that is, unity – rather than toleration of differing confessions. This was Henry IV's clear intention and served as his *modus operandi* for the rest of his reign, though he clearly hoped this religious unity could be achieved peacefully and he vowed to protect the rights of the Huguenots in the meantime. Second, it is often claimed that the edict was a victory of modern *raison d'état* over religious dogmatism, that Henry IV and his 'politique' supporters clearly viewed the salvation of the state as more important than religious unity. In other words, religious piety and zealous faith were forced to take a back seat to modern secular politics. This view is not only anachronistic – there was no such thing as secular politics in the sixteenth century – but it also completely overlooks Henry's goals of religious concord and unity as well as his own understanding of confessional politics. The Edict of Nantes was, to be sure, a forced settlement like most of the earlier edicts of pacification. It resulted from the particular circumstances of the 1590s: Henry's abjuration, the submission of the League, and his politics of appeasement. But the edict was also a product of Henry's commitment to the Gallican monarchy of his predecessors. Rather than religious toleration or modern reason of state, the underlying principle of the Edict of Nantes was the restoration of 'one king, one faith, one law'.

The Edict of Nantes actually consisted of four separate documents: 92 general articles, 56 so-called 'secret articles' dealing with particular towns and individuals that were exempt from the general articles, and two royal *brevets*.[12] The principal difference between the articles and the *brevets* is that the two sets of articles were registered in the Parlements and could

---

[12] The entire text of all four documents is in English translation in Roland Mousnier, *The Assassination of Henry IV: The Tyrannicide Problem and the Consolidation of the French Absolute Monarchy in the Early Seventeenth Century*, trans. Joan Spencer (London, 1973), pp. 316–63. For a good summary of these documents, see ibid., pp. 144–51, and Sutherland, *Huguenot Struggle for Recognition*, pp. 328–32.

only be countermanded by another edict registered in the Parlements. Royal *brevets*, issued by an individual monarch, could be withdrawn at the whim of the king, and in any case could be overturned by a later king. In the case of the Edict of Nantes, Henry realized full well that the most significant concessions granted to the Protestants would likely never be registered by the Parlements, so these were granted in the royal *brevets*. Finally, the general and secret articles were explicitly labeled 'perpetual and irrevocable', while the most significant of the *brevets* was clearly intended to be provisional, expiring in eight years.

One of the most striking elements of the edict to modern readers is that it mentioned nothing about belief or doctrine. Like all the earlier edicts of pacification throughout the religious wars, beliefs were not mandated. This does not mean that Henry was unconcerned with what his subjects believed, but it underscores the central fact that in the sixteenth century religion was perceived in social rather than intellectual terms. This religious settlement, then, focused on religious co-existence and attempted to deal with the very real problem of trying to integrate a corporate body of Huguenots into a Catholic state. Belief and doctrine were important, but they were perceived as the inevitable products of an ordered Christian society. So, for sixteenth-century Christians the extirpation of false doctrine and heresy necessitated healing the divisions in the body social. It was exactly these fissures the Edict of Nantes attempted to remedy.

That religious unity was Henry IV's ultimate goal rather than permanent toleration of the Huguenots was made clear in the preamble to the general articles. Here at the very beginning of the public edict Henry lamented the religious division of his subjects:

But now that it hath pleased God to give us a beginning of enjoying some Rest, we think we cannot imploy ourself better, to apply to that which may tend to the glory and service of his holy name, and to provide that he may be adored and prayed unto by all our Subjects: and if it hath *not yet* pleased him to permit it to be in one and the same form of Religion, that it may at the least be with one and the same intention ... and that we and this Kingdom may alwayes conserve the glorious title of most Christian, which hath been by so much merit so long since acquired.[13]

So even though Henry declared the edict to be 'perpetual and irrevocable' later in the preamble, all he meant by that was that it could only be countermanded by another edict registered in the Parlements. It clearly did not condone a permanent and lasting religious settlement based on religious toleration.

---

[13] This quotation is from the seventeenth-century English translation in Mousnier, *Assassination of Henry IV*, p. 317 (my emphasis added).

The 92 general articles of the edict resemble most closely the Edicts of Beaulieu (May 1576) and Poitiers (September 1577), and many of the articles were reproduced nearly word for word from these earlier settlements. Organized as a general amnesty, the edict did recognize and provide for the enforcement of many Protestant rights, above all the complete freedom of conscience (article 6). It also allowed freedom of worship in all cities and towns controlled by the Huguenots in August 1597, in all towns so designated in earlier peace edicts, and in the private homes of Protestant nobles (articles 7–10). This last article reinforced the position of nobles in the Huguenot movement, who already dominated its political assemblies. Although the Huguenots were forbidden from worshipping in Catholic churches, they could build their own in the areas they controlled (article 16). They were also accorded full civil rights in respect to eligibility for admission to schools, colleges, and universities (article 22) as well as to holding any public or royal offices including the posts in the Parlements (article 27). Much of the remainder of the general articles (articles 30–81) focused on the sovereign courts and regulated fair treatment of Protestants, principally through the bi-partisan chambers (*chambres mi-parties*) first introduced in the Peace of Monsieur in 1576. Although such bi-partisan chambers were not created in every Parlement, and the chamber in the Parlement of Paris would eventually be reduced to just one Protestant judge, the justice clauses of the edict were crucial in order to secure the edict's enforcement. Although this was a long way from the comprehensive and general freedom of conscience and worship the Huguenot assembly at Châtellerault had demanded, it was far more than most Catholics had ever imagined their Most Catholic King would be willing to give them.

The general articles were far from a total Huguenot victory, however. On the contrary, they underscored the Catholicity of the crown and the realm. The Catholic mass was restored 'in all places and quarters of this Kingdom', including all those areas where it had been banned under Huguenot control (article 3). Thus, French Catholics enjoyed the complete freedom of conscience and worship everywhere in the kingdom, whereas the Huguenots' freedom of worship was severely restricted. Moreover, the edict introduced the mass into some Protestant-controlled areas for the first time in forty years. When mass was restored to the Huguenot stronghold of La Rochelle, for example, the future saint François de Sales exclaimed: 'Would to God that [Catholic] worship could be made as free in Geneva as it is in La Rochelle.'[14] The Huguenots were also obliged 'to keep and observe' all the feast days of

[14] Quoted in ibid., p. 148.

the Catholic church and were forbidden from working on those and any other Catholic holidays (article 20). They were also forbidden from selling books outside the areas they controlled, anything they did print was subject to strict censorship (article 21), and they were required to observe the laws of the Catholic church regarding marriage and contracts (article 23). Finally, the Huguenots were still required to pay the ecclesiastical tithe, just like all Catholics (article 25). Given Henry IV's goal eventually to reunite all his subjects under the umbrella of the Gallican church, the Edict of Nantes was far from a total Protestant victory, despite the outraged reactions of many French Catholics to the terms of the settlement.

The 56 secret articles dealt with a number of exceptions to and omissions from the general articles, some favourable to the Catholics though most were more favourable to the Huguenots. Above all, the king granted them permission to hold their own consistories, colloquies, provincial and national synods in the towns they controlled (secret article 34). This is significant, largely because the general articles had forbidden the Huguenots from holding any further political assemblies, such as the recent ones at Saumur and Châtellerault (article 82). By allowing religious assemblies, however, the secret articles provided a forum that could easily be adapted to political purposes. Moreover, the secret articles did allow the Huguenots to have one official political representative at court to lobby the king.

The most significant Protestant gains of all came not in the general or secret articles, however, but in the two *brevets*. Issued within weeks of the former, the two *brevets* granted the Protestants unprecedented concessions. Henry was forced to issue these concessions in the form of a *brevet*, because he recognized very clearly that the Parlements would balk at registering them. The first provided an annual subsidy of 45,000 *écus* (or 135,000 *livres tournois*) to pay the salaries of Huguenot pastors, and was clearly designed to take the sting out of being forced to pay the ecclesiastical tithe. The second was far more important, as it guaranteed the Huguenots a strong military presence in the kingdom. It allowed them to maintain troops in about 200 towns in their jurisdiction. Roughly half of them were designated fortified towns, garrisoned with troops paid for by the crown, for which Henry provided an annual subsidy of 180,000 *écus* (or 540,000 *livres tournois*). The remaining towns were to be manned by a local citizen militia. Allowing the Huguenots to remain armed and in control of a number of prominent towns was not one of Henry's objectives, as it clearly imposed on his own authority. His politics of appeasement meant that peace was bought at a price, however, and the large number of fortified towns garrisoned with Protestant soldiers paid for by the crown was the price exacted from the Huguenot nobles to get them to lay down their arms. By allowing the Huguenots to remain armed and in possession of so many fortified towns, Henry was indirectly endorsing the Huguenot 'state within the state'. The king made it very clear, however, that this concession of fortified towns was purely temporary, as the *brevet* expired eight years after its publication. Therefore, religious co-existence, like the Protestant 'state within the state', was never meant to be permanent. They were purely concessions granted to restore peace to the kingdom, after which time Henry could get on with his ultimate aim of healing the divisions in the body social and the body politic and restoring the concord of his people under 'one king, one law, one faith'.

Even though the concessions Catholics found most intolerable were in the two royal *brevets*, the Parlement balked at registering the two sets of published articles. Several clergy in Paris organized so many religious processions and popular demonstrations against the edict, in fact, that they were banned for threatening sedition. Ultimately, Achille de Harlay, First President in the Parlement of Paris, led a delegation of judges to the Louvre in February 1599 to petition the king in person against the edict's registration. Henry's response to the magistrates was firm and to the point:

You see me in my study, where I have come to speak to you, not dressed in royal attire with sword and cape like my predecessors, nor like a prince who has come to speak with foreign ambassadors, but dressed in a simple doublet, like the father of a family speaking intimately with his children. What I have to say is that I want you to verify the edict I have granted to those of the [reformed] religion. What I have done is for the cause of peace, which I have already secured abroad and now desire within my own kingdom. You owe me your obedience, even if for no other consideration than my rank [*qualité*], and for the duty all my subjects owe me, particularly you members of my Parlement ... Do not make any allegations about my Catholic religion. I love it more than you do, and I am more Catholic than you. I am the eldest son of the church, which none of you are or can be.

In addition to underscoring his devotion to the Catholic religion, Henry made it very clear that he granted the Huguenots concessions in order to achieve peace. 'Those who want to block the passage of my edict want war', he stressed, since 'necessity led me to draft this edict'.

My last word to you is to urge you to follow the example of Monsieur de Mayenne. When he was asked to undertake some intrigues against my will, he replied that he was too obliged to me, as were all my subjects, and that he would always be among those willing to risk his life to please me, because I have restored France [in peace] despite those who want the contrary. And if the leader of the League, who in the past made every effort to overthrow the state, has spoken in this manner, what say you whom I have re-established [in Parlement], both those loyal to me as well as those whose estates were restored to them [after the submission of the League]?

The king concluded his stern lecture to the stunned magistrates by invoking his politics of appeasement, the carrot rather than the stick: 'Grant to my prayers what you would not grant to my threats, since I am no longer threatening you. Just do as I command you, or rather what I beg you. You will be doing it not only for me but also for yourselves and the cause of peace.'[15]

Although the Parlements did eventually give in to the royal will, it was a very grudging acceptance of the edict. The Parlement of Paris registered it on 25 February 1599 just two weeks after their visit to the Louvre. The provincial Parlements were more recalcitrant, raising further objections and delaying for as long as possible. The edict was not registered in the Parlement of Grenoble until September 1599, while the Parlements of Dijon and Toulouse held out until January 1600 and the Parlements of Aix and Rennes until August 1600. Finally, the Parlement of Rouen steadfastly refused to register the Edict of Nantes in its entirety until August 1609, a full ten years after it was first promulgated. Like many Catholics, all the Parlements feared that the temporary religious coexistence afforded the Huguenots by the peace would allow them to regroup and eventually to advance the Calvinist cause anew.

One final bit of historical mythology that is in need of revision concerns the so-called 'politique' party. In the first place, there never was any organized party of 'politiques'. This was as true in the 1570s, when such a group was thought to exist in the household of François, duke of Alençon and Anjou, as it was in the 1590s, when a very different group of moderate Catholics and Protestants rallied to the cause of the king in opposition to the Holy League. A number of individuals were certainly referred to pejoratively as 'politiques' by their enemies in both periods, and the epithet was intended as a term of derision indicating a lack of religious zeal and piety. But there was never any organized group of such individuals. Moreover, much like the Edict of Nantes itself, these so-called 'politiques' were champions of neither a permanent peace settlement of religious toleration nor any modern notion of reason of state. The figures usually categorized as 'politique' supporters of Henry IV in the 1590s – men like Achille de Harlay, First President of the Parlement of Paris; Jacques-Auguste de Thou, historian and also a member of the Parlement of Paris; Etienne Pasquier, another *parlementaire*; and the

---

[15] Berger de Xivrey, ed., *Recueil des lettres missives de Henri IV*, V (Paris, 1850), pp. 90–4, 'Les paroles que le roy a tenues à messieurs de la court de Parlement le vii février 1599.' There is an English translation of the complete speech in Mousnier, *Assassination of Henry IV*, pp. 364–7, though I have made my own translation from the French in the quotations here.

diarist Pierre de l'Estoile, a clerk in the Parlement – were certainly moderate Catholics, enemies of the League, as well as ardent supporters of Henry IV's cause. They were not by any stretch of the imagination champions of permanent religious toleration, however, and all four of them explicitly sought a peace settlement restoring the Huguenots to the Catholic faith. In other words, like Henry himself they sought religious concord and unity rather than toleration. And as it happened, all four individuals complained bitterly about the Edict of Nantes when it was published, because they felt it granted the Protestants too many concessions. So whatever else the 'politiques' were, they clearly did not favour a policy of permanent religious toleration nor any concept of putting the state above religious unity; they were deeply religious Catholics who championed the cause of 'one king, one faith, one law'.[16] One of the reasons Henry IV was able to defeat the League after his abjuration, in fact, was that these 'politiques' shared so much in common with many moderates of the League. Both groups shared many common goals, and it was upon this broad base of support – moderate Leaguers, 'politique' Catholics, and peaceful and loyal Huguenots – that the polity of Henry IV's authority rested.

Henry's promises to protect and maintain his former co-religionnaires, the Huguenots, could, of course, have undermined his commitment to religious unity. The king's strength, however, was in enforcing the Edict of Nantes evenhandedly, and above all, in maintaining the peace settlement. Thus, he shied away from doing anything that would jeopardize the peace. In practice, this meant that Henry had to fight for the rights of the minority Protestants much harder than he did for Catholics. It meant that he maintained public and visible ties with the Huguenot community even

---

[16] Although full evidence for the religious views of Harlay, De Thou, Pasquier, and L'Estoile is provided in Nancy Lyman Roelker, *One King, One Faith: The Parlement of Paris and the Religious Reformations of the Sixteenth Century* (University of California Press, forthcoming), see Etienne Pasquier, *Ecrits politiques*, ed. D. Thickett (Geneva, 1966), pp. 127–77 and 287–309; Jacques-Auguste de Thou, *Histoire universelle ... depuis 1543 jusqu'en 1607*, 16 vols. (London, 1734), XIII, 375; Christopher Bettinson, 'The Politiques and the Politique Party: A Reappraisal', in Keith Cameron, ed., *From Valois to Bourbon: Dynasty, State, and Society in Early Modern France* (Exeter, 1989), pp. 35–49; Mario Turchetti, 'Concorde ou tolérance? de 1562 à 1598', *Revue historique*, vol. 274 (1985), 341–55; and idem, 'Religious Concord and Political Tolerance in Sixteenth- and Seventeenth-Century France', *Sixteenth Century Journal*, vol. 22 (1991), 15–25. Although some historians claim that Pasquier was an advocate of religious freedom, this is usually due to mistaking him as the author of the anonymous *Exhortation aux Princes et aux Seigneurs au Conseil Privé du Roy* (1561), whose author does call for religious toleration. It has been convincingly demonstrated by Vittorio de Caprariis, however, that Pasquier could not have written this work and that his other writings completely contradict it. See Vittorio de Caprariis, *Propaganda e pensiero politico in Francia durante le guerre di religione, 1559–1572* (Naples, 1959), pp. 153–4 and 290–1.

as a Catholic king. It meant that Henry had to endure the taunts of many Catholics that he was in fact just a Nicodemite, who was publicly a Catholic while privately still a Calvinist. Yet Henry was very faithful to the Huguenots and never sold them out. This does not mean, however, that he had abandoned his ultimate goal of religious unity. In a conversation with the cardinal of Florence in September 1598, the king made it clear that the garrisoned towns given to the Huguenots were only temporary, as he hoped to see all Protestants abjure and return to the Catholic church by 1606.[17] Even opponents of the Edict of Nantes, such as the magistrates in the Parlement of Rouen, recognized Henry's goal of religious unity; they just did not believe it could be accomplished under the edict. As they informed him in 1609 when they reluctantly and belatedly registered it, 'His Majesty's intention is to reduce [the Protestants] little by little to the Church ... which certainly would not happen if they were made on all points equal to the Catholics.'[18] Although his day to day decisions make clear that he was only trying to placate both Protestants and Catholics in an evenhanded and neutral manner, his religious sentiments ultimately lay in reuniting all his subjects within the Gallican church. There were numerous Huguenots at court and Henry even had a number in his council, none more important than the baron de Rosny, who was made duke of Sully in 1606. But the fact that Henry continued to support them throughout his reign should not obscure the fact of his ultimate goal of religious unity.

Henry had already supported one such effort, in fact, in the 1590s. Just after his abjuration and coronation he lent his support to an effort at reunification of the two churches by the Calvinist theologian, Jean de Serres. Although this effort never came to much, largely because it was denounced from Geneva, Henry clearly believed the policy was the only solution for a lasting peace.[19] A far more serious effort at religious unity was made in 1607 by Jean Hotman de Villiers, son of the Huguenot political theorist, François Hotman, and this effort was also strongly supported by Henry IV, according to the diary of Pierre de l'Estoile:

[17] Raymond Ritter, *Lettres de cardinal de Florence sur Henri IV et sur la France* (Paris, 1955), pp. 247–50.
[18] Quoted in Jonathan Dewald, *The Formation of a Provincial Nobility: The Magistrates of the Parlement of Rouen, 1499–1610* (Princeton, 1980), p. 49.
[19] W. B. Patterson, 'Jean de Serres and the Politics of Religious Pacification, 1594–98', in Derek Baker, ed., *Church, Society and Politics* (Oxford, 1975), pp. 223–44; and Pierre de l'Estoile, *Journal pour le règne de Henri IV*, ed. L-R. Lefebvre, 3 vols. (Paris, 1948–60), I, 521.

Monday, the 24th [of September 1607] M. de Hotman-Villiers came to see me and gave me a list of books and other writings to find, if I could, for the reformation of the church and the reunification of the two religions. Hotman and many other worthy men are working very hard toward this end, and he passed on to me a number of interesting details and said that he was working under the king's authorization. He told me that he found the king strongly in favour of this project. And just in the last few days the king has asked Cardinal Berberini to present to His Holiness [the Pope] a book on this subject written by one of his archbishops.[20]

Although this effort ultimately failed like the earlier one – in the end both churches saw the compromises necessary for reunion as apostasy – they indicate that Henry's seeming ecumenicism was oriented much more to a policy of concord than toleration.

And if concord were ever going to be a reality, Henry realized that it could only be within the traditional framework of the Gallican church. To this end, he made repeated efforts to convince many of the Huguenot nobility that they ought to emulate his example of 1593 and abjure their religion in order to reunite all French men and women under 'one king, one faith, one law'. He was not particularly successful in these efforts, and he did not pressure at all some of his closest and longest-serving Huguenot friends, such as Rosny. One notable failure was his own sister, Catherine de Bourbon, princess of Bar. Henry even assigned his own confessor, the Jesuit Father Coton, to work on his sister, but she remained steadfast in her Calvinist convictions. The point to underscore here is that Henry's efforts were vigorous even if his success was fairly modest. There were a number of successes, however, as a brief perusal of his published correspondence makes clear. One example among many that could be cited is the noble Jacques d'Hilaire, seigneur de Jovyac, who was governor of the town and château of Rochemaure in the Vivarais. Jovyac had served as a captain of a company of *gens d'armes* with Henry when royal forces captured Rochemaure from the League in December 1591. When Jovyac along with his entire family abjured Protestantism in April 1607, the nobleman wrote a short pamphlet about the experience and dedicated it to the king: *The Happy Conversion of the Huguenots* (Lyon, 1608). When he sent the king news of his family's conversion to Catholicism along with a copy of the pamphlet, Henry was obviously delighted:

Monsieur de Jovyac, I have received such joy and happiness from the news of your conversion to the Catholic church, along with a number of other persons, as well as from all the good work you have performed toward the same end, that I had to

---

[20] L'Estoile, *Journal pour le règne de Henri IV*, II, 271–2. Also see Mark Greengrass, *France in the Age of Henri IV* (London, 1984), p. 82; and Corrado Vivanti, *Lotta politica e pace religiosa in Francia fra Cinque e Seicento* (Turin, 1963), pp. 189–324.

write to tell you. And by the same token, I thank you for the book you have dedicated to me, seeing how it might bear a lot of fruit, not only those who might want to imitate you in this sacred and praiseworthy action, but also those who might just want to read it. You have made me recognize that you are, depending on what the situation requires, as handy with a pen as you are with a sword.[21]

Although Henry could not afford to alienate the majority of Huguenots who refused to abjure by overly rewarding those who did, Jovyac was nevertheless made a *gentilhomme ordinaire* of the king's bedchamber with a considerable stipend. Once again, Henry chose to use the carrot rather than the stick to get the Huguenots to rejoin the Catholic church. And even though the 1620s rather than the reign of Henry IV was the period of the most significant Protestant abjuration since St Bartholomew's Day, Henry hoped that the politics of appeasement could succeed where nearly four decades of civil war had failed to reunite the two faiths.

There was certainly opposition to Henry's attempted policy of reconciliation after the Edict of Nantes, none so more visible than several Huguenot leaders, chief among them being Philippe du Plessis-Mornay. Mornay bristled at the king's attempts to woo French Protestants back into the Catholic fold. And in an effort to disrupt any further abjurations, in 1598 just a few months after the publication of the Edict itself he published an incendiary treatise on the Catholic Mass titled *On the Institution, Usage and Doctrine of the Holy Sacrament of the Eucharist.*[22] In more than 1000 pages of text and using more than 5000 references to the Bible and the writings of the Church fathers and other sources on the early Christian Church, Mornay set out to prove that the Catholic Mass was a recent invention that had no basis in Scripture, and which was founded upon errors of interpretation as well as on the willful ignorance of several Popes. French Catholic reaction was immediate and unequivocal. The Sorbonne censured the book, while preachers throughout the capital of Paris attacked the work from the pulpit. Jesuits in Bordeaux urged the Parlement to burn all copies of the work. Even moderate Catholic intellectuals complained that Mornay's polemic had gone too far. Mornay's language made it very clear that the Catholic Mass was fit only for pigs and dogs in the street:

What kind of injury, then, does [the doctrine of] transubstantiation do our Lord, the precious pearl of the Gospel, inasmuch as it is offered [by Catholic priests] to hypocrites and unbelievers just as it is thrown out to dogs and swine, as if it were

---

[21] Berger de Xivrey, ed. *Recueil des lettres missives*, VII, 516–17.
[22] Philippe Duplessis-Mornay, *De l'Institution, usage et doctrine du Sainct Sacrement de l'Eucharistie, en l'Eglise Ancienne, Ensemble, Comment, Quand, & par quells Degrez la Messe s'est introduite en sa place* ([Genève]: Gabriel Cartier, 1599).

only a question of having a mouth into which to pour or a stomach into which to swallow.

Moreover, Mornay claimed that the Mass was 'just a heap of words and a variety of gestures', which did not truly unite Catholics to Christ as the Lord's Supper did. Instead, he claimed that Catholics 'neither eat nor drink either corporally or spiritually. They simply stare and gaze at the priest, who eats and drinks [for them], remaining all the while both deaf and dumb as they ponder this so-called mystery.'[23]

Thus, Mornay attacked the Catholic mass in terms designed to tear at the social fabric of France after the publication of the Edict of Nantes. Just as Henry IV and many moderate Huguenots as Catholics were attempting to forge a new social cohesion wherein Catholics and Protestants could live together peacefully, and where former Leaguers and Huguenots could work side by side at court and in the institutions of the nation, Mornay's treatise on the Catholic Mass argued forcefully and extensively that such social cohesion and religious co-existence was neither desirable nor, in fact, even possible. The unmistakable message of Mornay's book was that French Catholics – 'dogs and swine' – were not just outside the community of Christ, but that they were still enemies who threatened this community. The publication of Mornay's book was thus far more consequential than simply an erudite attempt to use Biblical scholarship to support a particular theological point of view. It was much more than that. Catholics viewed it as an unsheathed sword drawn to continue the very confessional battle that the Edict of Nantes was designed to bring to a close. By attacking the Catholic Mass, Mornay was also attacking the heart of Catholic society and public life in France. For those Huguenots who were attempting to become part of this public life, Mornay's treatise put them in a difficult position.

Mornay's treatise on the Catholic Mass attracted immediate responses in print from a variety of Catholic voices. One of the loudest of these voices was Jacques Davy du Perron, bishop of Evreux, a former Huguenot recently converted to Catholicism. In an effort to defend himself, Mornay reluctantly agreed to respond publicly to Du Perron's charge that he had discovered 500 errors of citation in the treatise. Henry IV himself condoned the exercise and even appointed four scholarly figures to adjudicate the debate, which took place at Fontainebleau on 4 May 1600. Of the 500 errors previously claimed by Du Perron, only nine were actually presented for Mornay to defend at Fontainebleau. And in the end, this august group could find fault in only two of the nine citations

---

[23] Ibid., pp. 939–40 and 1108–10.

defended by Mornay. Thus, of the more than 5,000 citations in the text, two were found not to be fully accurate. The king nevertheless decided that Du Perron had proved his case against Mornay, and the governor of Saumur's fall from grace was now complete. This aristocratic leader of the Huguenots during the religious wars was thus forced to retire from public life at court to his château at Saumur. Fighting back against the king's efforts at religious reunification could thus have serious consequences.

What might have happened had Henry IV not been struck down by an assassin in May 1610 is one of the most intriguing counter-factual questions of French history. His goal of 'one king, one faith, one law' by 1606 was overly ambitious, which even he recognized, as he was forced to renew the royal *brevet* guaranteeing the Huguenots' fortified towns for another eight years. Although he remained on very close terms with the Huguenots, the radicals in the Protestant assemblies were already becoming much more distant from the king even before his death. He certainly underestimated his former co-religionnaires' resistance to the pressures of abjuration, and it is doubtful that his efforts at reunification of the two churches were ever going to produce a sudden breakthrough.

But the Edict of Nantes did achieve what none of the previous peace settlements had managed: a lasting peace. For all its weaknesses, exceptions, and contingencies, the Edict of Nantes did result in Protestants and Catholics agreeing to lay down their arms. To be sure, the peace depended on the delicate balance of Henry's politics of appeasement. Wary Catholics, especially former Leaguers, were placated less by royal patronage than by Henry's commitment to a France reunited under the Gallican church. That same commitment worried the Huguenots, however. Although they were appeased by the knowledge that the king would never *force* them to abandon their religion, they clearly recognized that their legal recognition and protection depended entirely on royal largesse. That largesse was seriously jeopardized in May 1610 when Henry was murdered, by another zealous Catholic unhappy with the religious commitment of the king (just as in Henry III's murder in 1589). He had long since received papal dispensation to divorce his Protestant wife Marguerite of Navarre and had married a Catholic, Marie de Medici, daughter of the Grand Duke of Tuscany and niece of the former Queen Mother. Henry's only legitimate son was the dauphin Louis, not yet even nine years old. Thus, the Huguenots found their fate in the hands of a Catholic dowager-queen as regent and a royal council dominated by Catholics, including a number of former Leaguers. The parallel with the situation half a century earlier at the death of Henry IV's grandfather, Henry II, was striking, and Huguenots all over France could not help wondering what would become of the fragile peace.

7   Epilogue: the last war of religion, 1610–1629

The previous chapter attempted to revise the traditional view that the Edict of Nantes was intended to be a permanent settlement of religious toleration. Equally untenable is the notion that the Huguenot 'state within the state' would have survived intact only had Henry IV not been assassinated and replaced by first a regent and then a new monarch, neither of whom was as sympathetic to the Protestants as was Henry. To begin with, when Henry reluctantly renewed the *brevet* guaranteeing the Huguenot fortified towns, he halved the annual subsidy provided by the crown to garrison them. Moreover, the annual subsidies were already well in arrears, and nowhere near the sums promised in the *brevet* were ever disbursed to the Huguenots. Second, the judicial components of the edict, particularly the bi-partisan *chambres mi-parties*, proved not to be as effective in enforcing the rest of the edict as the Protestants had hoped. Not only did the magistrates in the various parlements procrastinate and drag their feet in implementing the new chambers, but there was institutional resistance to the Protestant judges throughout the sovereign courts. Although Henry himself never made any advance against the Huguenots' freedom of conscience, it is simply not true that the many concessions they won in the edict only began to erode after Henry's assassination.[1] The irony, of course, is that to Henry's murderer, François Ravaillac, and many ultra-Catholics, the king had not done nearly enough to force the Huguenots' return to the mother church.

With Henry's young son not yet even nine years old, the king's widow, Marie de Medici, became sole regent until Louis XIII reached his majority. Reared a devout Catholic in Italy, she could never be the kind of patron to the Huguenots that Henry IV had been. Even more injurious to the Protestant cause, however, was the fact that the Huguenots' ally on the royal council, the superintendent of finances, the duke of Sully, found

---

[1] For a superb analysis of the problems with the bi-partisan *chambres mi-parties*, see Diane C. Margolf, *Religion and Royal Justice in Early Modern France: The Paris Chambre de l'Edit, 1598–1665* (Kirksville, 2003).

himself isolated and virtually powerless to influence affairs. Those with the closest ear of the new regent, in fact, were the grey-bearded former Leaguers like Pierre Jeannin, Nicolas de Neufville, seigneur de Villeroy, and the chancellor Nicolas Brûlart, sieur de Sillery. Although these councillors had been moderate Leaguers in the 1590s, a more radical, and ultramontane (pro-papal) faction was already in the ascendant. While the king's privy council had been dominated by Catholics during Henry's reign, at least the Huguenots felt they had a spokesman at court. When the beleaguered Sully resigned from the council in disgust in early 1611, however, Protestants all over France had good reason to wonder whether the Edict of Nantes would ever be enforced again.[2]

The Huguenots' own position after the murder of Henry IV was thus one of perceived insecurity. And though the nobility had managed to wrest control of the movement already by 1610, this insecurity only underscored the aristocratic dominance. The noble leadership among the Protestant ranks was anything but united, however, on what policies to pursue. With the resignation of Sully from the council in 1611, there remained only a few natural aristocratic leaders. Henri II de Bourbon, prince of Condé, grandson of Louis de Bourbon, the first prince of Condé in the 1560s, had as a young child abjured the Protestant religion during the reign of Henry III. Moreover, he would become one of the most severe persecutors of the Huguenots over the next two decades. Henri de la Tour d'Auvergne, duke of Bouillon, a much older military warrior who fought alongside Condé's father during the 1570s and 1580s, and Henri, duke of Rohan, who grew up during the height of the Catholic League, were almost by default the only two Hugenot noblemen able to wield significant influence after the forced resignation of Sully. There were a few old hands around, such as Philippe du Plessis-Mornay, but they, like Sully, found themselves to be hostage to a new era of leadership. The experienced duke of Bouillon, who was a less than loyal servant of Henry IV, urged the Huguenots to trust the regent as they had trusted her husband. His pleas for support fell on deaf ears, however, as the Protestants were seeking a more militant voice to protect them from further encroachments against the Edict of Nantes. Thus, at the Huguenot assembly held at Saumur in 1611, ostensibly a religious assembly to elect two deputies to reside at court to supervise the enforcement of the peace, the Huguenots turned over the political and military leadership of their cause to the thirty-two year old Henri, duke of Rohan.

---

[2] On the council under the regency see Richard Bonney, 'Was There a Bourbon Style of Government?', in Keith Cameron, ed., *From Valois to Bourbon: Dynasty, State and Society in Early Modern France* (Exeter, 1989), p. 173.

Supported by a number of other grandees such as La Force (royal governor in Béarn), Soubise (Rohan's younger brother), and Châtillon (grandson of Admiral Coligny), Rohan's policy of militancy won out over Bouillon's pleas for caution. Moreover, the Saumur assembly underscored the total re-politicization of the Huguenot movement led by the grandees, something the Edict of Nantes had been designed explicitly to prevent.[3]

Over the next three years two related developments served to exacerbate even further the tensions between the crown and the Huguenots. The first was the rise at court of the Italian Concino Concini, husband of one of Marie de Medici's closest friends. Not only was the Catholic Concini overtly hostile to the Huguenots, but he favoured a much closer relationship between France and the Papacy. This favourite of the regent soon replaced the old guard of Jeannin, Villeroy, and Brûlart as the strongest influence on policy at court, and his sudden rise to prominence was viewed with apprehension by most Protestants. Second, the rise to prominence of Concini alienated many of the other aristocratic grandees at court, such as Condé, resulting in increased tension between many of the traditional nobles at court and the regency government. The end result of both these developments was a revolt by a significant number of the court nobility against the regency government in January 1614. Condé, the nominal leader of the rebels, was particularly upset by the marriage negotiations going on on behalf of the young Louis XIII. Marie de Medici and Concini had both sought an alliance with Spain by trying to arrange marriage pacts between Louis and the daughter of Philip III of Spain, Anne of Austria, as well as between Louis's sister Elisabeth and Anne's brother. Condé issued a manifesto in the name of the young king, declaring that 'the Queen, your mother, was from the beginning constrained for the health of your State to accord to the most powerful unjust benefits, contrary to your authority'. He called for the king to convoke the Estates-General in order to restore a proper balance of power to the council and for the public good. As the princes began trying to mobilize support for their cause, both they and Marie de Medici sought the support of the Huguenots.[4]

---

[3] Victor-L. Tapié, *France in the Age of Louis XIII and Richelieu*, trans. D. M. Lockie (London, 1974), pp. 68–9.

[4] Manifesto of 1614 quoted in Jeffrey K. Sawyer, *Printed Poison: Pamphlet Propaganda, Faction Politics, and the Public Sphere in Early Seventeenth-century France* (Berkeley, 1990), p. 31. Also see Arlette Jouanna, *Le devoir de révolte: La noblesse française et la gestation de l'Etat moderne, 1559–1661* (Paris, 1989), pp. 212–44.

Although the Huguenots managed to avoid becoming involved in the revolt of the princes directly, the fact that many of the Protestant princes supported this revolt meant that the fate of the Protestant cause in France was inevitably tied to the aristocratic rebellion. The Estates-General was convoked shortly after Louis reached his age of majority – his fourteenth year – in October 1614, but it did not resolve the unpopularity of the regency government. Nothing really changed, since Louis made his mother head of his council. Moreover, at the meeting of the Estates the few Protestant deputies in attendance discovered that there was an explicit move afoot to deprive them of their remaining privileges. Although a deputy from the first estate, the young bishop of Luçon (the future Cardinal Richelieu), seemed to imply that the Catholic clergy only desired their conversion, the general *cahier* (list of grievances) of the clergy sounded a much more ominous note. It called for the banning of the 'so-called reformed religion' outright as well as the suppression of the Huguenots' fortified towns. Moreover, the clergy demanded that the Protestants return all church property they had seized as well as rebuild all churches they had destroyed. Finally, the Estates-General did nothing to settle the revolt of the princes, as they continued their dispute with Marie de Medici and Concini the following year. The Huguenots were still caught in the middle. They did not desire a return to civil war, yet they could only lament their declining status at court.[5]

The revolt of the princes came to a head in April 1617 when, amidst the propaganda war aimed at Marie de Medici and Concini, the young Louis XIII decided to assert his own authority. He had Concini imprisoned and later killed, while he exiled his mother to the royal château at Blois. Dismissing all his mother's councillors, he recalled all the former servants of Henry IV that she and Concini had previously discarded. The removal of the regent and Concini did not mean a reprieve for the Huguenots, however, for Louis himself vowed to 'work towards the ruin of the Huguenots, if given the opportunity'.[6] And the opportunity that presented itself was that of reuniting the principality of Béarn to the French crown. The restoration of Catholic worship and all church property in the independent Bourbon principality of Béarn had been one of the conditions of Henry's absolution by the pope in 1595. As this territory was technically not covered by the Edict of Nantes, many French Catholics (including Henry IV) considered the anomaly of Béarn in the extreme southwest to

[5] J. Michael Hayden, *France and the Estates General of 1614* (Cambridge, 1974), pp. 181–2.
[6] Quoted in Christian Desplat, 'Louis XIII and the Union of Béarn to France', in Mark Greengrass, ed., *Conquest and Coalescence: The Shaping of the State in Early Modern Europe* (London, 1991), p. 69.

be in need of correction. In fact, Henry IV had made an effort to correct it in 1595 with the Edict of Fontainebleau, which allowed the relocation of Catholics in a limited number of areas. Enforcement of this edict was extremely slow in coming, however. Encouraged by his Catholic clergy, Louis XIII issued an Edict of Restitution in June 1617 requiring all church property seized since 1569 to be restored to the Catholic church. When opposition to this edict emerged in the Béarnese capital of Pau in the spring of 1618, Louis was forced to put together a royal army to enforce it upon the recalcitrant Protestants. It was even more troubling for the king when he learned that just as some of his own Protestant subjects were rebelling against royal authority in Pau, a similar rebellion by Protestants in Prague threatened Habsburg rule in Bohemia.

The military campaign of the king's army through the southwest in the summer of 1620 (Map 9) was an exercise in establishing royal authority. Although most French Protestants had been loyal to the crown throughout the regency and reign of Louis XIII, the king was determined to expose and root out those few Huguenot militants who might be able to rouse significant opposition to the crown. And even though the army he led to Béarn was pitifully undermanned and ill-equipped to deal with much serious opposition, Louis was determined to show those Huguenot militants that he was prepared to uphold the laws governing religious coexistence for Catholics as well as Protestants. Fortunately, his army never had to fight. First the Protestant governor of Béarn, the duke of La Force, recognized the danger of resisting the king and obediently submitted. And with the king's rag-tag army on the outskirts of Pau in October, local magistrates hastily registered the Edict of Restitution and turned over the city's large church of St Martin to Catholic clergy for the first time in fifty years. Louis XIII entered the city of Pau on 15 October 1620 without a shot being fired, and five days later he attended mass and participated in a procession of the Holy Sacrament through the city. Thus, Catholicism as well as royal authority were re-established in Pau without bloodshed. And though legally the royal campaign to Béarn in 1620 did not alter the crown's relationship with the other French Huguenots, news and propaganda of the event sent shockwaves rippling throughout the Protestant community.[7]

Nowhere was the news of the submission of Béarn received with greater alarm than in the fortified port city of La Rochelle, the Huguenot stronghold that was dominated by some of the most militant voices in the Protestant movement. 'I believe', wrote Anne de Rohan, 'that soon they [the royal army] will besiege La Rochelle ... certainly they have sworn to

[7] Ibid., pp. 71–5.

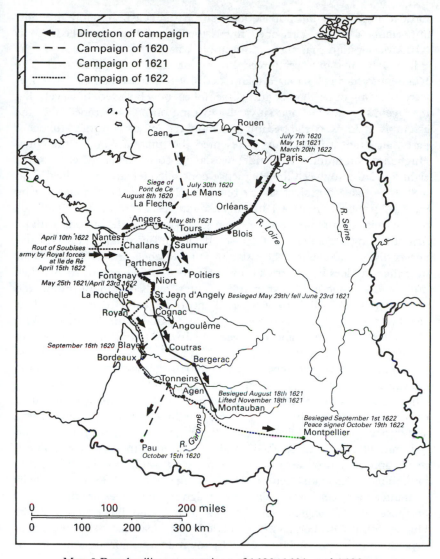

Legend:
- Direction of campaign
- Campaign of 1620
- Campaign of 1621
- Campaign of 1622

Rouen

Caen

July 7th 1620
May 1st 1621
March 20th 1622
Paris

Siege of
Pont de Ce
August 8th 1620

July 30th 1620
Le Mans

La Fleche

Orléans

R. Loire

R. Seine

Angers
May 8th 1621
Tours

Blois

April 10th 1622 Nantes

Rout of Soubises
army by Royal forces
at Ile de Ré
April 15th 1622

Challans
Saumur

Parthenay

Fontenay
May 25th 1621/April 23rd 1622
Niort
Poitiers

La Rochelle

St Jean d'Angely *Besieged May 29th/ fell June 23rd 1621*

Royan
Cognac

Angoulême

September 16th 1620 Blaye
Coutras

Bordeaux
Bergerac

Tonneins

Agen

*Besieged August 18th 1621
Lifted November 18th 1621*
Montauban

R. Garonne

*Besieged September 1st 1622
Peace signed October 19th 1622*
Montpellier

Pau
October 15th 1620

R. Garonne

0   100   200 miles
0   100   200   300 km

Map 9 Royal military campaigns of 1620, 1621, and 1622

finish us'.[8] Just six weeks after the submission of Béarn, the Huguenots decided to strengthen their military readiness there as well as bolster their political organization by calling for an assembly at La Rochelle, the most

---

[8] Quoted in David Parker, *La Rochelle and the French Monarchy: Conflict and Order in Seventeenth-century France* (London, 1980), p. 31.

fortified and, given its strategic location on the coast, arguably the most important of all the garrisoned towns the Huguenots controlled. Louis XIII's declaration that such an assembly was illegal and contrary to the Edict of Nantes only reinforced Protestant fears of royal reprisal. The Huguenots, having long since abandoned any pretence that their assemblies were anything other than political assemblies, now believed, however, that they were fighting for their survival. Opening on 28 November 1620 the assembly at La Rochelle became the supreme authority of the Huguenot party, although it really only represented the militant wing of the entire Huguenot community. A grandee was assigned to safeguard each of the eight 'circles' into which the Huguenot-controlled territory was divided, as well as to take control of all tax revenues. None of these nobles – who included Rohan, Soubise, Châtillon, Lesdiguières, La Force, and Bouillon – was permitted to make peace or even sign a truce with the king without first obtaining the consent of the assembly itself. According to the contemporary historian Malingre, the assembly at La Rochelle 'ruled like a republic over the grandees who carried on its war, recognising no one higher than itself, and keeping in its own hands all the threads of administration and absolute power'.[9] Malingre was overtly hostile to the Huguenots, and his views were part of the royal propaganda campaign that the Huguenots were clearly seditious rebels and deserved royal retribution. Nevertheless, his perception that the political assembly at La Rochelle had gone well beyond the bounds of loyal subjects was true enough. Louis had no hesitation in declaring all involved in the assembly as guilty of *lèse-majesté* (high treason). The Huguenots had indeed trespassed upon royal authority by issuing their own commissions for the levying of troops, administering their own justice, and setting up their own fiscal and political machinery of government. Louis did warn all those at La Rochelle of his intentions to treat them as seditious rebels and offered protection to all those who would remain obedient to him. The Huguenots' refusal of the king's offers, however, virtually guaranteed another royal military campaign in 1621. Despite the rhetoric of those like Malingre about the Huguenot 'republic', however, the Huguenots' political organization made it very clear that they were still as dependent on their nobility as ever. In any military confrontation with the crown, their fate would necessarily rest in aristocratic hands.

Unlike the campaign of the previous year, the 1621 expedition resulted in some resistance and eventual military confrontation in the form of two extended sieges. The fortified town of St-Jean d'Angély, where Rohan was governor, fell to royal forces on 23 June 1621 after a month-long

[9] Quoted in A. D. Lublinskaya, *French Absolutism: The Crucial Phase, 1620–1629*, trans. Brian Pearce (Cambridge, 1968), p. 173.

siege. St-Jean d'Angély was the principal fortress guarding the land side of La Rochelle and its submission to the king only foreshadowed what lay in store for the Rochelois. The other major conflict of 1621 was at Montauban, which was besieged in August. After La Rochelle, Montauban was the largest Protestant stronghold and it served as a bulwark to protect most of lower Languedoc. Moreover, after the fall of St-Jean d'Angély the dukes of Rohan and La Force made it the base of their resistance to the crown. Unlike the siege of St-Jean d'Angély, however, the royal army proved susceptible to disease and lack of pay. After only six weeks the royal army was reduced to one-fourth its original size due to defections, and Louis was forced to lift the siege in mid-November due to the oncoming winter. The respite was only temporary, as royal pressure on the Huguenots continued the following spring.

There were voices at court that tried to persuade the king that his forced suppression of the Huguenots might be counterproductive. Some of the old guard who had been around in the wars of the League thirty years before tried to remind him that four decades of civil war had not resulted in the total defeat of the Protestants, and there was no reason to think a policy of suppression would work now. One of the most vocal critics of royal policy was Pierre Jeannin, a president in the Parlement of Paris and comptroller of finances during the regency. Jeannin had been a moderate Leaguer in his native Burgundy in the 1590s, where he was a member of the Parlement of Dijon. Having supported the surrender to Henry IV in 1595, Jeannin was rewarded with a promotion to the Parlement of Paris and further perquisites under Henry and the regency government of Marie de Medici. This senior magistrate urged Louis to emphasize that the campaign against the Huguenots was the result of sedition rather than their religion. Any effort to make the campaign a 'war of religion' was likely to unite the Protestants as well as push them into the arms of Protestant powers abroad. Given the nature of the war in Germany, this was no remote possibility. 'We should fear lest France becomes the theatre for the acting out of this bloody tragedy which will decide the religious issues at stake for the whole of Christendom', Jeannin lamented.

It is certain Sire that as long as there is a faction amongst those of the 'religion prétendue réformée' which is powerful enough to trouble the state and resist your commands, that your authority will never be absolute, nor the peace of your subjects assured; that is why it is necessary above all to work incessantly and with great diligence to weaken them and to bring them back to their duty and to the obedience of good subjects.

The best way to do this, however, was not with force. Jeannin believed in Henry IV's politics of appeasement as well as letting God and the clergy work to try to encourage the Huguenots to abjure of their own free will. This policy was actually working, he argued, until it was 'disrupted by the indiscreet zeal of a number of naive and short-sighted Catholics and the ambitious designs of others'.[10]

Encouraged by the Catholic clergy as well as a number of *dévots* at court, Louis reminded those such as Jeannin that it was well and good to leave the conversion of the Huguenots up to God. However, he was God's anointed sword on earth and he could hardly stand by idly having promised in his coronation oath to eradicate all heresy from the kingdom. More to the point, Louis could single out the many Protestant nobles who had abjured their faith and sided with the king ever since the opening of the Huguenot assembly at La Rochelle. The prince of Condé had long since made his peace with the king and had permanently abandoned the Huguenots for royal service. But in 1621 Marshal Châtillon, grandson of Coligny, abjured his faith and entered royal service, closely followed by the duke of Lesdiguières, the leader of the Protestant party in Dauphiné. With the dukes of Bouillon and La Force choosing to remain neutral (which effec- tively meant they had abandoned the Huguenots at La Rochelle as well), only Rohan and his brother Soubise remained of the grandee leadership on which the Huguenots were so reliant. Louis XIII rewarded Lesdiguières for his submission to the crown and the Catholic faith with the position of Constable of France (the highest military appointment in France). The king also used the large annual sums provided by the Catholic clergy as pensions to offer to any Huguenot pastors who would abjure. Thus, Louis had determined to make use of the carrot and stick simultaneously.[11]

The spring of 1622 saw the renewal of the military campaign against the Huguenots begun the previous summer, and this time royal pressure resulted in the total isolation of the citadel of La Rochelle. The first major confrontation occurred just south of Nantes on the Atlantic coast at the Ile de Ré. Here in the marshes of Poitou a Huguenot army under the command of the Duke of Soubise was cut off and routed by royal forces on 15 April 1622. Two to three thousand Protestant soldiers were killed, nearly a thousand others drowned in the marshland, and seven hundred were taken prisoner. Thus, not only was Poitou lost to the Huguenots, along with all the resources and revenue that it generated, it began the process of royal recovery of one Huguenot town after another. After the stunning victory at the Ile de Ré the royal army headed south- ward once again for the third summer in a row. The target this time was

---

[10] Quoted in Parker, *La Rochelle and the French Monarchy*, pp. 139–40.
[11] On the abjurations and conversions of nobility and clergy, see ibid., pp. 141–3; and Lublinskaya, *French Absolutism*, pp. 158–9.

not Montauban but Montpellier, where Rohan was making a final stand. En route dozens of towns willingly submitted to royal authority, and others such as the town of Royan, gave in after only token resistance. By the end of August Louis and his forces had reached Montpellier to begin the siege. Having lost one fortress after another over the previous six months, and having been depleted of nearly all its aristocratic leadership, the Huguenots were in a much weaker position than they had been the year before. When the assembly at La Rochelle finally granted Rohan its consent to negotiate a peace with the king, the siege quickly came to an end. The peace edict published at Montpellier on 19 October 1622 was a total defeat for the Protestants. They were required to give up all the fortified towns that had submitted to the king – nearly a hundred, roughly half of those they controlled – while the garrisons guaranteed in the remaining Huguenot towns by the royal *brevet* from the Edict of Nantes would expire in 1625 without renewal. Louis had at last conquered the Midi so long dominated by the Huguenots. All Protestant political assemblies were explicitly forbidden, and the loopholes allowed by the Edict of Nantes were duly eliminated. Thus, the Huguenots lost much more than just a war: they lost their military and political organization. After the Peace of Montpellier there was no more 'state within the state'. In fact, the sole remaining resistance was in the isolated citadel of La Rochelle.[12]

The final phase of the last war of religion focused explicitly on recovering this last bastion of Huguenot strength. That it would take another six years to accomplish was largely due to political circumstances both domestic and foreign to which the Protestant cause was tied. It ought to be stressed, however, that it was the campaigns of 1620–22 that broke the back of the Protestant state and army. Indeed, had there not been further outbreaks of explicit rebellion against royal authority within La Rochelle in 1625 and 1627, the final siege may not have even been necessary. As it happened, La Rochelle recognized that it could not hold out against the king alone, and its determined isolation from 1622 to 1628 rested on the hope of assistance from abroad, most likely from England. This hope was not without some justification, as James I, the king of England, had often promised the Huguenots English support. But due to the political

---

[12] For terms of the Peace of Montpellier see Lublinskaya, *French Absolutism*, pp. 210–11. For a good summary of the Huguenot position after the Peace of Montpellier, see N. M. Sutherland, 'The Crown, the Huguenots, and the Edict of Nantes', in Richard M. Golden, ed., *The Huguenot Connection: The Edict of Nantes, Its Revocation, and Early French Migration to South Carolina* (Dordrecht and Boston, 1988), pp. 45–8.

situation in France and elsewhere in Europe in the 1620s, this long-sought English aid never materialized.[13]

On the domestic side the political event in France that most dramatically affected the status of the Huguenots in La Rochelle was the appointment to the royal council in 1624 of Armand-Jean du Plessis, Cardinal de Richelieu. Richelieu was a protégé of Marie de Medici, and his earlier career had been in the church. Appointed as bishop of Luçon when he was only 22, he had studied at the Sorbonne where he developed a serious interest in Gallican reform. And although he was no *dévot*, Richelieu was a serious reformer who conscientiously tried to introduce some of the post-Tridentine reforms of the Counter Reformation into his diocese. That he was largely unsuccessful was due more to the endemic problems he faced in Luçon than to his commitment to reform. It is often overlooked, however, that Richelieu had been a committed bishop and had established his career through the church before he ever entered politics. He grew up during the heyday of the Catholic League and his perception of the Huguenots was clearly tainted by the legacy of the Wars of Religion of the sixteenth century. For him, heresy and sedition went hand in hand, and this was always part of his permanent distrust of the French Huguenots.[14] While Richelieu could not totally dominate the council (at least until his appointment as first minister on the Day of Dupes in 1630), his influence was very great from the beginning despite his being a creature of the Queen Mother rather than the king. In the long run, his appointment to the king's privy council in 1624 did not bode well for the Huguenots.

Richelieu was a man of much broader vision than a mere Huguenot fighter, however, and he recognized that the authority and security of the French crown hinged to some degree on the outcome of international events that were quickly overtaking most of Europe. The rebellion in Bohemia against the Habsburg Emperor soon escalated into a pan-European war – the Thirty Years' War – as pro-Habsburg and anti-Habsburg states joined the struggle. Indeed, the crisis had almost become a referendum on the Habsburg domination of central and southern Europe. French hostility to the Habsburgs went back to the Italian wars of the late fifteenth and early sixteenth centuries, a rivalry that was intensified by Spanish support of the Catholic League in the 1580s and

---

[13] See Simon Adams, 'The Road to La Rochelle: English Foreign Policy and the Huguenots, 1610–1629', *Proceedings of the Huguenot Society of London*, vol. 22 (1975), 423–5; and idem, 'Foreign Policy and the Parliaments of 1621 and 1624', in Kevin Sharpe, ed., *Faction and Parliament: Essays on Early Stuart History* (Oxford, 1978), pp. 139–71.

[14] See Joseph Bergin, *The Rise of Richelieu* (New Haven, 1991), esp. pp. 86–106.

1590s. And it was Spanish Habsburg preponderance rather than Austrian Habsburg hegemony in Bohemia that most concerned Louis XIII and Richelieu. By 1625 Spanish troops were already occupying much of northern Italy and threatening the French border. While other ministers were counselling the king to stay out of the war against the Habsburgs, Richelieu made it very clear that Louis's own authority in France could be jeopardized if Habsburg expansion went unchecked. It was nevertheless obvious that Louis could hardly wage a war at home against the Huguenots while waging war abroad against the Spanish. The crisis escalated even further that same year when Soubise fled to England to seek support for the Huguenots, and at the same time began negotiating with Catholic Spain, who were only too glad to try to exacerbate French problems. When Soubise managed to seize the islands of Ré and Oléron off the coast of La Rochelle, making foreign intervention much easier by sea in January 1625, Louis XIII was faced with a serious problem. Spanish action in Italy as well as their intrigues with Soubise demanded an immediate response. But how could France engage in a foreign war while still trying to put down rebellion at home?

Ignoring the pleas of some on the council to stay out of any foreign dispute, Richelieu was in no doubt of what was necessary. Some kind of immediate accommodation with the Huguenots was required to enable Louis to engage the Spanish abroad. In early May 1625 he wrote a long memorandum to the king on the subject:

> As for the Huguenots, they are accustomed to advance their cause at the expense of the State, and to seize their opportunity when they see us occupied against those who are our declared enemies. They did so during the siege of Amiens [in 1597 during the reign of Henry IV]. We must fear that they will do the same on this occasion. Their taking to arms and insolent demands remove all doubt about it. However, it is necessary to see whether or not their power is sufficient to stop the King from following his plans for foreign war ... As long as the Huguenots have a foothold in France, the King will never be master at home and will never be able to undertake any glorious action abroad ... His Majesty may give [some temporary] satisfaction to the Huguenots. He will thus be able to create unity for the war against the Spaniards.[15]

This same advice was repeated more forcefully in another memorandum later that same year:

> It is certain that as long as the Huguenot party subsists in France, the King will not be absolute in his kingdom, and he will not be able to establish the order and rule

---

[15] Memorandum of Richelieu to the King, May 1625, in Richard Bonney, ed., *Society and Government in France under Richelieu and Mazarin, 1624–1661* (New York and London, 1988), pp. 4–6.

to which his conscience obliges him and which the necessity of his people requires. It is also necessary to destroy the pride of the great nobles, who regard La Rochelle as a citadel in whose shadow they can demonstrate their discontent with impunity. It is besides certain that no one will dare to undertake anything glorious abroad, nor even to oppose foreign ambitions, because the Huguenot party will seek to profit from the situation, as it did in the last war … [However,] prudence does not permit the undertaking of two wars at the same time. It is not known when the war in Italy will end. However, it would seem that one should settle the civil war, chiefly because the occasion to deal with the Huguenots will return, whereas if one loses the opportunity to deal with the foreigners' ambitions it will not be possible to do so again in a single attempt … If we make peace within the kingdom, there is nothing to be feared if they [the Spanish] invade, and it is likely that they will not undertake this course of action. But if we are well embarked on the siege of La Rochelle, they would certainly do so with impunity, and in such circumstances we would have to abandon the siege.[16]

Richelieu's proposal eventually swayed the king, who agreed to a temporary truce with the Huguenots of La Rochelle in order to escalate French reprisals against Spain in northern Italy.

Thus, anxieties about the Huguenots resulted not in an immediate siege but in yet another peace edict. The Edict of La Rochelle, signed on 6 February 1626, virtually ended any chance of a revival of Huguenot independence. Unable to acquire any meaningful aid from either England or Spain, Soubise was forced to submit to the king's terms: his life was spared and he was pardoned for his past rebellion in return for loyal service in the king's army. Any forthcoming aid from England was eliminated by the marriage pact between Louis XIII's sister Henrietta and Charles I of England in 1625, as the pact required Charles to desist from any further negotiations with the Huguenots. More importantly, the oligarchy of merchants and shipbuilders who had been temporarily replaced in La Rochelle by the Huguenot militants was restored to power. Catholic worship was restored throughout the city, and all ecclesiastical property seized by the Huguenots was restored to the church. The Edict of La Rochelle seemingly made any siege of the city unnecessary.[17] The prince of Condé wrote to the king that 'La Rochelle is without land, without islands, without sea, without soldiers, without vessels; there remains only six months without real fighting. She is yours.'[18]

That a siege of La Rochelle became necessary, however, was again the result of explicit rebellion against the crown. When Charles I of England caved in to Puritan appeals to aid the Huguenots in 1627 despite the

---

[16] Memorandum of Richelieu to the King, 25 November 1625, in ibid., pp. 7–8.

[17] For details of the edict, see Lublinskaya, *French Absolutism*, pp. 216–17.

[18] Quoted in Parker, *La Rochelle and the French Monarchy*, p. 15.

marriage agreement with Louis XIII, Rohan and Soubise quickly seized the chance. Although the two princes had difficulty attracting much support either from the Rochelais or elsewhere in the Protestant south-west to support their rebellion, they managed to get Charles I to send an English fleet under the command of the Duke of Buckingham in July. Buckingham attacked the royal garrison at St Martin on the Ile de Ré, though the French troops managed to hold off the initial advance. Having concluded a truce with Spain the year before – the irony of all Richelieu's polemic about the necessity of a foreign war against Spain was that it ended in a matter of months – Louis was able to send reinforcements to La Rochelle to supplement the royal garrison on the Ile de Ré. By the end of August 1627, there were about 15,000 French troops surrounding the citadel of La Rochelle and the final siege was officially underway. Even though the militant Huguenots seized control of the city once more, signed their own treaty with England in September, and thus joined in Rohan's and Soubise's rebellion, the outcome was never in doubt.

The turning point for the Rochelais came in November, when the English fleet was finally driven into the sea and permanently repelled. Without foreign support, the citadel's thick walls and proud towers that had safeguarded and protected the city for so long became its prison as siege warfare took its toll on the incarcerated population. Cut off on the land side by the royal army and on the seaward side by the royal fortresses on the islands as well as a large dyke Richelieu ingeniously constructed, the isolated city of La Rochelle quickly felt the ravages of famine and disease. Its predicament was much like that of the capital of Paris in 1590 when the capital was besieged by Henry of Navarre and a royalist army. Because the Rochelois had no duke of Parma to come to their rescue, however, the siege of La Rochelle lasted much longer than the siege of Paris and proved far deadlier as a result. For fourteen long months the Rochelois held out and resisted the many overtures of peace, as the very young and the very old, the weak and the ill died of famine and starvation. Out of a population of more than 25,000 at the outset of the siege in August 1627, nearly half died before the final submission came. Since about 5,000 more fled in the process, there were only about 5,000 to 8,000 Huguenots still remaining in the starving citadel when necessity forced a surrender on 28 October 1628. Four days later, on All Saints Day, about two o'clock in the after-noon, Louis XIII and Cardinal Richelieu personally escorted the royal army into the beleaguered city. As one contemporary remarked, what they discovered there was 'a city of ghosts, not people'.[19]

[19] Quoted in Lublinskaya, *French Absolutism*, p. 219. For details of the siege, see ibid., pp. 217–20, and Parker, *La Rochelle and the French Monarchy*, pp. 15–17.

Although the duke of Rohan managed to escape before the surrender and was at large seeking shelter in one Huguenot town after another throughout Languedoc for another eight months, the siege of La Rochelle was the final nail in the coffin of an already weakened and defenceless Huguenot republic. Rohan too eventually gave in to royal pressure to submit, and the result was the peace edict of Alais signed on 16 June 1629. Ending the ten-year effort by Louis XIII to force the Huguenot rebels to submit to royal authority, the edict also was the last in the long line of peace edicts that the crown made with the French Protestants starting with the first in January 1562. Its terms were surprisingly simple: the edict simply recognized the articles of the original text of the Edict of Nantes, that is, shorn of the royal *brevets* that gave the Huguenots their political and military independence. In effect, this final peace underscored the ideal of Catholic concord and unity spelled out in the Edict of Nantes, but it totally destroyed the corporate existence of the Huguenots, leaving them as heretics in a Catholic world. Although they had managed to hold out heroically against the force of suppression used by Louis XIII for so long, the fact that the Edict of Nantes was still upheld after such a catastrophic defeat only underscores how much of a Catholic vision Louis XIII and Richelieu had in attacking the Protestants' political privileges and legal violations. In sum, then, the final defeat of the Huguenot militants was the result of neither Machiavellian machinations of Louis XIII and Richelieu nor any abandonment of the policies of Henry IV; ultimately, it was three decades of living under the Edict of Nantes and its goal of 'one faith, one king, one law' that ultimately brought about the Huguenots' defeat. One is forced to agree with Professor N. M. Sutherland's conclusion that 'for thirty years they [the Huguenot rebels] had flouted the Edict [of Nantes], claiming more than it accorded. Now their corporate existence was extinguished and their defences destroyed, but quite as much by time and their own failings as by any action of the crown.'[20]

Although the last of the Wars of Religion ended with a stinging defeat for the rebellious Huguenot strongholds, the destiny of the entire Protestant community until 1685 when Louis XIII's son, Louis XIV, revoked the Edict of Nantes was surprisingly stable. To be sure, they were forced to exist as a heretical minority in a Catholic world, and by 1629 they were an even smaller minority than they had been in 1598. But after the siege of La Rochelle the numbers of Huguenots throughout the kingdom declined only slightly, as the faith held on to a majority of its

---

[20] Sutherland, 'The Crown, the Huguenots, and the Edict of Nantes', p. 48.

adherents. Moreover, they remained a very stable community institution-
ally, even without the benefit of their political assemblies. As Philip
Benedict has recently noted, 'the rapid rejection of prohibitions against
Lent and Advent marriages, the steady advance of a Protestant understanding of baptism, and the low rates of extramarital sexual activity all
suggest a religious community in which the moral and theological princi-
ples articulated by the church leaders were widely shared among the
faithful'.[21] At the same time, the evidence suggests that Protestants and
Catholics were better able to co-exist in the seventeenth century than they
had been in the sixteenth. This was partly due to the fact that by 1629,
with the Huguenots soundly defeated and disarmed and the Gallican
mantra of 'one king, one faith, one law' publicly restored, the
Huguenots were no longer perceived as the demons and pollutants of
Catholic culture they had once been. The demographic evidence even
suggests that in areas where Protestants were a minority, they were as
receptive as their Catholic neighbours to the wide variety of folk beliefs
about lucky and unlucky seasons to marry (customs and habits that both
the Protestant and Catholic churches were doing their best to destroy).
On the other hand, in Protestant regions where Catholics were a minority, Catholics also showed a tendency to postpone the baptism of their
children by a week or more as was the Protestant custom. Thus, 'a degree
of interpenetration of religious practices clearly occurred between the two
confessional groups living side by side in seventeenth-century France.
They were not [the] hermetically sealed communities of belief and practice' they may have once been.[22] Although this was not the complete
assimilation and religious unity that most French Catholics had hoped
for, it was certainly close to the kind of co-existence that Catherine de
Medici and some 'politiques' had sought since the 1560s.

Louis XIV's revocation of the Edict of Nantes in 1685, largely the
result of royal paranoia and insecurity, did alter this quasi-stable
Huguenot community, however. By forcing Protestants underground or
abroad, it had just the opposite effect that Louis intended: it not only
guaranteed the minority's survival, but introduced it into the New World.
Although other forms of Calvinism had already been established in
Puritan New England since the early seventeenth century, after 1685
the French Huguenots joined other religious minorities such as the
Moravians along the Carolina coast. And Protestantism even survived

---

[21] Philip Benedict, *The Huguenot Population of France, 1600–1685: The Demographic Fate
and Customs of a Religious Minority* (Philadelphia: Transactions of the American
Philosohical Society, vol. 81, pt. 5, 1991), p. 103.
[22] Ibid., pp. 103–4.

underground in France despite the revocation. When religious toleration was finally introduced in the eighteenth century, there was a thriving community of maybe several hundred thousand Huguenots who emerged from their underground churches.

Finally, it ought to be noted that the fate of the defeated Protestant leaders of La Rochelle in 1629 paralleled the leaders of the League when they were forced to surrender to Henry IV in 1594–95. That is, Louis XIII and Richelieu, far from being the bigots and bogeymen of traditional Protestant historians, practised the same politics of appeasement that worked so successfully for Louis's father in the 1590s. Soubise and Rohan were both pardoned and entered service in the royal army and fought admirably for Louis XIII and Richelieu in the Thirty Years War. The militant mayor of La Rochelle, Jean Guiton, who helped to overthrow the old guard once the siege began in 1628, was also pardoned and served for fifteen years in the royal navy under the very commander who had routed Buckingham and the English fleet in November 1627. Indeed, when Guiton died in 1654, his last will and testament listed among his belongings portraits of both Louis XIII and Richelieu.[23] The last of the religious wars was indeed over.

[23] Parker, *La Rochelle and the French Monarchy*, p. 169.

8   Conclusions: economic impact, social change, and absolutism

In the final analysis what are we to make of the French Wars of Religion? I have attempted in the preceding pages to demonstrate that religion – understood by contemporaries as something more social than intellectual – played a central role in these civil wars. Above all, the wars were experienced against the backdrop of the Reformation, where confessional division was common in many parts of sixteenth-century Europe. So, in this sense I have attempted to put religion back into the story that nineteenth- and early twentieth-century historians left out.[1] Throughout the Wars of Religion I have tried to show that time and again the principal – though clearly not the sole – motivating force behind the violence of the civil wars was the perception of safeguarding and defending a sacred notion of community defined by religion, whether that be the Gallican and traditionally Catholic community of most French men and women, or the minority community of the saints of the Protestant faith. Each community sought to define – or for the Huguenots to redefine – the boundaries between the sacred and the profane for the whole. As a result, at various times each group viewed the other with great suspicion and as a clear threat to its own survival. The Catholic reaction to the series of peace edicts, the St Bartholomew's massacres, the mentality of the Catholic League, and even the Edict of Nantes itself all seem to me to accentuate the importance of religion: defined as a community of believers rather than a body of beliefs. It is this social definition of religion that, in my view, best explains why the Wars of Religion happened the way they did, or indeed, happened at all. Ultimately, the fate of Henry of Navarre shows that the monarchy's ties to Catholicism as well as the deeprooted popular commitment to Catholic culture were too powerful to be swept away.

But by 'putting religion back' into the story, it is equally clear that politics, economics, intellectual trends, and other social forces still have their proper place. Moreover, I do not mean to suggest that explicitly

---

[1] For bibliographic details, see my 'Putting Religion Back into the Wars of Religion', *French Historical Studies*, vol. 18 (Fall 1993), 524–51.

political decisions – such as the decision by the royal council to murder the Huguenot nobles on St Bartholomew's Day, Henry III's decision to assassinate the Guises, or Henry IV's abjuration of Protestantism – did not significantly shape the outcome of the religious wars. While the sense of religious community that was endemic throughout society from top to bottom may have been the foundation of the conflict, political decisions at court were clearly crucial in triggering the popular violence as well as the military campaigns. Without high politics there is, in fact, no story at all, since it was politics that was responsible for both beginning and ending the long conflict. Moreover, the socio-economic tensions that were so much a part of the hierarchical society of the pre-modern world were also exacerbated by the civil wars, and these tensions occasionally spilled over into the arena of warfare: the popular uprisings in 1579 and 1593 being the most visible examples. Thus, I have not tried to downplay the impact of other factors that were clearly crucial to the Wars of Religion by emphasizing the social importance of religion; I have simply tried to restore a crucial piece of the puzzle that has been missing for far too long.

Another objective of this book has been to show that despite the political and economic domination of the ruling elites – and a very small percentage of the population obviously dominated the remainder in the pre-modern world – the feelings, behaviour, and actions of the popular classes were not only significant, but in some cases they were crucial to the story of the civil wars. The popular violence in Paris and several other cities in August and September 1572 that made up the St Bartholomew's massacres is evidence enough that the elites wielded power, but they could not always impose their own will. Moreover, it is equally clear that in the many cities the Huguenots controlled in the south, as well as in the cities controlled by the Catholic League in the 1590s, that the political elites relied in large part on the support of the popular classes for their success. There would have been no Protestant movement in France at all, nor any Catholic League for that matter, without the support of the people at nearly every social level. And certainly Henry IV – despite his politics of appeasement – would never have been as successful as he was in ending the fighting had he not enjoyed the groundswell of popular support and recognition following his abjuration of Protestantism in 1593. It would be naive to imagine that French artisans and peasants of the sixteenth century were free agents empowered to shape and mold their own world as they saw fit. But it seems equally simplistic to deny the significant role that non-elites played in defining the outcome of the conflict. How the popular classes adapted to the structures of power that restrained them is at least as important as the structures themselves.

But why was France the only state in sixteenth-century Europe to experience such a violent and protracted series of civil wars? The French were neither more religious nor necessarily more violent than other Europeans, so why were there not such extended civil wars elsewhere? Religious settlements were imposed from above by the state without much significant violence or bloodshed in states such as England, Sweden, and countless cities, duchies, and territories in the German empire. Moreover, other large Catholic states such as Spain managed to maintain Catholic preponderance without any kind of civil war. The closest parallel to the French experience was in Germany, where Charles V waged a protracted war against the Lutheran princes from 1530 to 1555. These were not truly civil wars, however, as the fighting was waged primarily by soldiers. Despite some singular exceptions like the Peasant Revolt of 1525, the German Reformation experienced nothing like the protracted civilian involvement and popular violence that was so characteristic of the French Wars of Religion. So, why was the experience of France so unique in Reformation Europe?

Two factors above all others seem most crucial. First of all, the proximity of Calvin's Geneva, both geographically and linguistically, resulted in a far more significant and concentrated infusion of Protestantism in France, particularly in the south, than in other Catholic territories such as Spain and Italy. While there was certainly as vibrant a strain of Christian humanist reformism in Spain and Italy as in France in the early sixteenth century, neither of those two territories experienced a wave of missionary evangelism emanating from Geneva. In the less than twenty-five years between Calvin's arrival in Geneva and the outbreak of the civil wars in France, more than a million French men and women had been converted to Protestantism, with pastors sent from Geneva playing a significant role in the process. In short, France had a much larger and more concentrated community of Protestants in its midst than either Spain or Italy.[2]

Second, unlike the smaller Protestant states of England and Sweden, where a state religion from above was imposed on the population with relatively little bloodshed or violence, royal religious policy in France vacillated and changed throughout the second half of the sixteenth century. No reformation was imposed from above because no French king embraced Protestantism. Yet, after 1559 no prolonged policy of

---

[2] The role of Genevan pastors in spreading Protestantism in France is best explored through Robert M. Kingdon, *Geneva and the Coming of the Wars of Religion in France, 1555–1563* (Geneva, 1956).

repression worked any better because of the large numbers of Protestants in the kingdom. It did not help, either, that at the height of Protestant growth in France – around 1560 – the accident of death left the kingdom of France in the hands of boy-kings, first Francis II (1559–1560) and then Charles IX (1560–1574). From the time of the accidental death of Henry II in 1559 to the majority of Charles IX in 1563, there was never really an established authority at court strong enough to prevent the noble factions from using the confessional divide to their advantage. And finally, the vacillating policies of the Queen Mother, Catherine de Medici, during this regency government to pursue a policy of religious co-existence and toleration of the Huguenots resulted in the reverse of her intentions, as the toleration edict of January 1562 actually made civil war more likely. While the aims of those like the Queen Mother and Michel de l'Hôpital to pursue peace through religious toleration rather than persecution are commendable, they were unrealistic in the 1560s (though by that time a renewal of the repression of Henry II would not have been any more effective). Any policy of religious settlement that was going to pass muster with the overwhelming majority of the Catholic French population was going to have to accommodate itself to the Gallican principle of 'one faith, one king, one law'. This was the lesson that the 'politiques' of the 1590s – such as Henry IV – learned from the 'politiques' of the 1560s. Thus, vacillating royal policy from 1559 to 1598 implemented by largely ineffective monarchs contributed greatly to the civil wars in France.

As for the impact of the French Wars of Religion, there are several key questions that require a more extended discussion. First, what was the economic impact of the wars on the French populace? That is, in what specific ways did the civil wars affect the way most French men and women carried on their daily lives? Who suffered most and how? And finally, how did the wars affect France economically? Were they as disastrous as the final phase of the Hundred Years' War in the fifteenth century? And if so, how long did it take for economic recovery? Second, in what specific ways did the wars affect the social structure of France? Did the wars, as many contemporaries believed, result in the decline of the old military aristocracy, or witness the rise of new bourgeois classes? How did the wars affect gender relations and the social roles for women? In short, did the extended period of civil war result in any significant changes in the French social structure? Third and last, in what manner did the Wars of Religion contribute to any significant political change in France? Specifically, what role, if any, did the civil wars play in helping to bring about a more centralized absolute monarchy in the seventeenth century?

Economic Change

The principal difficulty in attempting to assess the economic impact of
more than half a century of civil war lies in distinguishing between what
was the result of the civil wars and what was simply the result of half
a century. This is all the more difficult because of the vast economic
changes much of Europe experienced during the last half of the sixteenth
and early seventeenth centuries. When the Wars of Religion began in 1562
most of western Europe had just seen the end of a period of extended
economic growth. The population of France was still expanding and
had just about made up the demographic losses of the Black Death
and Hundred Years' War of the fourteenth and fifteenth centuries. The
standard of living of most Europeans in the century preceding the outbreak
of the Wars of Religion was relatively high. Professor Emmanuel Le Roy
Ladurie has demonstrated that even peasants in Languedoc and the Midi
had more meat in their diet, drank more and better wine, and overall
consumed more calories in this period than at any time before the twentieth
century. Moreover, there was more arable land per capita available to
them, so that peasants in the period 1450–1550 not only ate well, but
they were also better able to own their own land than under the earlier
feudal system of land tenure.[3] Aiding and abetting this economic expansion were the large sums of currency being pumped into Europe in the form
of silver from New World mines. Led by the Spanish, ships of New World
silver were arriving on a regular basis by the mid-sixteenth century, passing
through the port of Seville to expand the money supply of much of Europe.
Although this increase in the money supply did eventually result in significant inflation, which the political theorist Jean Bodin noticed as early as
1575, at mid-century its impact was still largely beneficial. Thus, for most
French men and women on the eve of the religious wars the economy was
expanding and economic growth had been perceived as a way of life for
nearly a century.

This rosy picture deteriorated rapidly by the 1570s and 1580s, however, and ended even sooner in many parts of Europe. The unrestrained
population growth since the end of the Hundred Years' War had by then
already approached the ceiling of the available arable land and food
supply. Prices of all goods, but especially foodstuffs, were already running
significantly ahead of wages, with the inevitable decline in living standards for many. Moreover, the 1580s and 1590s – which coincided with
the wars of the League – also witnessed the most severe and closely spaced

---

[3] Emmanuel Le Roy Ladurie, *The Peasants of Languedoc*, trans. John Day (Urbana, IL,
1974), pp. 11–145.

series of harvest failures and food shortages in the entire sixteenth century. This resulted in widespread famine and economic distress not only in France, but in much of Europe.[4] All of these economic forces, both the positive and the negative, were independent of the civil wars and would have occurred whether the Wars of Religion had broken out in 1562 or not. So, any attempt to distinguish the effects of war from these economic changes is bound to be problematic.

One contemporary made such an effort in 1581, however, even while the wars were still raging. He published his findings, *The Secret of the Finances of France*, under a false name – Nicolas Froumenteau – because the whole purpose of his endeavour was to suggest that the king had more than enough cash to finance the wars without further increases of taxation on the population. The author was clearly a financial official who worked in the royal treasury, as is evident from his familiarity with the royal tax receipts, and his findings are very detailed. Froumenteau calculated that in the period 1550–80, the royal treasury had taken in 1,453,000,000 *livres tournois*, while royal expenses (including all military expenses for the religious wars) had totalled only 927,206,000 *livres tournois*, thus leaving a surplus of 525,794,000 *livres tournois* (or 175,264,666 *écus* 40 *sous* at 3 *livres* per *écu*).[5] More astoundingly, Froumenteau calculated that the civil wars alone had resulted in the death of 765,200 French men and women as a result of the wars: 8,760 clergymen, 32,950 nobles from both religions, 36,300 civilian male commoners, 1,235 civilian female commoners, 656,000 French troops, and 32,600 foreign troops. Moreover, he went on to calculate that as a result of the civil wars 12,300 women and girls had been raped, nine cities had been burned or razed, 252 villages had been burned or razed, 4,256 houses had been burned, and 180,000 other homes had been destroyed.[6] It is obvious that these latter figures are nothing but invention (and even the figures on total royal receipts and expenses are probably fictitious), since there were no records kept on any national or local basis, official or unofficial, for things like the number of females raped or the number of houses destroyed. What is significant about Froumenteau's work is not, however, the specific figures he gives,

---

[4] See particularly Philip Benedict, 'Civil War and Natural Disaster in Northern France', and Mark Greengrass, 'The Later Wars of Religion in the French Midi', both in Peter Clark, ed., *The European Crisis of the 1590s: Essays in Comparative History* (London, 1985), pp. 84–105 and 106–34, respectively.

[5] N[icolas] Froumenteau, *Le secret des finances de France ... pour ouvrir les moyens legitimes et necessaires de payer les dettes du Roy, descharger ses suiets des subsides imposez depuis trente un ans et recouvrer tous les deniers prins a Sa Maiesté* ([Paris,] 1581), part i, p. 142. (The work is in three parts, and each part is paginated separately, forming a total of 1063 pp.)

[6] Froumenteau, *Le secret des finances*, part iii, pp. 377–80.

but the fact that he underscores the double-edged sword of warfare for the civilian population. They not only had to endure the pressures of economic change described above, but they had to overcome the dual threat of death and destruction from the soldiers themselves, as well as the pressure and hardship of royal taxation which the king needed to pay for the military destruction. Thus, for many French men and women, as Froumenteau's analysis makes clear, the experience of civil war was marked by the threat of death and physical annihilation from the military as well as fiscal hardship and the threat of financial ruin meted out by the crown's tax collectors. It was a double danger from which many could not recover, and a variety of different economic indicators shows the extent of these threats and their impact on the population.

Available mortality figures show, for example, that the 1580s and 1590s were the period of the highest death rates in the century. To be sure, these high mortality rates were not all the result of war, as outbreaks of the plague and famine caused by harvest failure were also on the increase, particularly in the 1580s. This is clear from the mortality figures in the rural area around Nantes in Brittany, where there was little fighting in the 1580s but where plague was rampant, as well as in the city of Rouen, where the wars of the League and particularly the siege of the city in 1592 were responsible for the rise in mortality figures there (see Figure 8.1).[7]

A second economic indicator is prices. As already mentioned, the inflation of the second half of the sixteenth century caused by an expanded money supply was a general trend that was exacerbated by harvest failure and warfare. A poor harvest of cereal grains could send the price of bread skyrocketing, but the effects of war should not thus be ignored. The scarcity of the supply of bread for any reason could easily be a cause of severe inflation as well as famine, as the sieges of Paris (1590), Rouen (1592), and La Rochelle (1627–28) demonstrate. Whenever marauding troops billeted themselves on the civilian population, they invariably seized all livestock and grain stores as a matter of practice. Thus, the rural population could be equally vulnerable to scarcity of food, famine, and the resulting inflation. As exact figures tend only to survive from cities, the price series for Paris, Toulouse, and Dijon (chosen from very different parts of the kingdom) all suggest not only inflationary prices for

---

[7] The documentation for the area around Nantes comes from Alain Croix, *Nantes et le pays nantais au XVIe siècle: Etude démographique* (Paris, 1974), chap. 5, and the figures for Rouen come from Philip Benedict, 'Catholics and Huguenots in Sixteenth-century Rouen: The Demographic Effects of the Religious Wars', *French Historical Studies*, vol. 9 (1975), 209–34. The graph of Figure 8.1 is based on that in Philip Benedict, 'Civil War and Natural Disaster in Northern France', p. 85.

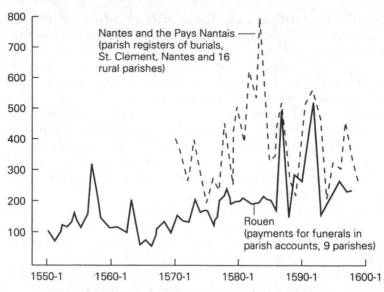

Figure 8.1 Mortality rates in Nantes and Rouen

bread and wine generally during the wars, but they show the significant disruption and oscillation of prices during the wars of the League particularly (see Figures 8.2 and 8.3).[8] It is equally clear, however, that in the long run, wages ran considerably behind the rising prices of the second half of the sixteenth century. While there are very few records of wage rates for most professions in the period, it is clear from the few examples that have survived that nominal wages were easily eroded by rising prices, resulting in an even more serious decrease in the overall ability to fight the economic effects of the civil wars, as well as a decrease in the standard of living (see Figure 8.4). Day labourers in Lyon, for example, France's second largest city, suffered a serious crisis during the period of the Catholic League as the cost of living rose while their real salaries declined, putting one inhabitant in five on poor relief.[9]

[8] The prices for Paris come from Micheline Baulant and Jean Meuvret, *Prix des céreales extraits de la mercuriale de Paris (1520–1698)*, 2 vols. (Paris, 1960); the prices for Toulouse from Georges and Geneviève Frêche, *Les prix des grains, des vins et des légumes à Toulouse (1486–1868)* (Paris, 1967); and the prices for Dijon from the Archives municipales de Dijon, B 188 to 242. Because different monetary units and different measuring units of wheat and wine were used in the three cities, I have indexed all the prices for comparison.

[9] The figures for real wages of day labourers in Lyon come from Richard Gascon, *Grand commerce et vie urbaine au XVIe siècle: Lyon et ses marchands*, 2 vols. (Paris, 1971), II, 933–6; and the graph is based on Charles Wilson and Geoffrey Parker, eds., *An Introduction to the Sources of European Economic History, 1500–1800* (London, 1977), p. 183.

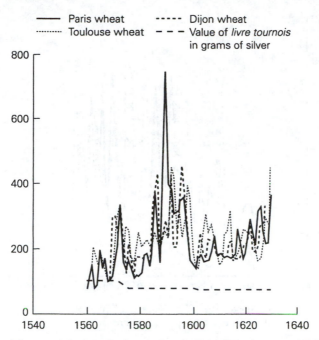

Figure 8.2 Index of wheat prices in Paris, Toulouse and Dijon

A third economic indicator is agricultural and economic production. Agricultural production was necessarily tied to harvest failure and the disruption of warfare. As outlined above, rural peasants, unprotected by city walls, often found themselves the easiest of targets for pillaging troops. But the seizure of their livestock not only meant they might be unable to bring in their harvest or to replant the following year, it also reduced the fertilization of what crops they were able to continue to harvest. In terms of agricultural yields, livestock was just as important for natural fertilizer as it was for ploughing the fields. The tithe records for the region around Beaune in Burgundy show the disruption in agricultural output due to the twin causes of harvest failure and the disruption of troops. Once again, the 1590s during the wars of the League show a marked decline in agricultural output, with lower yields by far than any other period in the sixteenth or seventeenth century (see Figure 8.5).[10] Industrial production could be equally affected. In times of vastly

[10] Albert Silbert, 'La production des céréales à Beaune d'après les dîmes', in J. Goy and E. Le Roy Ladurie, eds., *Les Fluctuations du produit de la dîme: Conjoncture décimale et domaniale de la fin du Moyen Age au XVIIIe siècle* (Paris, 1972), pp. 134–52; the graph is based on that in Benedict, 'Civil War and Natural Disaster in Northern France', p. 86.

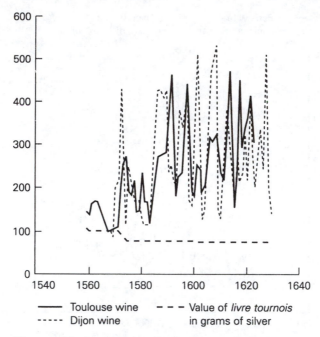

Figure 8.3 Index of wine prices in Toulouse and Dijon

escalating food prices, most French men and women were forced to spend much more, if not all, their household income on food, resulting in a significant decrease in demand for manufactured goods. Warfare could also disrupt the supply of materials as well as the distribution of finished goods to consumers, both of which made inroads on industrial output. Again, while few sets of continuous figures exist from the sixteenth century, those that do show that warfare helped to exacerbate other economic factors to diminish manufacturing capacity during the civil wars. Textile production in Amiens rose sharply in the first half of the century to meet a rising demand, where it remained on a fairly stable plateau from about 1530 to 1580. The 1580s and 1590s, however, witnessed a sharp reversal as production fell off precipitously after 1586. What little documentation survives from other cities suggests a similar pattern.[11]

---

[11] The figures for Amiens come from Pierre Deyon, 'Variations de la production textile aux XVIe et XVIIe siècles: Sources et premiers résultats', *Annales: Economies, Sociétés, Civilisations*, vol. 18 (1963), 948–9; while information about industrial production from other cities is in Benedict, 'Civil War and Natural Disaster in Northern France', pp. 87–90.

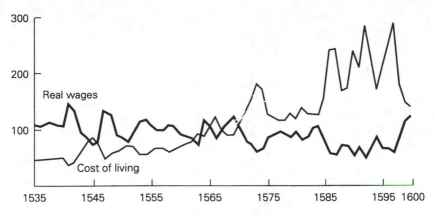

Figure 8.4 Real wages and the cost of living at Lyon

Finally, we ought to look at the tax demands of the crown and the fiscal pressure from other sources put on almost every type of community in the kingdom, whether rural or urban, during the civil wars. The royal tax called the *taille* had long since become a permanent source of revenue for the crown by the sixteenth century. While in some parts of the realm it was assessed on land (from which noble fiefs were exempt) and in other areas based on personal wealth (regardless of whether one lived on a fief or not), this tax was one of the crown's principal sources of revenue; and in general only the aristocracy were exempt from paying it. As the crown's debts mounted after the outbreak of civil war in 1562, and as military costs escalated with each civil war with the failure of the royal army to achieve a total military victory over either the Huguenots or the League, the successive kings of France turned to the only remedy they had in their control: levies of new subsidies or imposts, or an increase in the levy of the *taille*. An increase in the amounts the crown sought and the actual amounts it managed to collect varied widely over the course of the wars, and no monarch or tax collector ever for a moment believed that all subsidies owed would ever be paid in full. From the perspective of the poor taxpayer, already hard-hit by the inflation of food prices and other economic hardships, an increase in taxes proved to be the last straw. In the worst of times, as has already been seen in 1579 and again in 1593, such fiscal pressure could result in peasant revolts. The sight of royal officers arresting and imprisoning those who could barely meet their needs of subsistence, much less pay increased subsidies, was enough to rouse any peasant to revolt.

Though it would be naive to assume that these amounts were ever fully paid, a brief look at the amounts the crown levied and attempted to collect

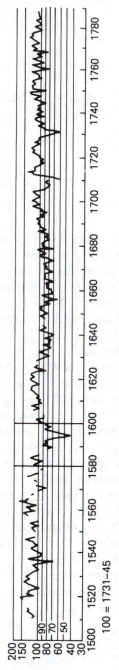

Figure 8.5 Index of agricultural yields derived from the tithe in the region of Beaune

100 = 1731–45

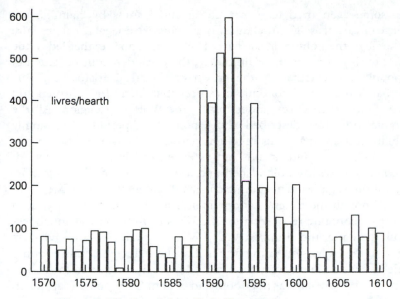

Figure 8.6 Levies of the taille in Dauphiné

in Dauphiné during the civil wars is a good example of the kind of fiscal pressure many communities were under. From 1570 to 1588, this region was rarely levied more than 100 *livres* per hearth (not the number of actual hearths, or households, in the region, but a number assigned purely for tax assessment purposes to each village, community, and town). Between 1589 and 1600, however, the levy was never below 100 *livres* and was usually considerably above it. In 1589 the levy rose to more than 400 *livres* per hearth, while in 1592 it rose to a record 600 *livres* per hearth. Even in 1600, long after all the fighting had stopped in Dauphiné, the royal levy of the *taille* was still around 200 *livres* per hearth, more than twice what it had been during the 1570s and early 1580s (see Figure 8.6).[12]

Despite the steep increases in fiscal demands by the crown, most French men and women were nevertheless inclined to grant the king his due. Even towns and communities made every effort to try to meet royal tax demands, at least minimally. To do so, they often had to borrow from wealthy nobles, and it was the increased fiscal pressure from the nobility in times of crisis that was ultimately the most severe cause of urban and rural unrest. Not only did many nobles demand exorbitant interest for

[12] These figures come from Mark Greengrass, 'The Later Wars of Religion in the French Midi', p. 124.

loans, some even tried to extort unwarranted sums by claiming the privilege of various seigneurial dues. It was this extra-legal fiscal pressure from some of the nobility in the early 1590s, for example, that led to the peasant uprisings of 1593.[13] Ultimately, the fiscal demands on much of the population, whether by the crown or the local aristocracy, only exacerbated the other economic pressures that many French men and women found themselves under during the Wars of Religion. All the economic indicators described above point to a period of economic instability and, for many, distress. The period of the wars of the League in the 1580s and 1590s stands out as an especially uncertain period, where not only was the bloodshed and loss of life of the fighting at its apex, but the vagaries of economic change threatened the subsistence of many. Although these same economic indicators point to a fairly rapid recovery – economic recovery after the Wars of Religion was much less difficult than after the Hundred Years' War, for example – the civil wars did curtail the expansion of the first half of the sixteenth century sooner and delay economic recovery for France longer in relation to the rest of Europe. To be sure, all was not doom and gloom. Economic expansion in cities such as Lyon and Rouen continued despite the civil wars, and investment in foreign trade actually increased.[14] Moreover, despite the general demographic slowdown in the second half of the sixteenth century, some towns and cities actually experienced population increases. Between 1550 and 1600, for example, Marseille grew from around 30,000 to 45,000 people, Nantes and Angers both increased from about 17,000 to 25,000 people, and Grenoble nearly doubled from 6,000 to 10,000 people.[15] For the majority of the French population, however, the Wars of Religion were a time of economic uncertainty, and for many a time of real economic distress.

Social Change

Did the Wars of Religion alter the structure of French society? Some historians have argued that the civil wars resulted in the beginning of a

[13] J. H. M. Salmon, *Society in Crisis: France in the Sixteenth Century* (London and New York, 1975), pp. 282–91.

[14] See Richard Gascon, *Grand commerce et vie urbaine au XVI siècle*, 2 vols. (Paris, 1971); Philip Benedict, 'Rouen's Foreign Trade in the Age of the Religious Wars (1560–1600)', *Journal of European Economic History*, vol. 13 (1984), 29–74; and Gayle K. Brunelle, *The New World Merchants of Rouen, 1559–1630* (Kirksville, MO, 1991).

[15] See Philip Benedict, 'French Cities from the Sixteenth Century to the Revolution: An Overview', in idem, ed., *Cities and Social Change in Early Modern France* (London, 1989), pp. 7–68.

long-term decline of the nobility, as seigneurial rents and dues were unable to keep pace with the rising prices of the sixteenth century. As a result, many nobles, particularly the rural ones without other sources of income, either went bankrupt or were forced into trade and commerce. Many others were forced to sell off portions of their estates simply to survive. Accompanied by a concomitant rise in wealth and economic power of a royal officer class, as well as significant segments of the middle classes generally, it has been argued that the Wars of Religion began a long-term decline of the French aristocracy that was exacerbated by the absolutist powers of the crown of the seventeenth century.[16]

The sources do show a significant increase in noble land sales in the late sixteenth and early seventeenth centuries, but this should not be taken on its own as *prima facie* evidence of a decline of the aristocracy. Doubtless there were many nobles who did suffer a loss of economic and political power during the civil wars, but there were just as many others who profited. In an unusually complete series of notarial records of land sales in the region around Toul in Lorraine, Guy Cabourdin has shown that even if some nobles were forced to sell off portions of their estates, they were selling them in large part to other nobles. Moreover, the pattern of land sales was tied directly to the harvest. When a poor harvest resulted in higher grain prices, the volume of land sales increased significantly, as many, particularly peasants, were forced to sell land in order to survive. Cabourdin also shows that the volume of land sales in Toulois escalated most sharply in the period from 1586 to 1600, the period of most serious economic disruption. From all land sales in the region during this period, it is clear who profited most from the plight of those forced to sell: nobles acquired 35 per cent of the land, urban elites such as merchants and lawyers acquired 29 per cent, prosperous peasants acquired 17.5 per cent, and members of the clergy acquired 13.5 per cent (with 5 per cent unknown).[17] Burgundy experienced a very similar pattern.[18] Thus, sales of noble land do not necessarily reflect a decline in the economic power of the nobility, as other nobles were the ones most likely to profit from such sales.

[16] For example, see Lucien Romier, *Le royaume de Catherine de Médici*, 2 vols. (Paris, 1922), I, 160–216; Davis Bitton, *The French Nobility in Crisis, 1560–1640* (Stanford, 1969); and J. H. Mariéjol, *La Réforme, la Ligue, l'Edit de Nantes, 1559–1598* (Paris, 1904).

[17] Guy Cabourdin, *Terre et hommes en Lorraine (1550–1635): Toulois et comté de Vaudémont* (Nancy, 1977), pp. 377–424. There is a good English summary of this material in Benedict, 'Civil War and Natural Distaster in Northern France', pp. 96–8.

[18] Pierre de St Jacob, 'Mutations économiques et sociales dans les campagnes bourguignonnes à la fin du XVIe siècle', *Etudes rurales*, vol. 1 (1961), 34–49; and Gaston Roupnel, *La ville et la campagne au XVIIe siècle: Etudes sur la population du pays dijonnais* (Paris, 1955).

Many of the French nobility even profited from the fighting and military campaigns, some making fortunes by the wars' end. While the great
military commanders did often have to dip into their private wealth to
advance large sums to their troops simply to keep them from mutinying,
most of them also received generous pensions from the crown by 1598. It
should be remembered that Henry IV's politics of appeasement rewarded
Leaguer and Huguenot alike. It was the lesser nobility who were more
often unable to profit from the war. Some like Jérome de Luc, sieur de
Fontenay-le-Comte, returned from the wars virtually broke. He was
forced to borrow a ransom of 200 *écus* a few years earlier from a merchant
in Orléans and was completely in debt. While his case was not unique, it
was nevertheless true that the nobility as a whole was better able to survive
the disruptions of warfare and economic change than any other social
group in the kingdom. Even the most rustic of rural nobles, as has already
been shown, could invent new tolls, dues, and exactions on the local
peasantry when times got tough. And they also had the military force to
exact payment. While the distress and bankruptcy of many individual nobles was in fact a reality, as a social cohort the aristocracy was still
firmly atop the social ladder in France in 1629 just as they had
always been.[19]

It was equally clear, however, that other groups were attempting to join
them on the top rung. This was especially true of the royal officer class
that expanded considerably during the Wars of Religion. Although not
all offices carried with them the title of nobility as did many of those in the
sovereign courts (the Parlements, Chambers of Accounts, and Courts of
Aides), it was this 'nobility of the robe' that the traditional military aristocracy, the so-called 'nobility of the sword', found intimidating. The
sheer expansion of the royal officers during the civil wars was noticeable
by almost everyone, and it was the overall growth of this group that
appeared to be so threatening to many aristocrats. For just one example,
in Montpellier there were only 112 royal officers in the city in 1500
who earned a total of 14,885 *livres tournois* in total salaries. By 1550 this
group had expanded slightly to 125 officers earning 33,350 *livres* in total
salaries. The number of officers doubled by 1575 to 253, earning 67,520
livres in total salaries, and nearly doubled again by 1600 to 442 royal
officers, who earned 265,791 *livres tournois* in total salaries.[20] This was an
enormous expansion of numbers and salaries (even after adjustment for

---

[19] Benedict, 'Civil War and Natural Disaster in Northern France', p. 98; and J. Russell
Major, 'Noble Income, Inflation, and the Wars of Religion in France', *American Historical
Review*, vol. 86 (1981), 21–48.
[20] Greengrass, 'The Later Wars of Religion in the French Midi', p. 122.

inflation), and the pattern in Montpellier was common in many other cities and towns throughout the kingdom. And although many older noble families were naturally suspicious and condescending to these nobles of the robe, and did in fact feel threatened by them, the growth of royal officers during the religious wars did not threaten the social domination of the aristocracy at large. After all, the royal officers hoped to join the ranks of the aristocratic class, not overthrow it.[21]

There were other ways of joining the ranks of the nobility than the purchase of venal office, however. For those wealthy enough, letters of ennoblement could be purchased directly from the crown. Although these were not easy to obtain, since one usually needed some social standing already, there was an increase in such letters in the sixteenth century.[22] By far the most common method of joining the ruling classes, however, was simply to begin to live nobly if one could afford to. After a generation or two, if the façade was well maintained, a general public acceptance was possible. Perhaps the most famous example was Michel de Montaigne, mayor of Bordeaux and essayist during the civil wars. For all his complaints and hostile remarks about those who claimed false titles and pretended to be what they were not, his great-grandfather was a very successful fish and wine merchant on the Bordeaux docks. He acquired enough wealth to purchase a noble fief, which included the château at Montaigne, and added the 'de Montaigne' to the family name of Eyquem, providing the veneer of noble heritage. So, the essayist who excoriated false nobles in his essays was himself only three generations removed from much humbler social origins.[23] Like the nobility of the robe, these *parvenu* nobles wanted to join the ranks of the nobility, not undermine them, so their threat to the noble domination of society was in fact less serious than the litany of aristocratic complaints might suggest. Moreover, for the most part the ridiculously unsuccessful attempt of Molière's *Bourgeois gentilhomme* to pass himself off as a noble was much more common than the rapid social ascent of the Eyquems. What is true is that although the same social elites dominated society at the end of the Wars of Religion as at their beginning, the noble elites themselves were expanding and undergoing changes of composition. By the end of the civil wars, daughters and second sons of families of the older military nobility had intermarried with

[21] The best study of the growth of venal offices is still Roland Mousnier, *La Vénalité des offices sous Henri IV et Louis XIII* (Paris, 2nd edn, 1971), esp. chaps. 1–2.

[22] Ellery Schalk, 'Ennoblement in France from 1350 to 1660', *Journal of Social History*, vol. 16 (1982), 101–10.

[23] For Montaigne's excoriation of false nobles, see Donald M. Frame, ed. and trans., *The Complete Essays of Montaigne* (Stanford, 1958), pp. 276–7. Also see Frame's biography, *Montaigne: A Biography* (New York, 1965), chap. 1.

families from the newer robe nobility. Whatever losses the aristocratic classes suffered during the economic dislocation of the civil wars – and there clearly were some – they were more than offset by these newer additions. So, however much the nobility as a class may have changed in the process, it was still an intimidating social and political force that even Louis XIV would have to accommodate in the seventeenth century.[24]

As the land sale records from Toulois suggested, if there was any significant social change during the Wars of Religion, it occurred at the bottom of the social ladder rather than at the top. The poor and the destitute were among the least able to withstand the dual pressures of population growth and the disruption of civil war. Far more peasants were forced to sell land to survive than nobles, but even below them were the sharecroppers and day labourers who had no land to sell when subsistence became uncertain. Without the ability to raise money for food and without collateral to secure loans, they were the first to succumb to starvation when bread prices skyrocketed after a series of poor harvests. Even one poor harvest might be enough to threaten the poorest of share-croppers. The most destitute in city and country alike clearly suffered more during the civil wars and had fewer economic weapons to defend themselves than any other social group. All the sources suggest that welfare problems in every type of community escalated rapidly, especially during the later stages of the wars, as the numbers of the poor increased beyond the capacity of all forms of charity and poor relief. The English ambassador in France recounted the crisis in 1586:

Here have been with the King two deputies, one from Xaintonge and the other of Périgord, who, upon their knees have humbly desired the King to make a peace and to have pity upon his poor people, whose want was such as they were forced to eat bread made of ardoise and of nut-shells, which they brought and showed to the King. They told him also that the famine was so great as a woman in Périgord had already eaten two of her children and the like had been done in Xaintonge ... Many thousand there [are] already dead for hunger, and, in that extremity ... that they feed upon grass ... like horses and die with grass in their mouths.[25]

About the same time François Robert, a winegrower from the village of Couchey in Burgundy, reported a similar story. 'Over the last few years the poor were so ruined that their houses were completely empty, so that there was nothing standing but four bare walls ... The soldiers, who were

[24] See William Beik, *Absolutism and Society in Seventeenth-century France: State Power and Provincial Aristocracy in Languedoc* (Cambridge, 1985).
[25] Quoted in Greengrass, 'The Later Wars of Religion in the French Midi', p. 117.

everywhere in the vicinity, ate all the grain, so there was nothing left to harvest.'[26]

Everywhere the story was much the same. While the social elites had means of adapting to the economic changes and conditions of warfare, those at the bottom of society suffered the most. If there was any significant social change that occurred during the Wars of Religion, it was an increase in the social cleavage between those at the top and those at the bottom of society. The social structure itself was not threatened; that would not occur until the French Revolution. The social tensions inherent in this hierarchical society were significantly increased in the second half of the sixteenth century, however, as the pressures of economic change and civil war widened the gap between rich and poor. The various popular revolts in 1593 are just one indication of how close to the surface these tensions always were.

One final, though perhaps less visible, social change concerns the role of women during the Wars of Religion. Like the hierarchical social order, the patriarchal order obviously survived the civil wars intact. Although nowhere in France, or elsewhere in Europe, did women gain political or economic power on anything close to an equal footing with men, and although no changes in the legal status and rights of women occurred, the experience of protracted civil war did result in some significant changes in the way women lived their lives in early modern France. The most striking statistic is the rising number of single women and widows who emerged on the tax rolls of the later sixteenth century. Although there were large numbers of men killed on the battlefield during the wars, other factors were equally responsible. With the economic dislocation of the civil wars, men tended to marry later in life than in the early sixteenth century, as it took them much longer to be able to provide for a wife. Thus, the gap in ages between men and women at marriage actually tended to increase during the latter stages of the wars, often resulting in husbands dying while their widows were still relatively young or middle-aged. So, both losses on the battlefield as well as the rising age of men at marriage resulted in many more widows by the 1580s and 1590s. One example that stands out is the town of Auxonne in Burgundy. Auxonne's population followed the pattern of most cities in the sixteenth century in terms of its demographic growth: a decline in the second half of the sixteenth century. A series of complete tax rolls for much of the later sixteenth century shows, however, that the increase in the number of widows was significant. Before 1580 the number of widows tended to fluctuate

---

[26] C. Oursel, 'Deux livres de raison bourguignons', *Mémoires de la Société bourguignonne de géographie et d'histoire*, vol. 24 (1908), 360.

around 5 per cent of the total number of heads of household. In 1551, for example, the tax rolls show that 11 households out of 206 (5.3 per cent) were headed by widows. The next tax roll in 1578 shows that four households out of 80 (5.0 per cent) were headed by widows or unmarried women. This figure escalated sharply thereafter, as the tax rolls for 1588 show that 37 households out of 125 (or 29.6 per cent) were headed by widows or unmarried women.[27] This latter year is significant, as in the spring of 1587 an army of German reiters marched through Burgundy, leaving everything pillaged and plundered in their wake. The unusually high number of widows is the result not only of those factors described above, but also because of the many widows in the surrounding villages who fled to the safety of Auxonne's fortified walls during the military campaign. Even though this was a temporary crisis, it shows how quickly the situations of women could change due to the military conflict. Thus, while these widows were never given the same legal and political rights as men, many were forced to provide for their children and enter the public sphere of the workplace in capacities normally operated by men. In some towns guild membership allowed widows of master artisans to retain membership in the guild, and in these towns women performed in the workplace where they would otherwise have been forbidden. These incidents only increased patriarchal pressures on widows from men, and in many places women were forced to rely on each other for survival. The tax rolls of Dijon, the Burgundian capital, show clearly that during the Wars of Religion, not only did the number of widow heads of household increase, but a clear majority of them lived together with other widows and single women. Two, three, or four single women living together at the same address was not uncommon in Dijon by the 1570s, such as the four widows of artisans who shared a house on the rue du College in St-Michel parish in 1577. As their tax assessments ranged from 40 sous down to 3 sous, clearly wealthier women were looking after their less fortunate counterparts.[28] This last example is all the more interesting because there were very likely a number of children who must have resided there (unfortunately, tax rolls did not list dependents). Thus, while many widows obviously remarried, those who either could not or chose not to remarry did manage to carve out a social space for themselves in the late sixteenth-century town. Although women never escaped the patriarchal domination of the pre-modern world, many of them experienced very different lives and social roles as a result of the Wars of Religion,

---

[27] Archives départementales de la Côte-d'Or (Dijon), C 4766, fols. 209v–213r for 1551; C 4767, fols. 37r–39v for 1578; and C 4768, fols. 6r–9r for 1588.
[28] Archives municipales de Dijon, L 205, fol. 46v.

experiencing the management of property and operating in the public sphere in ways they would not have done otherwise.[29]

A specific example is the case of an unknown noblewoman known only by her first name, Catherine. In an undated letter to Louis de Gonzague, duke of Nevers, Catherine wrote of the plight of her husband, besieged by a Huguenot captain in a fortress somewhere in France. Pleading for Nevers to go to the aid of her husband, Catherine also reported that the Huguenot captain had contacted her just two days previously, to see if she might be willing to pay a heavy ransom for the release of her besieged spouse.

Seeing him so close by, with all his troops and with eight cannon, even though I was ill I got myself into my litter and went to meet him ... And we were together for about an hour, and he began by haranguing me. And in one word I responded: that men give battle but that God gives victory, that I stand with my husband in such honor and repute that he could not threaten me without causing himself and his entire army shame, and that at this moment his face was giving him away, and that his men could see him sweat. He said that I was brave and resolute but that nevertheless he would overrun the fortress within ten days, even if it meant losing 3,000 men ... Whereupon he said that the best I could hope for my husband would be that he would be captured and have to pay an onerous ransom. And I answered that I would consider myself rich enough merely to have my husband back alive, and that I would gladly go about in my *chemise* if necessary in order to pay the ransom and have him back ... [30]

Even though we know neither the identity of this women nor the outcome of her request to Nevers, her letter makes it clear that many women carried on with the running of the estate or the shop in their husband's absence. While few women other than a noblewoman would ever encounter any military negotiation as did Catherine, her experience shows how expanded some women's roles became as a result of the Wars of Religion. To be sure, a sick woman on a litter making an enemy nobleman sweat in front of his men, willing to risk everything she owned including the shirt off her back, that is, baring herself to save her and her husband's honour, and then recounting the entire experience to another even more powerful nobleman like Nevers, was doubtless a unique event. Nevertheless, it was the protracted civil wars that put some women in this kind of situation. To sum up, while neither the legal status nor the ideas and perceptions about women changed very much

[29] See Barbara B. Diefendorf, 'Widowhood and Remarriage in Sixteenth-century Paris', *Journal of Family History*, vol. 7 (1982), 379–95; and Nancy L. Roelker, 'The Appeal of Calvinism to French Noblewomen in the Sixteenth Century', *Journal of Interdisciplinary History*, vol. 2 (1972), 391–418.

[30] Quoted from, and analyzed by, Kristin Neuschel, 'Noblewomen and War in Sixteenth-Century France', in Michael Wolfe, ed., *Changing Identities in Early Modern France* (Durham, NC, 1997), pp. 124–44 (quote on p. 133).

during the civil wars, the lives and experiences of many of them did alter considerably as their roles in society broadened and expanded.

Women were also significantly affected by the rising tide of penitential piety and ascetic spirituality that was a direct outgrowth of the Catholic Reformation at the end of the religious wars. The result was a new spiritual involvement that manifested itself in both the founding of dozens of new religious orders and convents for women as well as a dramatic and explicit female role in the collection of alms for the poor and other charitable foundations. Fifty new religious houses and convents for women were established in the capital alone between 1600 and 1650. The first of these was the Discalced Carmelites, founded in 1604 by followers of Teresa of Avila's reformed order created in Spain a century earlier. The Carmelites were quickly followed by the Capucines, resulting from a desire by women to emulate the strictly reformed male order of Franciscans known as Capuchins, and the Ursulines, founded originally in Italy as an open order of women who went out into the community to catechize young girls, but who in Paris were cloistered in keeping with the wishes of the founder. The founders and financial patrons of these new orders were from the highest social rank, including even Marie de Medici and Michel de Marillac. Ultimately, all these new religious houses in the capital spawned lay confraternities for women such as the Dames de la Charité, whose work in providing charity for the destitute was part of the overall goal of post-Tridentine Catholicism to transform the ways in which a Christian society took care of its poorest members. Just as the Wars of Religion provided, even forced, some women into military roles previously reserved for men, so too did the Catholic renewal that swept through France in the early seventeenth century provide women with new and more significant roles to play, making it very clear that the Catholic Reformation was not exclusively the work of male bishops.[31]

Absolutism

Of all the traditional clichés about the French Wars of Religion, the one that perhaps still holds up the best is that the disorder of civil war in the sixteenth century led to the absolute monarchy of the seventeenth. Whether in creating new institutions to centralize further the power of the crown, or simply reinvesting older institutions with renewed efficacy in order not to repeat the chaos and disorder of the religious wars,

---

[31] This paragraph is based on Barbara B. Diefendorf, *From Penance to Charity: Pious Women and the Catholic Reformation in Paris* (Oxford and New York, 2004), especially pp. 7–26.

it has long been argued that the absolute monarchy under Louis XIII and Louis XIV was built in large part out of the necessity of restoring France as well as the authority of the monarchy after the ravages of the civil wars. Given that the traditional view of absolutism was also based on the king's emasculation of a declining aristocracy, shorn of its political and economic influence (which we have already seen not to be the case), we need to tread carefully in defining the political programmes of the absolute monarchy of the seventeenth century. Nevertheless, there is no doubt that the legacy of the Wars of Religion served as a constant reminder to all later kings of the necessity for a strong monarchy.

Obviously, Henry IV made explicit attempts to strengthen the authority of the crown and to aid the recovery of the kingdom generally, though whether he had any systematic plan for doing so is still a debated question. Nevertheless, there is little doubt that with some new initiatives as well as some reforms of older institutions, the reign of Henry IV was instrumental in restoring the fiscal health of the royal treasury as well as the political authority of the monarchy. His success in this area was partly due to the man he appointed as his superintendent of finances, Maximilien de Béthune, baron of (and after 1606 duke of) Sully. Sully recognized by 1596 that the French state could never function in war – and France was at war with Spain at the time – while running large annual budget deficits and with such an antiquated fiscal system. The debts of nearly four decades of war meant that by 1598 the crown was in debt to the tune of 300 million *livres*, and the annual deficits increased this amount every year. There was no uniform sytem of tax assessment or tax collection throughout the realm, as the fiscal machine was heavily decentralized in favour of the localities. Sully's agenda was not for more minor tinkering with the system to improve its operation, but a complete overhaul. In essence, he wanted to shift the main burden for crown revenue from direct taxation – the *taille*, for which the population was already heavily taxed – to indirect taxes (subsidies on salt and wine, customs duties, sales taxes, etc.) which could be more easily regulated and controlled than the *taille*. In addition, Sully wanted to overhaul the maze of tax collection procedures so that royal tax officers could centralize the system of revenue collection and remove it from the less reliable hands of local tax farmers. In this way, Sully sought a means to increase revenue and balance the state budget without increasing the direct tax burden on the population. Henry and Sully were so successful that they not only turned a huge deficit into a surplus by 1610, and lowered the *taille* for the bulk of the population, they also set up a fiscal system that made it

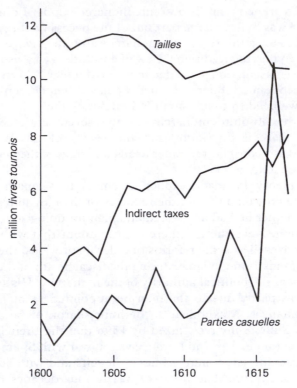

Figure 8.7 Royal income, 1600–171

possible for future generations of kings and superintendents of finances to increase royal revenues and royal authority in the process (see Figure 8.7).[32]

How did they do it? For a start Sully declared bankruptcy and either wrote off or renegotiated about half of the 300 millions in crown debt. Sully got the Swiss to accept payment of only one-seventh of the 36 million livres to clear the debt owed them, for example, and this was a common ploy with most of the foreign debt. The most obvious innovation, however, was the introduction of an annual tax on royal offices that all royal officeholders had to pay – one-sixtieth of the value of their office per year – in order to guarantee their right to pass on the office to their heirs. Revenue from this kind of inheritance tax had been so haphazard in the past, in fact, that it had always been referred to as 'casual revenue'

[32] This graph is based on the one in Mark Greengrass, *France in the Age of Henri IV* (London, 1984), p. 227.

(*parties casuelles*). Called the *paulette*, Sully introduced this mandatory tax on offices in 1604 and its impact was significant. Not only did it bring in a substantial annual sum into the royal coffers, it also brought political control and centralization of the system of venality of office under the crown's authority. The *paulette* was thus an annual reminder to every officeholder that he was beholden to the king rather than to any other powerbroker from whom he may have acquired the rights to that office. Between 1605 and 1609 it was so successful that it yielded on average 12 per cent of all ordinary revenues. As Richard Bonney has noted, the *paulette* 'may not have been a great money spinner under Henry IV but it was now a permanent revenue that could be more vigorously exploited in a later time of need'. And it was exploited almost immediately. As Figure 8.7 shows, it did not take long before the *paulette* brought in revenues that outstripped all the indirect taxes and on occasion even approached the levels of the *taille* itself. Henry and Sully thus put the crown firmly on a solid financial footing, allowing Henry and his successors much more power to enforce their authority throughout the kingdom.[33]

Henry and Sully were also successful in reforming and breathing new life into older, more traditional royal initiatives. The successful effort at introducing royal tax officials (*élus*) to supplant the provincial estates in the province of Guyenne, which both better enabled the crown to maintain control of tax collection there and weakened the power of the provincial estates, was not new. Henry III had tried the very same thing in Dauphiné in the 1570s and 1580s without any success whatsoever. And though the *élus* were not successfully introduced into the other *pays d'états* as Sully and Henry had hoped, it was nevertheless a significant first step on the road to a uniform tax-collection system.[34] Henry III and Henry IV also came to rely more and more on special commissions and royal commissioners to try to enforce the various edicts of pacification. Although compliance and enforcement of these edicts were never a major success in the provinces, the commissioners themselves became institutionalized over the course of the religious wars. And as Michel Antoine has shown very convincingly, these royal commissioners were the ancestors of the royal intendants that Richelieu and all later ministers found so useful in establishing royal authority throughout the kingdom in

---

[33] Much of this paragraph is based on Richard Bonney, *The King's Debts: Finance and Politics in France, 1589–1661* (Oxford, 1981), pp. 23–72.

[34] For Henry IV's initiatives, see J. Russell Major, 'Henry IV and Guyenne: A Study concerning the Origins of Royal Absolutism', *French Historical Studies* vol. 4 (1966), 363–83; and for Henry III's attempts see L. Scott Van Doren, 'The Royal *taille* in Dauphiné', in *Proceedings of the Western Society for French History*, vol. 3 (1976), 35–53.

the seventeenth century.[35] Indeed, what is most striking is that some of the same initiatives that emphasized the weakness of the crown during the civil wars proved to be more effective in the hands of Henry IV and Louis XIII. As has already been pointed out, weak monarchs and misguided political policies played a significant role in creating the civil wars, and stronger monarchs with better policies proved to be better able to maintain their authority. All French kings had sought absolute power and even acted as if they wielded it, but some proved much more efficacious in the process.

It is nevertheless true that no disorder and overt rebellion against the crown on the scale of the French Wars of Religion ever broke out again until the French Revolution; and Henry IV and Louis XIII were stronger than their predecessors. Moreover, the political rhetoric of the civil wars – resistance to tyrannical kings and an emphasis on the role of the Estates-General in the ancient constitution – quickly gave way in the early seventeenth century to the triumphal domination of theories of absolute monarchy. This was symbolized most visibly in the request by the third estate at the Estates-General of 1614, who insisted that it ought to be recognized as a fundamental law of the realm that all French kings held their crowns from God alone:

That, to arrest the course of the pernicious doctrine which was introduced several years ago by seditious spirits against kings and sovereign powers established by God and which troubles and subverts them: the King shall be asked to declare in the assembly of his Estates *as a Fundamental Law of the Kingdom, which shall be inviolable and known to all*: that since he is known to be sovereign in his state, holding his crown from God alone, that there is no power on earth whatever, spiritual or temporal, which has any authority over his kingdom, to take away the sacred nature of our kings, to dispense or absolve their subjects of the fidelity and obedience which they owe them for any cause or pretext whatsoever.[36]

The deputies of the third estate recognized that 'one king, one faith, one law' was a fundamental part of the unwritten French constitution. That they associated this in 1614 with a stronger king no doubt reflects the chaos and disorder of the Wars of Religion, and in this sense there clearly was a link between the civil wars and the so-called absolute monarchy that succeeded them. The perception that strong kingship and sacral monarchy went hand in hand was thus natural in the early seventeenth century and would remain so for some time. Moreover, the Estates-General,

---

[35] Michel Antoine, 'Genèse de l'institution des intendants', *Journal des savants*, (1982), 283–317.

[36] Quoted in J. Michael Hayden, *France and the Estates General of 1614* (Cambridge, 1974), p. 131 (italics in the original).

which met frequently in the sixteenth century during royal minorities or other periods of royal weakness, did not meet again after 1614 until 1789 at the outbreak of the French Revolution, by which time the sacral bonds of monarchy had been broken.

The political rhetoric of the early seventeenth century was thus altogether different from the cries (from Huguenots and Leaguers alike) for popular sovereignty, resistance to tyrannical kings, and regular meetings of the Estates-General. After the disorder of the religious wars, the new political discourse focused on order – an ordered society and a society of orders – as well as the necessity of an absolute monarch to maintain it. The writings of Charles Loyseau, a barrister in the Parlement of Paris, contrasted sharply with both Hotman's *Francogallia* and Boucher's *The Just Deposition of Henry III*. In three separate works published in the last years of the reign of Henry IV – *A Treatise on Lordships* (1608), *Five Books on the Law of Offices* (1609), and *A Treatise of Orders and Plain Dignities* (1610) – Loyseau outlined a theory of ordered society and absolute monarchy that went far beyond the very general prescription advocated by Jean Bodin in 1576. Loyseau's theory of absolute monarchy, unlike Bodin's, was based on formal rules of Aristotelian logic. For him Lordship (*seigneurie*), Office, and Order – the subjects of his three treatises – were all of the same genus, the genus of Dignity, but were species differentiated by power. Lordship was 'dignity with power in property'; office was 'dignity with public function'; and order was 'dignity with aptitude for public power'. Thus, even though the king of France was sovereign lord and seigneurial prince, he was also an officer. And 'this best-established monarchy that ever was' was in fact 'rather an office than a seigneurie'. The king was an officer of God, the 'minister Dei' and the people were 'bound by divine and human law entirely to obey' him. The offices of 'government, justice, and finance' were the king's prerogative alone. 'These three functions, or divers powers, are the three fleurons of the crown, or the three lilies of the arms of France', and the king had 'alone in his kingdom these three functions combined in his person, and this in all sovereignty'. The king alone, then, made 'absolute and immutable laws'.[37]

What Loyseau was building up to was order, the last part of his theory of absolute monarchy. In the preface to his *Treatise of Orders and Plain Dignities* he spelled out his argument very clearly:

---

[37] Quoted in Howell A. Lloyd, *The State, France, and the Sixteenth Century* (London, 1983), pp. 163–6.

In all things there must be order, for the sake of decorum and for their control ... For we cannot live together in a condition of equality, but of necessity it must be that some command and others obey. Those who command have several orders or degrees: sovereign lords command all those in their state, addressing their commandment to the great, the great to the intermediate, the intermediate to the minor, and the minor to the people. And the people, who obey all of these, are again divided into several orders and ranks, so that over each of them there may be superiors who account for their entire order to the magistrates, and the magistrates to the sovereign lords. And so, by means of these multiple divisions and subdivisions, one general order is formed out of many orders, and of many estates a well-ordered state where there are good harmony and consonance and a correspondence and interrelationship from the highest to the lowest: so that through order, an infinite number results in unity.

Thus, order and a well-ordered state could not exist without 'the sovereign lord' who governed absolutely at the top of this society of orders.[38]

The real legacy of the French Wars of Religion, however, was that this rhetoric of absolutism co-existed with the increased social polarization between rich and poor that resulted from the civil wars themselves (as outlined in the previous section). If we concentrate too much on the rhetoric, as some historians have done, we ignore the deep-seated social tensions that continued in French society long after the religious wars. Thus, absolutism did not automatically create order; it was a theory to combat disorder. Or as one historian has recently observed, absolutism 'was always in the making but never made'.[39] As the discourse of absolutism by jurists such as Loyseau intensified throughout the seventeenth century, so too did social tensions. If the reigns of Louis XIII and Louis XIV were the age of absolutism, as so many historians have long claimed, they were also the age of renewed and increased popular revolts like those of 1579 and 1593–94. The discourse of absolutism may have made Louis XIV confident enough to revoke the Edict of Nantes in 1685, but it was his inability to create the kind of dominant order outlined by Loyseau that made him think he needed to.

---

[38] Charles Loyseau, *A Treatise of Orders and Plain Dignities*, trans. and ed., Howell A. Lloyd (Cambridge, 1994), pp. 5–6.
[39] David Parker, *The Making of French Absolutism* (London, 1983), p. xvi.

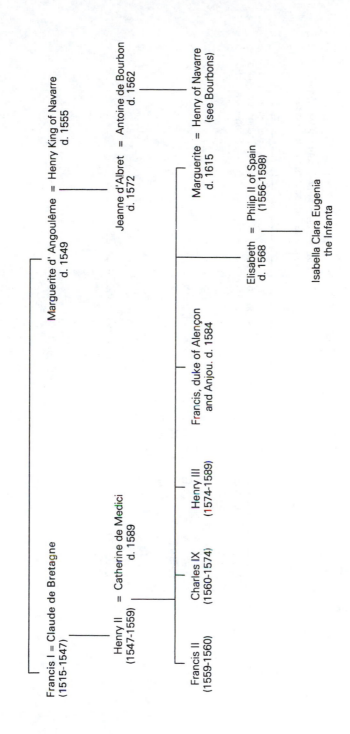

Genealogical chart: Valois

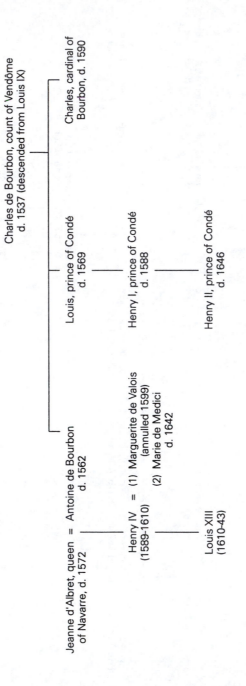

Genealogical chart: Bourbon

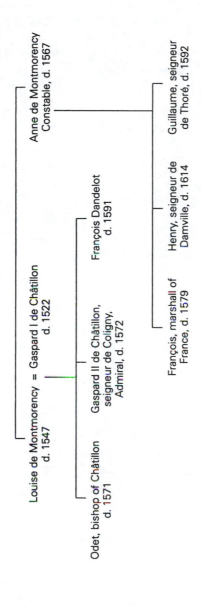

Genealogical chart: Montmorency

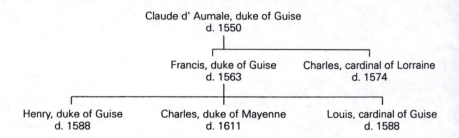

Claude d' Aumale, duke of Guise
d. 1550

Francis, duke of Guise   Charles, cardinal of Lorraine
d. 1563   d. 1574

Henry, duke of Guise   Charles, duke of Mayenne   Louis, cardinal of Guise
d. 1588   d. 1611   d. 1588

Genealogical chart: Guise

Brief biographies

ALBRET, JEANNE D', QUEEN OF NAVARRE (1528–1572)

Wife of Anthony of Navarre, she was a leading aristocratic figure in the early Protestant movement in France. Her support provided a refuge for Protestant growth in her lands in Béarn, and she was instrumental in arranging the marriage of her son Henry with Margaret of Valois in 1572.

ALENÇON AND ANJOU, FRANCIS, DUKE OF (1555–1584)

He was the youngest son of Henry II and Catherine de Medici, and although a Catholic, he sided with the Huguenots in the fifth civil war, leading to the Peace of Monsieur in 1576. His premature death in June 1584 left the Protestant Henry of Navarre as heir presumptive to the crown.

ANGOULÊME, MARGARET OF (1492–1549)

As the sister of Francis I, her patronage and protection of the circle at Meaux provided royal support to the humanist scholars and unorthodox theology of that group.

BRIÇONNET, GUILLAUME (1472–1534)

He was a Catholic abbot of St Germain-des-Prés, who was appointed bishop of Meaux in 1516. The circle of humanists and unorthodox thinkers who were attracted to him eventually came under the attack of the Sorbonne and the Parlement of Paris in 1525.

CALVIN, JOHN (1509–1564)

Although trained as a lawyer, he became enamored with Christian humanist scholarship which eventually led him to reformist ideology and unorthodox theology. After fleeing France, he went to Strasbourg, Basel, and eventually Geneva, where he established a reformed community after 1541. It was his teaching and ministry there that led to the spread of his reformist ideas into France in the 1550s.

CHARLES IX (1550–1574), King of France 1560–1574

He came to the throne when just a young boy, so a regency government headed by his mother, Catherine de Medici, governed until he came of age in 1563. He was partly responsible for the St Bartholomew's massacres in Paris in August 1572.

COLIGNY, GASPARD DE (1519–1572)

As Admiral of France, he was one of the leading French noblemen to convert to Calvinism. He was a nephew of Anne de Montmorency and the leader of the Huguenots after the death of Condé in 1569. It was his assassination in August 1572 that sparked off the St Bartholomew's massacres.

CONDÉ, LOUIS OF BOURBON, PRINCE OF (1530–1569)

An early convert to Protestantism, he was the leader of the Huguenots in the first three civil wars and was killed at the battle of Jarnac in 1569.

CONDÉ, HENRY I OF BOURBON, PRINCE OF (1552–1588)

He was the son of Louis of Bourbon and served the Protestant cause until his premature death. He was overshadowed first by Coligny then Henry of Navarre.

CONDÉ, HENRY II OF BOURBON, PRINCE OF (1588–1646)

As the posthumously born son of Henry I of Bourbon, he grew up during the League and eventually became a Catholic. He led several noble revolts during the reign of Louis XIII, for whom he also fought against the Huguenots.

DAMVILLE, HENRY DE MONTMORENCY, SEIGNEUR DE (1534–1614)

The son of Anne de Montmorency, he protected the Huguenots in Languedoc in the early 1570s, where he was royal governor. After 1576, however, he was won back over to the royalist cause.

FRANCIS I (1494–1547), King of France 1515–1547

He was on the throne when the Reformation began and initiated a policy of repression of Protestantism after the Affair of the Placards in 1534.

FRANCIS II (1544–1560), King of France 1559–1560

He was married to Mary Stuart of Scotland, and his short reign was dominated by his wife's uncles, the duke of Guise and the cardinal of Lorraine.

GUISE, FRANCIS OF LORRAINE, DUKE OF (1519–1563)

An ardent opponent of Protestantism, he dominated the short reign of Francis II and was later assassinated during the first civil war.

GUISE, HENRY OF LORRAINE, DUKE OF (1550–1588)

The son of Francis of Lorraine, he assumed the mantle of the leadership of the anti-Huguenot movement and ultimately challenged the authority of Henry III. His popularity in the capital in May 1588 on the Day of the Barricades forced the king to flee and eventually led to the king's decision to murder him in December 1588 at Blois.

HENRY II (1519–1559), King of France 1547–1559

He persecuted Protestantism during his reign and supported the 'Chambre ardente'. His premature death in a jousting accident in 1559 left his wife Catherine de Medici and his three young sons to deal with the growth of Protestantism in France.

HENRY III (1551–1589), King of France 1574–1589

Partly because he attempted to perpetuate the tolerationist policies of his mother, Catherine de Medici, he was ultimately opposed by Catholic militants and Henry, duke of Guise, whose entry into Paris on the Day of the Barricades in May 1588 forced the king's retreat from the capital. After assassinating Guise in December 1588, Henry himself was murdered the following summer. Because he died childless, he was the last Valois monarch, the succession passing to Henry of Navarre of the Bourbon family.

HENRY IV (1553–1610), King of Navarre, 1572–1610, King of France 1589–1610

After being reared as a Protestant, he came to the throne in 1589 upon the assassination of the childless Henry III. He was the first Bourbon monarch and brought a halt to the religious wars by abjuring Calvinism in 1593 and making peace with the Catholic League soon thereafter. He also was responsible for issuing the Edict of Nantes (1598), which served as the basis of the settlement with the Huguenots. He was assassinated in 1610.

LEFEVRE D'ETAPLES, JACQUES (1450–1536)

A humanist scholar who, like Erasmus, became attracted to Biblical scholarship, he was attracted to the circle at Meaux. Although he remained a Catholic, he held a number of unorthodox ideas that were later embraced by Protestants.

LORRAINE, CHARLES, CARDINAL OF (1524–1574)

The brother of Francis, duke of Guise, he was influential in heading the anti-Huguenot cause in the first four wars of religion. He also represented France at the Council of Trent.

LOUIS XIII (1601–1643), King of France 1610–1643

He succeeded his father Henry IV when only nine years old, necessitating a regency government. He eventually renewed the war against the Huguenots, culminating in their eventual defeat in the siege of La Rochelle (1627–28) and the Peace of Alais (1629).

LOUIS XIV (1638–1715), King of France 1643–1715.

He revoked the Edict of Nantes in 1685.

MAYENNE, CHARLES OF LORRAINE, DUKE OF (1554–1611)

He was the younger brother of Henry, duke of Guise, and succeeded him as the head of the Catholic League upon the latter's murder in 1588.

MEDICI, CATHERINE DE (1519–1589), Queen of France 1547–1559 and Queen Mother 1559–1589

She sought unsuccessfully to prevent civil war throughout the reigns of her three sons and was always a presence behind the throne. Her policies never achieved the lasting peace she desired, however, and she was implicated in the St Bartholomew's massacres in Paris in 1572.

MEDICI, MARIE DE (1573–1642), Queen of France 1600–1610

As the second wife of Henry IV, whom she married in 1600, she headed the regency government of her young son Louis XIII. She is significant for her patronage and support of Cardinal Richelieu.

MONTMORENCY, ANNE, DUKE OF (1493–1567)

As the Constable of France he headed the French military. Although he remained a Catholic and fought against the Huguenots in the first civil war, his three nephews, the Châtillon brothers, converted to Protestantism.

NAVARRE, ANTHONY OF BOURBON, KING OF (1518–1562)

Although he was only lukewarm to the Protestant movement, his wife Jeanne d'Albret and his son Henry became leaders of the Calvinist cause in France.

NAVARRE, HENRY OF.

See Henry IV.

PHILIP II (1527–1598), King of Spain 1556–1598

He provided significant military and financial support to the Catholic League in the eighth civil war.

RICHELIEU, ARMAND DU PLESSIS, CARDINAL OF (1585–1642)

He was a client of Marie de Medici who was appointed to the privy council of Louis XIII in 1624. He was instrumental in the defeat of the Huguenots in the last civil war.

ROHAN, HENRY, DUKE OF (1579–1638)

He was the principal Huguenot military leader during the last civil war.

SOUBISE, BENJAMIN DE ROHAN, SEIGNEUR OF (1583–1642)

As the younger brother of Rohan, he was a Huguenot military commander in the last civil war

SULLY, MAXIMILIEN DE BÉTHUNE, DUKE OF (1559–1641)

He was a Huguenot who fought under Henry IV in the 1590s and was later appointed as his superintendent of finances. After Henry's assassination in 1610, he was forced to resign from the privy council by the regency government of Marie de Medici.

VALOIS, MARGARET OF (1553–1615)

The daughter of Henry II and Catherine de Medici, she married the Protestant Henry of Navarre in 1572. The marriage was never conventional as she and Henry were never close, and it eventually ended in separation and divorce.

Suggestions for further reading

Virtually all the contemporary sources and much of the modern literature on the French Wars of Religion are written in French. So readers whose only language is English can have only a partial awareness of even the best work on the subject. What I have tried to do here is point the English-speaking reader to the most useful works written in or translated into English. Thus, this is only a partial and idiosyncratic list of works that I have found useful in trying to write about and teach the French Wars of Religion. It makes no pretence at being comprehensive, omitting works in French altogether, and is solely designed to point the reader who wants to know more in the right direction.

General works

The best general study of the Wars of Religion is J. H. M. Salmon, *Society in Crisis: France in the Sixteenth Century* (London and New York, 1975). Although it stops coverage in 1598, is far too detailed for beginners, and is now thirty years old, this is still the most comprehensive one-volume study of the civil wars in English, and my own book will not replace it. Other general narratives include two excellent books by Robert J. Knecht, a longer narrative called *The Rise and Fall of Renaissance France, 1483–1610* (London, 1996) and a shorter narrative called *The French Civil Wars, 1562–1598* (London, 2000). For the background to the Wars of Religion, there is the excellent book by David Potter, *A History of France, 1460–1560: The Emergence of a Nation State* (London, 1995). Other accounts include Frederic J. Baumgartner, *France in the Sixteenth Century* (New York, 1995), Mark Greengrass, *France in the Age of Henri IV: The Struggle for Stability*, 2nd edn. (London, 1994); and Mack P. Holt, ed., *Renaissance and Reformation France, 1500–1648* (Oxford, 2002), a collection of general essays by a team of specialists. Other works which can also be consulted with profit include N. M. Sutherland, *The Huguenot Struggle for Recognition* (New Haven, 1980), which is particularly strong on the various edicts of pacification; Philip Benedict, *Rouen during the Wars of Religion* (Cambridge, 1981) and Barbara B. Diefendorf, *Beneath the Cross*,

Catholics and Huguenots in Sixteenth-Century Paris (Oxford and New York, 1991), easily the best local studies; and Natalie Zemon Davis, *Society and Culture in Early Modern France* (Stanford, 1975), a book of essays that still inspires and bristles with new ideas.

Institutions

On the monarchy see Richard A. Jackson, *Vive le Roi! A History of the French Coronation from Charles V to Charles X* (Chapel Hill, 1984) and Marc Bloch, *The Royal Touch*, trans. J. E. Anderson (New York, 1989), both of which show the strong sacral and sacerdotal nature of French kingship. Three useful books on the Parlements are Jonathan Dewald, *The Formation of a Provincial Nobility: The Magistrates of the Parlement of Rouen, 1499–1610* (Princeton, 1980); Nancy Lyman Roelker, *One King, One Faith: The Parlement of Paris and the Religious Reformations of the Sixteenth Century* (Berkeley, 1996); and E. William Monter, *Judging the French Reformation: Heresy Trials by Sixteenth Century Parlements* (Cambridge, MA, 1999). The Estates-General and the provincial estates are admirably analysed by J. Russell Major, *Representative Government in Early Modern France* (New Haven, 1980) and the same author's *From Renaissance Monarchy to Absolute Monarchy: French Kings, Nobles, and Estates* (Baltimore, 1994). Two good books on the tax system and the fiscal machinery of the state are Martin Wolfe, *The Fiscal System in Renaissance France* (New Haven, 1972) and James B. Collins, *Fiscal Limits of Absolutism: Direct Taxation in Early Seventeenth-Century France* (Berkeley, 1988). Different perspectives on the Gallican church can be found in (from the top) Frederic J. Baumgartner, *Change and Continuity in the French Episcopate: The Bishops and the Wars of Religion* (Durham, NC, 1968); (on the parish level) Philip T. Hoffman, *Church and Community in the Diocese of Lyon, 1500–1789* (New Haven, 1984); and (a cultural view) Henry Phillips, *Church and Culture in Seventeenth-Century France* (Cambridge, 1997).

One area that has received virtually no attention until recently is the military, an oddity given the crucial role played by armies on all sides during the entire conflict. This void has been filled admirably by James B. Wood, *The Army of the King: Warfare, Soldiers, and Society during the Wars of Religion in France, 1562–1576* (Cambridge, 1996), a work which should be required reading for anyone who wishes to know why the wars lasted so long. And for the wars of the early seventeenth century, there is now the admirable book by David Parrott, *Richelieu's Army: War, Government, and Society in France, 1624–1642* (Cambridge, 2001).

Finally, though it covers primarily the seventeenth and eighteenth centuries, the two volumes of Roland Mousnier, *The Institutions of France under the Absolute Monarchy, 1598–1789*, trans. Arthur Goldhammer, 2 vols. (Chicago, 1979–84) is the most comprehensive survey of French institutions and has much to offer on the civil wars.

Reformation and religion

An excellent starting point is the brief but informative introduction by Mark Greengrass, *The French Reformation* (London, 1987). After reading that, one can turn with profit to Robert M. Kingdon, *Geneva and the Coming of the Wars of Religion in France, 1555–1563* (Geneva, 1956), still valuable after half a century, and Donald R. Kelley, *The Beginning of Ideology: Consciousness and Society in the French Reformation* (Cambridge, 1981). On the theological side, Calvin's *Institution of the Christian Religion* (there are many editions and translations) is a must, while social and moral discipline are introduced in E. William Monter, *Calvin's Geneva* (New York, 1967). On the Catholic side, excellent studies on preaching include Larissa J. Taylor, *Soldiers of Christ: Preaching in Late Medieval and Reformation France* (New York and Oxford, 1992) and the same author's *Heresy and Orthodoxy in Sixteenth-Century Paris: François Le Picart and the Beginnings of the Catholic Reformation* (Leiden, 1999). There is also Megan C. Armstrong, *The Politics of Piety: Franciscan Preachers during the Wars of Religion, 1560–1600* (Rochester, 2004). On Catholic lay piety see two articles by Virginia Reinburg, 'Liturgy and Laity in Late Medieval and Reformation France', *Sixteenth Century Journal*, 23 (Fall 1992) and 'Hearing Lay People's Prayer', in B. Diefendorf and C. Hesse, eds., *Culture and Identity in Early Modern Europe, 1500–1800* (Ann Arbor, 1993), 19–39, as well as the useful study of Anne T. Thayer, *Penitence, Preaching, and the Coming of the Reformation* (Aldershot, 2002). On the Jesuits, see A. Lynn Martin, *The Jesuit Mind: The Mentality of an Elite in Early Modern France* (Ithaca, 1988) and Eric W. Nelson, *The Monarchy and the Jesuits: Political Authority and Catholic Renewal in France, 1590–1615* (Aldershot, 2005). On the Protestant side, see Philip Benedict, *Christ's Churches Purely Reformed: A Social History of Calvinism* (New Haven, 2002); Glenn S. Sunshine, *Reforming French Protestantism: The Development of Huguenot Ecclesiastical Institutions, 1557–1572* (Kirksville, 2003); and two excellent collections of essays: Raymond A. Mentzer and Andrew Spicer, eds., *Society and Culture in the Huguenot World, 1559–1685* (Cambridge, 2002), and Philip Benedict, *The Faith and Fortune of France's Huguenots, 1600–1685* (Aldershot, 2001). Finally, for the interaction between Catholics and Huguenots, see the works cited above by Benedict, Diefendorf, and Davis (General Works).

Biographical studies

There are a number of informative studies on some of the major individuals in the Wars of Religion, and they are often useful entries in to the more specialized literature. Nancy Lyman Roelker's *Queen of Navarre: Jeanne d'Albret, 1528–1572* (Cambridge, MA, 1968) is a classic and shows how influential the patronage of noblewomen was during the civil wars. William J. Bouwsma's *John Calvin: A Sixteenth-Century Portrait* (Oxford and New York, 1988) is the best of the many studies of Calvin. For Calvin's lieutenant and successor, see Scott M. Manetsch, *Theodore Beza and the Quest for Peace in France, 1572–1598* (Leiden, 2000). R. J. Knecht, *Renaissance Warrior and Patron: The Reign of Francis I* (Cambridge, 1994) is the most comprehensive study of this monarch, while Frederic J. Baumgartner, *Henry II, King of France* (Durham, NC, 1987) provides a useful sequel to the reign of his successor. For Henry II's wife, there is now the excellent biography by R. J. Knecht, *Catherine De Medici* (London, 1998), though her sons Charles IX and Henry III still await good biographies in English. The troubled career of Charles IX's and Henry III's younger brother is explained in my own *The Duke of Anjou and the Politique Struggle during the Wars of Religion* (Cambridge, 1986), while Gaspard de Cologny can be approached through Junko Shimizu, *Conflict of Loyalties: Politics and Religion in the Reign of Gaspard de Coligny, Admiral of France, 1519–1572* (Geneva, 1970). Regrettably there are no biographies in English of either Henry, duke of Guise or his brother, Charles, duke of Mayenne. More books have been written about Henry IV than any other individual in the civil wars. In addition to the study of Greengrass mentioned above (General Works), see David Buisseret, *Henry IV* (London, 1982), which is very strong on military matters; Michael Wolfe, *The Conversion of Henry IV: Politics, Power, and Religious Belief in Early Modern France* (Cambridge, MA, 1993), which sets Henry's abjuration in context; Annette Finley-Croswhite, *Henry IV and the Towns: The Pursuit of Legitimacy in French Urban Society, 1589–1610* (Cambridge, 1999), which is very good on the politics of Henry's relations with the towns; N. M. Sutherland, *Henry IV of France and the Politics of Religion, 1572–1596*, 2 vols. (Bristol, 2002), which focuses on the international ramifications of Henry's abjuration and accession to the crown; and Ronald S. Love, *Blood and Religion: The Conscience of Henri IV, 1553–1593* (Montreal, 2001), which deals with Henry's religious beliefs and practices. Finally, Roland Mousnier's *The Assassination of Henry IV* (London, 1973) is a classic that everyone should read. For the seventeenth century, A. Lloyd Moote's *Louis XIII: The Just* (Berkeley, 1999) and Joseph Bergin's *The Rise of Richelieu* (New Haven, 1991) are both excellent introductions, though there is a need for a new study of the duke of Rohan to replace the outdated work by J. A. Clarke, *Huguenot Warrior: The Life and Times of Henri de Rohan, 1579–1638* (The Hague, 1966).

Local studies

In addition to the works by Diefendorf on Paris and Benedict on Rouen cited above (General Works), a number of useful local studies have appeared since the first edition of this book. Hilary J. Bernstein, *Between*

Crown and Community: Politics and Civic Culture in Sixteenth-Century Poitiers (Ithaca, 2004); Stuart Carroll, *Noble Power during the French Wars of Religion: The Guise Affinity and the Catholic Cause in Normandy* (Cambridge, 1998); Philip Conner, *Huguenot Heartland: Montauban and Southern French Calvinism during the Wars of Religion* (Aldershot, 2002); Mark W. Konnert, *Civic Agendas and Religious Passion: Châlons-sur-Marne during the French Wars of Religion, 1560–1594* (Kirksville, 1997); Kevin C. Robins, *City on the Ocean Sea: La Rochelle, 1530–1650* (Leiden, 1997); and Penny Roberts, *A City in Conflict: Troyes during the French Wars of Religion* (Manchester, 1996) are all well worth reading for the local and regional dynamics at work in the religious wars.

St Bartholomew's massacres

The St Bartholomew's massacres have generated much controversy ever since they occurred, and the historical debate does not appear to be letting up. N. M. Sutherland, *The Massacre of St. Bartholomew and the European Conflict, 1559–1572* (London, 1972) is good on the political and diplomatic background and offers a revisionist attempt to absolve Catherine de Medici of any responsibility in the initial attempt on Coligny's life. This view has drawn a good deal of criticism, especially from French scholars. Diefendorf's acount (see General Works) is now the most reliable guide, while the provincial massacres are expertly explained in Philip Benedict, 'The Saint Bartholomew's Massacres in the Provinces', *The Historical Journal*, 21 (1978), 205–25. And for propaganda after the massacres, see Robert M. Kingdon, *Myths About the St. Bartholomew's Day Massacres, 1572–1576* (Cambridge, MA, 1988); and Luc Racaut, *Hated in Print: Catholic Propaganda and Protestant Identity in the French Wars of Religion* (Aldershot, 2002).

The Catholic League

The best introduction to the League in the capital are the articles of J. H. M. Salmon, 'The Paris Sixteen, 1584–1594: The Social Analysis of a Revolutionary Movement', in Salmon's collection of essays, *Renaissance and Revolt: Essays in the Intellectual and Social History of Early Modern France* (Cambridge, 1987), pp. 235–66; and Denis Richet, 'Sociocultural Aspects of Religious Conflicts in Paris during the Second half of the Sixteenth Century', in R. Forster and O. Ranum, eds., *Ritual, Religion, and the Sacred: Selections from the Annales* (Baltimore, 1982), pp. 182–212. Ann W. Ramsey, *Liturgy, Politics, and Salvation: The Catholic League in Paris and the Nature of Catholic Reform, 1540–1630* (Rochester, 1999) is the most comprehensive study of the League in Paris. In addition, see the book by Armstrong cited above

(Reformation and religion) on the role Franciscan preachers played in radicalizing the capital during the wars of the League.

Political thought

For a good introduction to political ideas during the Wars of Religion, see the relevant chapters of J. H. Burns and M. Goldie, eds., *The Cambridge History of Political Thought, 1450–1700* (Cambridge, 1991). More detailed accounts can be found in Quentin Skinner, *The Foundations of Modern Political Thought: The Reformation* (Cambridge, 1978) chaps. 7–8; Julian H. Franklin, *Jean Bodin and the Rise of Absolutist Theory* (Cambridge, 1973); Frederic J. Baumgartner, *Radical Reactionaries: The Political Thought of the French Catholic League* (Geneva, 1975); and on Gallican ideology, Jotham Parsons, *The Church in the Republic: Gallicanism and Political Ideology in Renaissance France* (Washington, DC, 2004). To get the true flavour of political discourse during the Wars of Religion, however, one must read some of the original works written in the period. Several of the most important have been translated into English, and a good contrast is the Huguenot resistance theory of François Hotman, *Francogallia*, ed. and trans. R. E. Giesey and J. H. M. Salmon (Cambridge, 1973), which has a superb introduction; and the royalist ideas of Jean Bodin, *The Six Bookes of a Commonweale*, ed. K. D. McRae (Cambridge, MA, 1962), which is a facsimile edition of a 1606 English translation, also with an excellent introduction. And for the rhetoric of absolutism after the Edict of Nantes, see Charles Loyseau, *A Treatise of Orders and Plain Dignities*, ed. and trans. H. A. Lloyd (Cambridge, 1994).

Index

NEW APPROACHES TO EUROPEAN HISTORY